The CONFIDENT COLLECTOR™

MARILYN MONROE
Collectibles

D1023857

The CONFIDENT COLLECTOR™

MARILYN MONROE

Collectibles

A Comprehensive Guide to the Memorabilia of an American Legend

CLARK KIDDER

AVON BOOKS ◆ NEW YORK

AVON BOOKS, INC.
1350 Avenue of the Americas
New York, New York 10019

Copyright © 1999 by Clark Kidder
Cover photo by Debbie Fischer
Published by arrangement with the author
Library of Congress Catalog Card Number: 99-95271
ISBN: 0-380-79909-X
www.avonbooks.com

First Avon Books Trade Paperback Printing: November 1999

Printed in the U.S.A.

OPM 10 9 8 7 6 5 4 3 2 1

For Linda, Robby, and Nathan

ACKNOWLEDGMENTS

Without the generous help of my dear friends, Debbie Fischer, Ceasar Vasallo, Richard Vorpagel, Pat Austin and Bill Altman, this book would not have been possible. Sincere gratitude is due to my literary agent, Claudia Menza, for all her hard work and perseverance on my behalf. Thanks as well to Skip Drew for his diligent and expert photography of the items pictured in this book. My thanks to my friend George Zeno for agreeing to write the foreword. Thank you to my family for putting up with all my indulgences and interruptions in compiling this book and in my pursuits of the eternal blonde. And last, but not least, thank you to my editor Tia Maggini and Avon Books for believing in me and my book.

CONTENTS

FOREWORD

By George Zeno

I first saw Marilyn Monroe's image when I was seven years old. It was in January 1953 on a trip to visit my aunt in New York City. My family and I were riding the subway on an elevated track entering the Williamsburg Bridge from Brooklyn. Outside the window of the car I saw this billboard advertising the motion picture *Niagara*. A waterfall cascades over the bigger-than-life reclining figure of Marilyn Monroe. At that point, I had no idea who she was, and little did I know how much a part of my life she would become.

Later on that same year, I heard a lot of talk about this woman named Marilyn Monroe. I heard about her in school, at home, and around the neighborhood. Naturally, I was curious. One day, my older cousin came to visit. He had a magazine entitled *The Marilyn Monroe Story*. He was showing my father some of the photos that ran in the magazine. Finally, I got to see who this Marilyn Monroe was. What I remember most was that blond hair and that fantastic mouth. Her image stayed with me, but nothing really clicked until I saw *Gentlemen Prefer Blondes*. That did it! From that point on, she lived in my mind always. A few months later, I was playing in the park with a friend and I found a movie magazine on the ground. It was a copy of *Motion Pictures* dated October 1953. Janet Leigh was on the cover. I looked through it and came across a small color photo of Marilyn from *Gentlemen Prefer Blondes*. I kept the magazine and later cut out the photo. That was the start of my collection.

Between late 1953 and early 1954, Marilyn was on almost every magazine cover you could imagine. All my allowance went to buying as many as I could afford. I only bought magazines with her on the cover, or with full-page color pictures inside.

I also remember my first Marilyn newspaper front page. My father came home from work on the night of January 15, 1954, and handed me the paper. "Your girlfriend got married," he said. There she was in the *New York Daily News* with Joe DiMaggio. Another day, I saw the *Golden Dreams* nude calendar. It was hanging in the window of some repair shop. I can remember how different she looked and how strange it was seeing her naked. To make sure it was her, I read the small print: "posed by Marilyn Monroe." Even at the age of nine, I never thought of it as something that was cheap or embarrassing. As the years went by, there were fewer magazines to buy that featured Marilyn. The quality of magazines in which she appeared was not the same; they were more like "teen" magazines. By 1957, there was little being written about Marilyn. So the next thing for a collector to do was go back to even earlier years. By accident, I found a store near where I had seen the *Niagara* billboard. It was an old bookstore, but it also sold magazines going back to the forties. I found many magazines that I never knew existed, such as *Laff, Glance, Gala,* and *Hit.* The photos in these magazines were of Marilyn the "Pin-Up Girl" or Marilyn the model. I loved and enjoyed collecting even more, always wondering what I would find next. By 1959, following the success of *Some Like It Hot,* Marilyn was on top again and back in the news. About that time, I discovered the only store in New York City that sold foreign magazines. I was able to buy these otherwise hard to get magazines. Foreign countries seemed to put Marilyn on the cover more than America did.

In March 1959, I finally saw Marilyn Monroe in person. It was at the premiere of *Some Like It Hot* in Times Square. It was the only time I saw her; I was fourteen. I thought then that there would be many more times in the future. It was very cold, and my father and I waited about two hours for Marilyn to show up. When she did arrive, there was so much confusion from people pushing and fans cheering and screaming with so much excitement that we could see only her head through the crowd. At that point, the barricades were knocked down, and she was rushed into the theater. But that short moment in which I got to see her face will stay with me forever. She was even more beautiful than I had expected and was somehow unreal. I've never seen anyone with skin like hers; she was almost like a ghost. After that night, I knew that I would never stop collecting memorabilia on this wonderful human being who always brought happiness to me just by looking at her image.

In 1961, I wrote a letter to Marilyn. I wrote because I was very concerned about what I'd been reading in the newspapers about how she had been in and out of hospitals and how she was living alone. I wrote that it made me feel sad for her and that I feared that someday I'd read that something terrible had happened to her. I wrote about my collection and how I had collected for many years. I added a P.S. asking her to send me an autographed photo of herself and thanked her. Months later she did send me a beautiful photo taken by Cecil Beaton. She wrote: "To George, Best Wishes, Marilyn Monroe."

Naturally, after getting this photo I wanted to start some kind of communication with her again. It was Christmastime, and I wanted to send her a card. I found one with an illustration of four angelic faces on it. I thought of her the instant I saw it. There was something about those angelic faces that I knew she would like. They looked like little orphans. In the card, I wrote: "To Marilyn Monroe, the Most Beautiful and Best Actress in the whole world—May you have Happiness forever—From Your Fan, George Zeno."

I mailed the card to her New York address, not knowing it would be the last Christmas she would celebrate. Years later, someone who collects Marilyn memorabilia sent me a photocopy of that card. I was stunned. The collector said it had been found in her home where she had died. I asked him if I could have the card back because I didn't think it was of any value to anyone else, but he said that the card was now a valuable collectible.

This book by Clark Kidder, who for me is a true collector and a collector who loves the person he collects, is a treasure full of Marilyn Monroe gems to save and collect and preserve for the next century.

George Zeno's incredible collection of Marilyn Monroe memorabilia was featured in the October 1981 issue of Life *magazine in its article on collectors. In 1982, George coauthored a book on Marilyn with James Spada:* Monroe: Her Life in Pictures *(Doubleday/Dolphin). George is called on internationally to consult on Marilyn Monroe projects and supply photos for them, and was vice-president of the Marilyn Monroe Memorial Fan Club for four years. Born in Puerto Rico, he now lives in New York.*

INTRODUCTION

The need for a comprehensive price guide covering Marilyn Monroe collectibles has been long overdue. Why? Ask any paper dealer who their fastest-selling star is and they'll tell you Marilyn Monroe every time. Her career spanned just sixteen years but it was long enough to create a myriad of collectible items. In fact, new Monroe collectibles are being made at a feverish pace to this day, over thirty-five years after her untimely death in 1962. At auction houses around the world, Marilyn memorabilia is fetching record prices. One of her dresses worn in *There's No Business Like Show Business* recently brought $57,500 at auction at Christie's.

Owning a piece of vintage Americana is something of a fad these days, both in the United States and abroad. Marilyn Monroe is about as close as you can get to true Americana. She's right up there with baseball, hot dogs, and apple pie.

In writing this book I have attempted to be as comprehensive as possible in my coverage of the vast array of Monroe collectibles that were produced both during and after her lifetime—not only in the United States, but in foreign countries as well. You'll find chapters on how a beginning collector gets started, and tips on dealing with foreign countries and storing your valuable collectibles, as well as on trading with fellow collectors. In addition, detailed information and price ranges are given for many of the hundreds of Monroe collectibles listed within, such as sheet music, movie posters, books, magazine covers, calendars, autographs, and much more. Such information will allow you to be better informed when purchasing or selling such items.

Whether you inherit an attic full of stuff from your great uncle, or stumble onto a Marilyn Monroe collectible at a local flea market, or even if you are a veteran collector of Monroe, you'll find informative and interesting information within.

Interest in Marilyn Monroe is universal, which you'll see as you scan the following pages. There are presently fan clubs in Germany, England, Australia, and France. With access to millions via the Internet, the ability to connect with other Monroe collectors around the world is at an all-time high. The sky is the limit, as they say, so get on out there and take advantage of it! Oh, and make sure you enjoy yourself along the way.

MARILYN
BIO/TIME LINE

Marilyn Monroe. Her very name evokes memories of a quieter, happier time in our not-so-distant past. Marilyn was a part of what we often refer to affectionately as the "fabulous fifties," the postwar boom in America. Spirits were high, and the public was yearning for new, fresh ideas. The time was never more right for a new "blond bombshell" to sweep the cinemas. Hollywood was desperately in trouble. With the advent of television, people were staying home and not going to the movies. There was a real worry that the movie industry would collapse, a concept difficult for us to comprehend today.

Screen vamps Jean Harlow and Mae West had reigned during the 1930s, and the 1940s brought Rita Hayworth and Betty Grable, but the 1950s called for a new and more exciting presence on the screen. Enter Marilyn Monroe, born Norma Jean Mortenson in Los Angeles, California, on June 1, 1926, daughter of Gladys Baker and an unknown father, presumed to be C. Stanley Gifford. Gladys was a film cutter for the studios, but would soon be committed to an institution for mental instability. Little Norma Jean had a miserable childhood, growing up in nearly a dozen foster homes and two orphanages. One foster family made her pray all day and told her it was a sin to go to a movie. Yet another family had her playing "soldiers" with empty whiskey bottles strewn across the floor.

Finally, at age sixteen, Norma Jean married her first husband, James Dougherty, a merchant marine and a friend of the family. While Jim was at sea, Norma Jean took a job assembling parachutes at a nearby factory, doing her part to aid in the war effort. One day army photographer David Conover was sent to the factory to take photos that would help lift the morale of the troops. Norma Jean donned a red sweater for the occasion, and Conover thought her so photogenic that he encouraged her to pursue modeling, advice that she enthusiastically took.

Before long, Norma Jean had signed with the Blue Book Modeling Agency and was on her way to a modeling career. Meanwhile, Jim was receiving her "Dear John" letter, along with divorce papers. The way was clear now for the metamorphosis to take place from Norma Jean to Marilyn Monroe.

Between 1946 and 1952, Marilyn was given roles in a series of films for the various Hollywood studios. Her parts were generally small ones, but she was gradually earning a name for herself in Hollywood. One of her most pivotal roles career-wise was in the 1950 film *The Asphalt Jungle*. Another equally important role was in *All About Eve*, also in 1950; this film's star was none other than Bette Davis, and the film won much critical acclaim.

During this time, Marilyn supplemented her income by posing for various glamour photographers, such as André de Dienes and Laszlo Willinger. Many of the resulting photos found their way to the covers of magazines throughout the world and later in calendars.

After several more films in 1951 and 1952, Marilyn's career was in high gear, until, that is, the press had discovered that a nude photo of her was gracing a calendar in wide circulation! Marilyn, as well as many others, thought that the ensuing scandal could very well spell the end of her career. Marilyn admitted that she posed for the nude session in 1949 for photographer Tom Kelley. She was out of work at the time and needed the fifty dollars he had offered. Luckily for Marilyn, the tide began to turn when *Life* magazine decided to feature her on the cover of its April 7, 1952, issue, even including the famous calendar as part of the article. Luckily, the public was sympathetic to Marilyn's reasons for posing, and soon people were lined up in droves to see her next film. Instead of ending her career, the nude photos had only bolstered it! And, in December 1953, one of the nude photos became the very first centerfold in the premiere issue of *Playboy* magazine. She was now truly a "star."

The year 1953 brought great success in films for Marilyn. She now had top billing and was on her way to building the legendary status that she would later attain. A romance soon began with baseball great Joe DiMaggio, and the couple were married in San Francisco on January 14, 1954. They spent their honeymoon in Japan, where Marilyn stole the show from Joe among even the baseball-loving Japanese. One Japanese radio announcer referred to her as the "honorable hip-swinging blonde." Against Joe's wishes, Marilyn decided to accept an offer to entertain the troops in Korea. Braving the bitter cold, she won the admiration of thousands of battle-weary soldiers. She later called the experience the highlight of her life.

In 1955, Marilyn flew to New York to film a scene for her upcoming movie, *The Seven-Year Itch*. It was in this movie that the now famous series of photos of her in the billowing white skirt were taken. During numerous retakes, husband Joe stood seething on the sidelines, appalled that his wife was baring her legs and underpants before thousands of spectators. He stormed off in a rage, and not long afterward the two divorced. They would remain friends, however, until the end, even planning to remarry shortly before Marilyn's death in 1962.

By 1956, Marilyn, disgusted at Fox for casting her in nothing but dumb-blonde roles, decided to form her own production company. Appropriately it was called Marilyn Monroe Productions. Her partner was her well-known friend and photographer, Milton H. Greene. Never before had a star so boldly challenged the studio system. Yet, Marilyn emerged victorious, gaining critical director approval, among other things. The next film Marilyn would do would be *Bus Stop*. In this film she could put to use the new system of method acting that she had just studied at the famed Actors Studio in New York City. Marilyn's performance in the film gained her much critical acclaim and it would be lauded as her finest performance ever.

In 1956, a romance began to blossom between Marilyn and the famous playwright Arthur Miller. Marilyn seemed on top of the world, and before long the couple were married. The pair were affectionately referred to as "the egghead and the hourglass." The wedding took place first in a civil ceremony on June 29, 1956, and then in a Jewish ceremony on July 1, 1956.

But the marriage was not a happy one. Marilyn's dreams of having a child were dashed after she had several miscarriages. And Arthur, unable to live up to the expectations that Marilyn had placed upon him, realized that the marriage was slowly dissolving. Indeed, it ended in divorce in January 1961.

In the fall of 1956, Marilyn and Arthur had flown to England to shoot her next film, *The Prince and the Showgirl*, which would costar Sir Laurence Olivier. There was much tension between Marilyn and Olivier during filming, but the end result was a fine movie that showcased the tremendous comedic abilities of Marilyn. The film was released in 1957 and is another favorite among today's Marilyn fans.

Marilyn's next film, *Some Like It Hot*, was released in 1959. Marilyn did not want to make the film, but she needed the money to help pay mounting bills. Despite her reluctance, the film, which costarred Tony Curtis and Jack Lemmon, proved to be extremely successful at the box office.

In 1960, still under contract with Fox to do three more movies, Marilyn accepted the role in a film entitled *Let's Make Love*. Her costar was French actor Yves Montand, with whom Marilyn had an affair both on and off screen. Unfortunately, the film proved to be a flop and prompted critics and industry officials to predict the end of Marilyn's reign at the top of the box office.

Sadly, Marilyn was to complete only one more film, *The Misfits*, in 1961. It costarred Montgomery Clift and Clark Gable, and its screenplay was written for Marilyn as a gift from her husband, Arthur Miller. It would be only a marginal success at the box office, but it proved that Marilyn could handle playing more serious roles. Marilyn became increasingly fragile during filming of *The Misfits* in the hot desert surrounding Reno, Nevada. To complicate things further, her marriage to Arthur Miller was falling apart during filming, and the two went their separate ways after completing it. Marilyn struggled through 1961, and in 1962 began work on her next film for Fox, *Something's Got to Give*, which would costar Dean Martin, a good friend of Marilyn's. Not long after shooting began, Marilyn came down with a serious sinus infection and was absent so often that it angered Fox enough to actually fire her and file a lawsuit. The studio became even more infuriated when Marilyn accepted an invitation to sing "Happy Birthday" to President Kennedy in Washington instead of continuing work on the film.

In a matter of weeks, Marilyn was rehired by Fox, but her downhill spiral continued. She drank heavily and took pills to fall asleep and pills to wake up. Everything came to a head on the evening of Saturday, August 4, 1962. Alone on a Saturday night, the greatest yet loneliest star in the world retired to her bedroom and, within hours, was dead of an overdose. Whether by her own hand, by an accident, or, as some have suggested, by the hands of others, an American legend was gone.

Although Marilyn Monroe was with us for only a brief moment, she left such an indelible impression on the world that she will be remembered for an eternity.

THE BEGINNING
COLLECTOR

Nearly all of us have collected something in our lifetime. Remember that baseball card or stamp collection you had as a child? Sooner or later such collections got tucked away in the attic, sold in a rummage sale, or simply (and sadly) tossed in the trash. It really takes a special sort of person to be a collector. You might say you have to be bitten by the "collecting bug."

Quite often, collections are started on a very small scale and at a slow pace. There are, of course, exceptions to this rule. Some people collect for monetary reasons exclusively—for investment purposes. There is certainly nothing wrong with collecting for investment purposes, and it makes great sense from a business standpoint. However, a true dyed-in-the-wool collector is one who cares little about the investment potential but instead derives an extreme amount of pleasure from the pursuit of collecting itself.

I tend to fall somewhere in the middle. There is the businessman in me who really cares about the long-term investment potential of my collection. However, I also derive great pleasure from my Marilyn collection; to me, that is the true meaning of collecting.

I began my Marilyn collection at a snail's pace in the early 1980s. My first purchases were a framed photo purchased at Kmart and a couple books that had just been published on Marilyn. After spying the *Life* magazine article on Marilyn collector George Zeno in the October 1981 issue, which featured a two-page spread on George's wall of Marilyn magazine covers, I was hooked! From then on I hunted at a more feverish pace for vintage Monroe items, primarily magazine covers.

My first finds were at local auctions, garage sales, and antique shops. They consisted mainly of Marilyn's 1950s and 60s magazine cover appearances on *Life* and *Look* magazines. I was soon extracting from the classified ads of collecting-related periodicals the names and addresses of people who dealt in old magazines or Hollywood memorabilia in general. From here my collection really took off via mail order. The sky was the limit, and I soon found myself dealing with foreign sellers and trading with foreign collectors who had also advertised in U.S. collecting periodicals. A list of such periodicals can be found in the last chapter of this book.

It's best to stick to a budget as closely as you can when amassing your collection. It's very easy and tempting to purchase every item that comes your way. Set some realistic goals and stick to them. Perhaps you'll wish to specialize in movie posters, books, or magazine covers. Stay focused, whatever your collecting objective may be, and you'll be just fine. Consider such things as how much space you have to store or display your collection effectively and safely. Visit your library. Surf the Internet! Read up and ask as many questions as you can from experienced collectors. The better informed you are from the start, the better your entire collecting experience will be. Most important of all, enjoy yourself along the way!

Storing Your Marilyn Paper Collectibles

After going to the trouble of hunting down a valuable and fragile Marilyn paper collectible, it is a very good idea to take some precautions to preserve it. One good rule of thumb is to never store magazines in deep stacks, as this can crush their already fragile spines. Ideally, one should secure acid-free backing boards and plastic sleeves to store and encase your paper collectibles. It's best to wear a pair of plastic gloves when you handle an item, as this will prevent the damaging oils and acids from your skin from blemishing its surface.

Always store your paper collectibles in an environment that is fairly dry but not overly dry. Avoid placing the items in the direct path of sunlight, or near registers and water pipes that can also damage them. It only takes exposure to a half hour of sunlight a day to badly damage an item. Use a commonsense approach, and you'll be fine.

Some collectors prefer to display their items, which allows them to enjoy their collectibles every day. If you choose to frame the pieces for display, it's always a good idea to use acid-free matting material. Some folks choose to shrink-wrap their items, which is fine as long as they don't forget to punch the occasional hole in the plastic so that the article can "breathe."

Ideally, collectible paper items should be stored in a temperature-controlled room. Short of this, one can utilize an air-conditioning system during the humid summer months and a humidifier during the super-dry months of winter. It's not uncommon for humidity levels in a home to dive to 13 percent during the winter.

Insuring Your Collection

It's a great idea to insure your collectibles, because before you know it you may have a considerable investment. Usually you can just simply contact the company you have your household insurance with and they will accommodate you. If this fails, ask your insurance agent to recommend someone who will insure your collectibles. I have found that the cost is minimal and, in my case, it costs just forty cents to insure each one hundred dollars' worth of collectibles per year. Usually an inventory list is required by the insurance company, and it's a good idea to go a step further and make a videotape of all of the insured items as well. Place a copy of the tape with your insurance company and put one in your safe-deposit box at the bank.

Here's a cautionary example: I have a friend with a sizable Marilyn collection who woke up one morning to discover that a water pipe had ruptured in the bathroom situated directly above his collectibles. The result was disastrous. Luckily he had insurance and was reimbursed for his loss, although the loss of such cherished items was very upsetting. Don't procrastinate! Get that insurance today!

Restoring Paper Collectibles

The thought of restoring collectible paper items tends to intimidate most of us, and justifiably so. However, one should not be afraid to consider either sending a certain item to a professional restorer or doing a little home restoration on a piece that has minimal problems. Restoration of such items as movie posters, lobby cards, etc., can actually increase their value substantially. With the passing of time, the collecting community is becoming more comfortable with the idea of purchasing restored pieces for their collections. After all, there are only so many of these items, and there are more collectors born every day!

In the case of minor scratches and creases on the surface of your paper collectible, you can fill crevices with good results by using pastel chalks. Watercolors are another option, though it's best to let a professional artist or restorer use these. Quite often a local artist will do the work for a fee. One should never use oil-based products for the restoration of paper items since they permeate the paper and are nearly impossible to remove if one desires to do so at a later date. In addition, collectors of movie posters often choose to have their posters either linen backed or backed with special removable and acid-free paper to help reinforce the item. You can also do this with old calendars.

To perfect your technique, it is best to experiment first on old magazines or on other items of no value. It takes time to get the hang of it, but like anything, practice makes perfect! You'll be amazed at the wonderful results you can achieve and, at the same time, you'll be increasing the value of your collection.

Note: Please see the list of professional restorers later in this book (see page 316).

Buying from Foreign Countries

I have amassed nearly half of my paper collection by dealing with foreign dealers and collectors. The rules are not much different from those for ordering from U.S. sources.

Sources for foreign Monroe material can be found on the Internet or in trade publications such as those listed in the back of this guide (see pages 317–20). It generally takes one week for a letter to reach a foreign destination and/or to receive one. If the items are not priced in U.S. dollars, you can call your local bank to get the current exchange rate for the specific currency you are dealing with. You may also request that the seller quote you the items in U.S. dollars. The method of payment is usually an international money order, which you can secure from your post office. You make the money order out for the U.S. dollar amount due the seller, and the post office converts it to the specified currency. Sending cash through the mail is, of course, a definite no-no, but something that is done quite often nonetheless. Some foreign sellers are able to take personal checks, but there will be a conversion charge you will be asked to pay in most cases.

You must instruct the seller to ship the items either via surface or airmail. There is an intermediate service available from certain countries that costs more than the surface rate but less than the airmail rate. Surface mail will take from one and one-half to three months, while airmail will take about one week. The price difference in postage is substantial, and you must decide which way you want to go. Instruct the shipper to sandwich the flat-paper items between two pieces of stiff cardboard and otherwise pack well, and you'll receive your precious collectibles in good shape.

Trading with Other Collectors

Just as sports card collectors do, collectors of Marilyn memorabilia often trade among themselves. This is usually done between friends who have established a rapport over a period of time. Trading is fun and a win-win situation for both parties involved, allowing them to trade duplicates in their collection for items they don't have. I have traded for years with many U.S. and foreign Marilyn collectors. Problems have only arisen when an item offered for trade is not fully and honestly described. It is best to make either a black-and-white or color copy of the item offered for trade, so that the other person involved has an accurate idea of the condition of at least the outside cover of the item. Be sure to describe any damage to the interior of the item, such as articles that have been clipped, or writing that is on the pages, or pages that are missing. Honesty is always the best policy, and for it you will be rewarded with many successful trades.

Mail-Order Buying

Without mail order, my collection would be tiny. It has opened doors that otherwise would have been closed and has given me access to exciting items the world over. After fifteen years of collecting, I have had only one bad experience in the hundreds of transactions I have made.

Certain precautions must, of course, be taken. When you first deal with a new person, you should purchase a lower-priced item on the list in order to get a feel for the kind of service the seller will give you. If the seller has a return policy, all the better. In fact, try to purchase only from those who are willing to provide this return policy, as it is a common courtesy. It's not a bad idea to request a photocopy of the item(s) you are interested in buying. It's also courteous to offer to pay for this service. Discuss who is going to pay for postage, especially if the items need to be returned. Explain to the seller that you want your merchandise to be insured and packaged very well. Insurance costs little and gives you peace of mind. Magazines should always be sandwiched between two pieces of stiff cardboard, and posters or calendars should be rolled and placed in mailing tubes. Fragile collectible items should be carefully wrapped in Bubble Wrap with thick layers of newspaper placed around them to avoid breakage. Don't allow a newspaper to come in direct contact with the collectible, however, since the newsprint can be transferred to the surface of your valuable item, tarnishing it.

It is a very good idea to pay with a credit card if you can. Some credit card companies do things such as reverse the charges on unsatisfactory purchases or offer a refund if you find lower prices elsewhere. Call your credit card issuer and ask what their policy is in this area. If the items are paid for with a personal check, the seller may opt to wait a few weeks before shipping the item to you to be sure that your check clears. Money orders or transfers will allow the seller to expedite your shipment.

Another good idea is to keep a record of your phone calls and correspondence regarding the order, so in the case of any questions or discrepancies, you can refer back to your notes to clear up any confusion.

If you are answering someone's ad, be aware of the time difference when calling. If you write, it's common courtesy to include a self-addressed stamped envelope (SASE). These rules also apply to any dealings over the Internet. If these tips are followed, you will greatly reduce the risk of having a bad experience with mail order.

MAGAZINES

Marilyn Monroe easily could be called the original cover girl. Her very appearance on a magazine cover insured a considerable increase in issue sales. Of course, this was true only after she had attained superstar status around 1952. Prior to this time she had graced the covers of many U.S. and foreign magazines as simply just another pretty model.

Marilyn began her career as a model in 1945 at the tender age of nineteen. She learned early on how to best use makeup, and would later be a photographer's dream come true. She took great pride in applying most of her own makeup. Fox studio photographer Frank Powolny once said of her, "She works fast, has her own ideas. She's good for twenty poses an hour."

Marilyn's first cover appearance (although not solo) was on the January 1946 issue of *Douglas Airview*, an in-house publication put out by Douglas Airlines. In late 1945, Norma Jean posed for photographer Larry Kronquist in one of her first paid modeling jobs, showing off the interior of Douglas's new DC-6 airplane. Marilyn's first solo cover appearance was on the April 26, 1946, issue of *Family Circle*, which was ironic considering the reputation she would later attain.

By this time, Marilyn had begun to appear on a number of foreign covers as well, often unidentified. Her early U.S. cover appearances tended to be on romance or men's types of publications. In some magazines, the more risqué photographs had to have clothing painted on in strategic areas in order to comply with censorship laws. Marilyn was really ahead of her time and continuously taunted the censors, more than three decades before Madonna was even heard of!

Marilyn's magazine cover appearances are some of the most popular Monroe collectibles, with some fetching prices in the hundreds of dollars. These appearances number well over one thousand to date, and she continues to grace covers in nearly every country in the world, over thirty-six years after her death.

In general, magazines with collectible Monroe covers come in four sizes: pocket (4 × 6"), digest (5½ × 7½"), standard (8½ × 11"), and large (10½ × 14"). In most cases, size makes little difference when determining the value of the magazines. The covers most sought after by collectors are those in which Marilyn occupies the entire cover.

Descriptions of Magazine Grades

MINT
Never used. Just as it came from the printer, regardless of its age. Appears to be new.

NEAR MINT
Looks perfect at a glance. Only minor imperfections evident in the form of tiny tears, corner creases, or spine stresses.

VERY FINE
An excellent copy. Minimal surface wear is evident. Staples may show discoloring through paper. Spine may show stress lines.

FINE
An above average issue with minor but noticeable cover wear. Some discoloring at staples. Minor wear at staples and spine, but not serious. Corner creases evident. Multiple creasing will drop it a grade. Cover may be slightly loose.

VERY GOOD
General wear evident. Staples may be rusty. A store stamp or name may be written on cover. Pages may be a bit brittle. A small amount of chipping may be evident, or a small piece of a corner may be torn. Cover may be stained, spine split, cover creased and slightly soiled. Minor tape repair may be noted.

GOOD
Below average copy. Numerous creases; light soiling and staining. Cover may be detached and have both small and large tears. Spine

may be split. Pages may be yellowed and a little brittle as well as displaying various areas of chipping.

FAIR

Complete issue but with a few pages missing, writing on cover, chunks missing. Cover may be detached and have tape repairs. A good reading copy. Pages brittle and also yellowed with age.

POOR

Much of the cover may be missing, as well as several pages. Heavily soiled with brittle pages. Good reading or research copy. Good copy to clip ads from.

U.S. COVER APPEARANCES

Year	Title	Date	Vol./No.	Description	Value
1946	*Douglas Airview*	1/46	v. XIII, n. 1	Norma Jean's first cover	$400–600
1946	*Laff*	6/46	v. 7, n. 3	Her third cover—given credit as Norma Jean Dougherty	$250–350
1946	*Laff*	8/46	v. 7, n. 5	Fourth major cover—given credit as "Jean Norman"	$250–350
1946	*Pageant*	6/46	v. 2, n. 5	An André de Dienes shot on this digest issue	$150–250

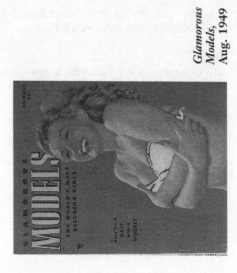

Glamorous Models, Aug. 1949

Douglas Airview, Jan. 1946

Year	Title	Date	Vol./No.	Description	Value
1946	Salute	8/46	v. 1, n. 4	A morale boosting issue for the soldiers serving in WWII	$300-400
1946	Family Circle	4/26/46	v. 28, n. 17	Norma Jean as a cute farmgirl	$250-350
1946	U.S. Camera	5/46	v. 1X, n. 4	Norma Jean on ¼ of the cover	$100-175
1947	Laff	1/47	v. 7, n. 10	Given credit as Norma Jean Dougherty	$250-350
1947	Laff	9/47	v. 8, n. 6	Introduced as Marilyn Monroe	$250-350
1947	Parade	2/16/47		Delivered with the Sunday newspaper	$250-350
1947	Personal Romances	6/47	v. 14, n. 2	Pictured in a wedding gown	$300-400
1947	Personal Romances	7/47	v. 14, n. 3	Pictured as a cute sailor girl	$300-400
1947	True Experiences	9/47		At the steering wheel of a boat	$400-600
1949	Film Humor	Spring, 49	v. 1, n. 4	As one of four swimsuit models	$50-75
1949	Foto-Parade	8/49	v. 1, n. 1	Classic cheesecake in a striped bikini	$150-250
1949	Hit!	9/49	v. 6, n. 6	In a yellow bikini Marilyn wore often	$150-250
1949	Glamorous Models	8/49	v. IV, n. 3	In a white bikini top	$150-275
1949	So-Rite Fall Fashions	Fall, 49		A catalog cover appearance	$400-600
1949	Sunday News	8/14/49		Stepping out of a pool in a green suit	$150-250
1949	Teen-Age Diary Secrets	10/49	v. 1, n. 6	In a red sweater on this comic book	$400-600
1950	Chicago Tribune	8/6/50		With long red hair and black lace gloves	$200-300
1950	Gala	May/June 1950	v. 1, n. 1	Posing with a polka-dot umbrella	$125-200
1950	Glance	5/50	v. 3, n. 1	A vivid cover, sitting on a diving board	$250-350
1950	Laff	2/50	v. 10, n. 11	Curled up with a powder puff and high heels	$150-225

Year	Title	Date	Vol./No.	Description	Value
1950	Man to Man	Feb./Mar. 1950	v. 1, n. 2	Posed in a lacy top with a telephone	$100–150
1950	True Experiences	5/50	v. 48, n. 6	With shorter bobbed hair	$125–225
1951	Focus (pocket)	12/51	v. 1, n. 5	Playing on the rocks in a swimsuit	$40–60
1951	People Today (pocket)	2/13/51	v. 2, n. 4	Publicity photo from All About Eve	$40–60
1951	Pittsburgh Press Roto Magazine	7/1/51		A full-blown glamour shot with hair up	$100–200
1951	Quick (pocket)	11/19/51	v. 5, n. 21	Cute cover with a comparison to Jean Harlow	$40–60
1951	True Romance	9/51	v. 54, n. 1	In a pink scarf and yellow sweater	$125–225
1951	True Story	11/51	v. 65, n. 4	With very short hair in a yellow turtleneck	$100–150
1951	Your Money Maker	9/51		In a two-piece striped bathing suit	$200–300
1952	Art Photography	3/52	v. 3, n. 7	A blue-tint cover, playing in the snow	$75–125
1952	Chicago Tribune Grafic	5/25/52		A sultry photo by Ernest Bachrach	$100–200
1952	Chicago Tribune Grafic	10/12/52		With a blue satin halter top	$100–200
1952	Down Beat	9/10/52	v. 19, n. 18	With Ray Anthony in a candid pose	$50–100
1952	Eye (digest)	11/52	v. 2, n. 8	Sitting on a diving board in a gold bikini	$50–80
1952	Focus (pocket)	9/52	v. 2, n. 8	In a gold bikini top	$50–80
1952	Gold Coast News Magazine	10/15/52	v. 3, n. 43	Published only in Florida	$80–120
1952	I Confess	9/52		A glamour shot in a black strapless dress	$100–175
1952	Look	9/9/52	v. 16, n. 19	As a cheerleader	$60–80

Year	Title	Date	Vol./No.	Description	Value
1952	Life	4/7/52	v. 32, n. 14	A classic image taken by Philippe Halsman	$60-80
1952	Movie Fan	12/52	v. 7, n. 3	In the red dress from *Niagara*	$100-150
1952	Movieland	7/52	v. 10, n. 6	In a blue satin halter top	$80-125
1952	Movieland	10/52	v. 10, n. 9	Curled up in a yellow bikini	$80-125
1952	Movie Life	11/52	v. 15, n. 12	In a red negligee	$75-100
1952	Movie Spotlight	10/52	v. 3, n. 6	Glamour shot in a brown fur	$75-100
1952	Movie Pin-ups	3/52	v. 1, n. 2	Sitting, wearing a bikini	$75-100
1952	Movie Pix	10/52	v. 3, n. 6	Classic Monroe: open mouth, half-mast eyes	$75-125
1952	Music Views (pocket)	10/52	v. 4, n. 13	With Ray Anthony	$40-60
1952	People Today (pocket)	6/18/52	v. 5, n. 12	In a white bikini on a ladder	$40-60
1952	People Today (pocket)	12/3/52	v. 23, n. 1	A b/w portrait holding a cigarette	$40-60
1952	Pic	2/52		A glamour pose looking up at the camera	$75-125
1952	Picture Roto Magazine	7/27/52	v. 56, n. 10	A sultry pose with reflection	$125-200
1952	Screenland	8/52		An *Asphalt Jungle*–era photograph	$75-125
1952	Ray Anthony & Co.	1952		Posing cheek to cheek with Ray	$50-75
1952	Scope	11/52	v. 1, n. 1	A long-haired cheesecake shot	$100-200
1952	See	7/52	v. 11, n. 4	With short red hair	$100-175
1952	Screen Fan	12/52	v. 1, n. 2	In a strapless black gown and earrings	$75-125
1952	Silver Screen	2/52	v. 22, n. 4	A well-known shot with jewels and a fur	$75-125
1952	Sir!	12/52	v. 8, n. 3	A young Norma Jean on a green barrel	$75-125
1952	Sunday News (N.Y.)	11/30/52		In a red dress before green drapery	$100-175
1952	Sunday Mirror (N.Y.)	9/7/52		A lovely dual image with a mirror	$125-250
1952	TV Forecast (digest)	10/4/52	v. 5, n. 23	A pre–*TV Guide* publication	$100-175

Year	Title	Date	Vol./No.	Description	Value
1952	*Vue* (digest)	9/52	v. 3, n. 2	Leaning back in a yellow swimsuit	$50–80
1953	*Bako News* (digest)	July/Aug. 1953	v. 13, n. 3	Sent to employees of Bausch & Lomb	$100–200
1953	*Brief* (digest)	12/53	v. 1, n. 8	In a black lacy negligee	$50–80
1953	*Cheesecake*	1953		Reclining in a yellow halter bikini	$75–125
1953	*Cue*	6/27/53		A shared cover with Jane Russell	$50–80
1953	*Cosmopolitan*	5/53	v. 134, n. 5	Smiling in a long, black lace negligee	$75–125
1953	*Eye* (digest)	2/53	v. 3, n. 2	In pink long johns warming by a fire	$40–80

Vue, Aug. 1952

Screen Fan, Dec. 1952.

Year	Title	Date	Vol./No.	Description	Value
1953	Eye (digest)	8/53	v. 13, n. 8	A wraparound cover in a yellow bikini	$40–80
1953	Films In Review (digest)	4/53	v. IV, n. 4	A b/w cover featuring Monroe reading	$100–150
1953	Focus (pocket)	3/53	v. 3, n. 3	A b/w cheesecake shot by Beauchamp	$40–60
1953	Focus (pocket)	5/53	v. 3, n. 5	Wearing a bow necklace	$40–60
1953	Hit Parader	1/53		Practicing the typical allure	$30–50
1953	I Confess	5/53	v. 3, n. 2	A young, long-haired early Marilyn	$100–150
1953	Laff	1/53	v. 14, n. 5	Sitting on the beach in a red suit	$75–125
1953	Leisure Time	12/20/53		With Jane Russell in *Gentlemen Prefer Blondes*	$75–125
1953	Life	5/25/53	v. 34, n. 21	With Jane Russell in *Blondes*	$40–65
1953	Look	6/30/53	v. 17, n. 13	With Lauren Bacall and Betty Grable	$75–125
1953	Look	11/17/53	v. 17, n. 23	In a gray sweater holding a cigarette	$75–125
1953	Marilyn Monroe's Beauty Secrets (digest)			B/w cover in a lamé halter dress	$100–300
1953	Marilyn Monroe Pin-Ups	1953		There are 2 versions of this issue with different inside photos. One was banned.	$100–200
1953	Milwaukee Journal (Sunday insert)	9/6/53		Glamorous image in a white fur	$100–200
1953	Modern Man	11/53	v. 3, n. 5–29	A de Dienes image, playing on the beach	$75–95
1953	Modern Screen	10/53	v. 47, n. 5	Pretty over the shoulder in a white fur	$75–100
1953	Motion Picture & TV Magazine	1/53	v. LXXXIV, n. 6	From *Niagara* in a white fur-trim robe	$75–100

Year	Title	Date	Vol./No.	Description	Value
1953	Motion Picture & TV Magazine	11/53	v. LXXXVI, n. 4	In a yellow suit sitting on a wire table	$75–100
1953	Motor World	6/19/53	v. 4, n. 13	A b/w shot atop a car	$100–150
1953	Movieland	1/53	v. 10, n. 12	Glamorous in black gloves and up-swept hair	$100–150
1953	Movieland	4/53	v. 11, n. 3	Sitting on the floor in a purple outfit	$100–150
1953	Movieland	10/53	v. 11, n. 9	Against a stool in a red negligee	$75–125
1953	Movie Life	12/53	v. 17, n. 1	In a white dress and diamond jewelry	$75–125
1953	3-D Movie Magazine	9/53		Inside photos printed in 3D; includes glasses	$75–125
1953	Movie Pix	4/53	v. 4, n. 3	Hand on her hip in a red outfit	$75–125
1953	Movie Pix	12/53	v. 5, n. 1	With Lauren Bacall and Betty Grable	$75–125
1953	Movies	2/53	v. 2, n. 6	In the red Niagara dress	$75–125
1953	Movie Stars Parade	10/53	v.13, n. 11	A still from Blondes	$75–125
1953	Movie World	9/53	v. 4, n. 5	A very short-haired MM in a bow necklace	$75–125
1953	People Today (pocket)	7/29/53	v. 7, n. 2	In a white fringe bikini, cross-legged on floor	$40–60
1953	People Today (pocket)	12/2/53	v. 7, n. 11	Hugging a white pillar in a red swimsuit	$40–60
1953	Photo (digest)	7/53	v. 2, n. 7	Sitting on her feet in a yellow bikini	$60–80
1953	Photoplay	2/53	v. 43, n. 2	In a black dress with a white collar	$75–125
1953	Photoplay	12/53	v.53, n. 2	In a white fur with a striped background	$75–125
1953	Photoplay Pin-ups		n. 4	Holding a mink stole in the air	$75–125

Year	Title	Date	Vol./No.	Description	Value
1953	*Pic*	5/53	v. 24, n. 3	In a black halter-style one-piece swimsuit	$75–125
1953	*Picture Scope*	7/53	v. 1, n. 5	Wearing one of the gowns from *Blondes*	$75–125
1953	*Playboy*	12/53	v. 1, n. 1	The first issue. MM is the centerfold.	$1000–2000
1953	*Pocket Pin-ups* (pocket)	1953		A cute b/w image in a short nightie	$50–100
1953	*Prevue* (pocket)	1/53	v. 2, n. 1	A b/w candid in the *Niagara* dress	$40–60

People Today,
Dec. 2, 1953

I Confess,
May 1953

Year	Title	Date	Vol./No.	Description	Value
1953	Redbook	3/53	v. 100, n. 5	Wearing a sequined cocktail dress	$75–125
1953	Screen Annual	1953		In one of the *Blondes* musical number costumes	$75–125
1953	Screen Fan	6/53	v. 1, n. 6	In a dinner jacket from *Blondes*	$75–125
1953	Screen Life	11/53	v. 6, n. 5	In a red suit with glass shoes and an umbrella	$75–125
1953	Screen Stars	2/53	v. 11, n. 1	In a low-cut dress and emerald earrings	$75–125
1953	Screen World	12/53	v. 1, n. 2	In the red *Blondes* dress	$75–125
1953	See	11/53	v. 12, n. 6	Lovely in the famous gold lamé gown	$75–125
1953	Show (pocket)	3/53	v. 1, n. 7	In a black nightie on a giant pillow	$40–60
1953	Silver Screen	10/53	v. 23, n. 12	One of the famous photos in a white fur	$75–125
1953	Song Hits	11/53	v. 17, n. 4	An earlier glamour image	$55–100
1953	3-D Star Pin-Ups	12/53	v. 1, n. 1	In a red swimsuit hugging a column	$100–150
1953	Sunday News (N.Y.)	2/15/53		With Jane Russell in a publicity pose	$100–200
1953	Sweet Hearts (comic)	1/53	n. 119	Embracing Richard Widmark	$100–200
1953	Tab (digest)	9/53		In a pink one-piece swimsuit	$60–80
1953	Tele-Views	9/53		A 1952 glamour shot	$80–110
1953	Tempo (pocket)	8/31/53	v. 1, n. 13	A b/w image with an inset of Joe DiMaggio	$40–60
1953	That Girl Marilyn! (pocket)	1953		Entire issue devoted to MM	$50–100
1953	The American News	5/53	v. 35, n. 4	A typical glamour photo	$125–250
1953	The Wiesbaden Shopping Guide	1/53		In a one-piece bathing suit	$125–175
1953	TV and Movie Screen	11/53	v. 1, n. 1	A typical sexy cover	$75–125

Year	Title	Date	Vol./No.	Description	Value
1953	*TV Digest*	3/21/53		A b/w pose on this Pittsburgh TV guide	$100–130
1953	*TV Guide* (digest)	Jan 23–29, 1953	v. VI, n. 4	A portrait from *Niagara* and an article on censors	$350–600
1953	*TV Starland*	11/53	v. 1, n. 2	Dancing with Walter Winchell	$75–125
1953	*TV Today*	5/8/53; 7/17/53; 11/13/53		Detroit's version of *TV Guide*	$100–150 each
1953	*Who's Who in Hollywood 1953*	1953	v. 1, n. 8	In a clinging lavender gown	$75–125
1953	*Why* (digest)	6/53	v. 1, n. 16	A b/w image and sex symbol article	$60–80
1954	*Art Photography*	10/54	v. 6, n. 4–64	Standing atop a globe	$75–100
1954	*Bold* (pocket)	1/54	v. 1, n. 1	A b/w image with Joe DiMaggio	$40–60
1954	*Film Stars Album* Winter	1953–4	v. 1, n. 1	A glamour shot with shorter hair	$75–125
1954	*Focus* (pocket)	6/54	v. 4, n. 7	In the *Niagara* dress with gold hoop earrings	$40–60
1954	*Hollywood Yearbook 1954*	1954	v. 1, n. 5	In a red dress and matching earrings	$75–100
1954	*Marilyn* (by Sidney Skolsky)	1954		Entire issue devoted to MM	$100–200
1954	*Miami Daily News*	5/7/54		Delivered with the Sunday newspaper.	$125–200
1954	*Modern Photography*	8/54	v. 18, n. 8	Sitting on her feet in a yellow bikini	$75–125
1954	*Modern Screen*	3/54	v. 48, n. 4	In a ruffled blouse with longer hair	$75–125
1954	*Modern Screen*	9/54	v. 48, n. 10	Holding up diamonds from *Blondes*	$75–125
1954	*Movie Fan*	7/54	v. 9, n. 4	A glamour image, wearing pearls	$75–125

Year	Title	Date	Vol./No.	Description	Value
1954	Movieland's Annual 1954	1954		In a one-strap fuschia gown	$75–125
1954	Movieland	2/54	v. 12, n. 2	In a rhinestone-studded black dress	$75–125
1954	Movieland	11/54	v. 12, n. 11	Smiling in the one-strap fuschia dress	$75–125
1954	Movie Life	8/54	v. 17, n. 9	Lowering one bathing suit strap	$75–125
1954	Movie Life Yearbook	1954		A b/w image in a white sweater	$75–100
1954	Movies	6/54	v. 3, n. 2	A publicity shot from *How to Marry a Millionaire*	$75–125
1954	Movie Spotlight	10/54	v. 5, n. 5	A wide-eyed Monroe with long earrings	$75–125
1954	Movie Stars Parade	3/54	v. 14, n. 4	In a gold lamé gown, tinted silver	$75–125
1954	Movie Stars Parade	9/54	v. 15, n. 1	Wearing a sexy black lace gown	$75–125
1954	Movie Time	2/54	v. 2, n. 6	Showing off a diamond necklace	$75–125
1954	Movie World	5/54	v. 5, n. 3	In a dark one-piece bathing suit	$75–125
1954	Night & Day	8/54	v. 6, n. 8	The first star to have a cover alone	$100–150
1954	Now (digest)	1/54	v. 1, n. 2	A candid photo with Joe DiMaggio at a restaurant	$40–60
1954	Pic	6/54	v. 25, n. 5	Singing to the troops in Korea	$75–125
1954	Picture Life (pocket)	4/54	v. 1, n. 3	Posing in a pair of red long johns	$40–60
1954	Prevue (pocket)	1/54	v. 4, n. 1	A close-up wearing emerald earrings	$40–60
1954	Roto Sunday Magazine	3/28/54		Wearing a corset, delivered with the paper	$100–200
1954	Screen Annual 1954	1954		Holding up a polka-dot scarf	$75–125
1954	Screen Stars	11/54	v. 12, n. 5	A pretty, close-up portrait	$75–125
1954	Screen Stories	11/54	v. 52, n. 5	In a white costume from *Monkey Business*	$75–100
1954	See	11/54	v. 13, n. 6	In a corset with fishnet stockings	$75–125

Year	Title	Date	Vol./No.	Description	Value
1954	Silver Screen	4/54	v. 24, n. 6	Sitting in a red lacy negligee	$75–125
1954	Sir!	4/54	v. 11, n. 7	In a red dress with green drapery behind	$75–125
1954	Song Fan	7/54	v. 1, n. 3	With Robert Mitchum in *River of No Return*	$50–75
1954	3-D Hollywood Pin-Ups	1/54		Cheesecake pose in a one-piece suit	$100–140
1954	Sunday Mirror (N.Y.)	3/21/54		Weekend Sunday section; sexy portrait	$125–200
1954	Tempo (pocket)	3/8/54	v. 2, n. 10	In a swimsuit, posed along jagged rocks	$40–60
1954	Tempo (pocket)	9/6/54	v. 3, n. 9	Almost full-body photo in red lace	$40–60
1954	Tempo (pocket)	11/8/54	v. 3, n. 19	A vivid image in the red *Niagara* dress	$40–60
1954–55	The Dynamo	1954–55		A Fox Studio Publication	$100–140
1954	The Hotel Dixie Host	12/18/54		A digest-sized weekly guide to New York	$50–100
1955	Behind the Scene (pocket)	7/55	v. 1, n. 8	Wearing a diamond necklace	$40–60
1955	Bold (pocket)	1/55	v. 2, n. 1	Sitting Indian-style in a white bikini	$40–60
1955	Boston Sunday Herald	1/23/55		Weekend Sunday section; sitting in a chair	$100–200
1955	Cabaret	7/55	v. 1, n. 3	B/w image, sitting in a bubble bath	$50–75
1955	Cartoon Cuties (digest)	9/55	n. 2	A young glamour shot from *Love Happy*	$75–125
1955	Down Beat	7/27/55		In the blowing white dress from *The Seven-Year Itch*	$50–75

Year	Title	Date	Vol./No.	Description	Value
1955	*Empire*	1955		Sunday Section with a candid from *Bus Stop*	$100–120
1955	*Focus* (pocket)	1/55	v. 5, n. 1	Sitting on a step in a nightie	$40–60
1955	*Focus* (pocket)	11/55	v. 5, n. 1	The classic gold lamé image	$40–60
1955	*He* (pocket)	2/55	v. 2, n. 3	Cute in a corset from *River*	$40–60
1955	*Inside Hollywood Annual*	1955	v. 1, n. 1	Coyly looking over her shoulder	$75–125
1955	*Modern Man*	3/55	v. 4, n. 9–45	Puckering up for the camera	$75–100
1955	*Modern Man*	5/55	v. 6, n. 6	With white skirt blowing up	$75–125
1955	*Modern Screen*	6/55	v. 49, n. 7	Modeling a black fur	$75–100
1955	*Modern Screen*	10/55	v. 49, n. 11	Wearing a white terry cloth robe	$75–100
1955	*Modern Screen Pin-Ups*	1955		Slipping a fur stole behind her back	$75–125
1955	*Movieland*	6/55	v. 13, n. 5	Reclining in a red chair	$75–125
1955	*Movieland*	12/55	v. 13, n. 12	Three images in a sweater	$75–125
1955	*Movie Life*	4/55	v. 18, n. 5	Looking over her shoulder	$75–100
1955	*Movie Play*	11/55	v. 9, n. 6	In the red *Niagara* dress	$75–125
1955	*Movies*	12/55		Sharing a cover with Kim Novak	$40–60
1955	*Movie Secrets*	2/55	v. 1, n. 1	In a red costume from *Blondes*	$75–125
1955	*Movie Stars Parade*	9/55	v. 15, n. 10	In a white dress with her arms up	$75–125
1955	*Movie World*	6/55	v. 6, n. 3	In her "Heatwave" costume from *Business*	$75–125
1955	*Parts Pups*	5/55		Put out by Napa Parts, riding an elephant	$100–175
1955	*Pic* (digest)	9/55	v. 26, n. 4	In her elephant-riding costume	$40–65
1955	*Picture Life* (pocket)	2/55	v. 2, n. 1	Holding a red cover-up to her side	$40–60

Year	Title	Date	Vol./No.	Description	Value
1955	Picture Scope (digest)	5/55	v. 3, n. 4	In a red negligee with a navy blue background	$50–75
1955	Picture Week (pocket)	2/26/55	v. 1, n. 1	A cute b/w image in a blouse and a smile	$40–60
1955	Picture Week (pocket)	6/4/55	v. 1, n. 14	Riding an elephant at Madison Square Garden	$40–60
1955	Picture Week (pocket)	7/16/55	v. 1, n. 17	In the tiger-stripe dress from *Itch*	$40–60
1955	Pin-ups Past and Present	1955	v. 1, n. 1	A b/w image on this historical look at sex symbols	$50–100
1955	Redbook	7/55	v. 105, n. 3	A close-up in the bathrobe from *Itch*	$75–125
1955	Screen Annual Pin-Ups	1955		Sitting on steps in a black nightie	$75–100
1955	Screen Hits Annual	1955		A full-length cheesecake pose in red lace	$40–60
1955	Screen Life	3/55	v. 8, n. 1	Sitting on a wire table in a yellow suit	$75–125
1955	Screen Stars	7/55	v. 13, n. 4	In a tight red clinging gown	$75–125
1955	Screen Stories	7/55	v. 54, n. 1	*Itch* is depicted	$45–65
1955	See	7/55	v. 14, n. 4	In a black one-piece swimsuit	$75–125
1955	Tab (digest)	8/55	v. 5, n. 3	In the red *Niagara* dress and earrings	$60–80
1955	Tempo (pocket)	2/14/55	v. 4, n. 7	Posing inside a large heart	$40–60
1955	Tempo (pocket)	7/4/55	v. 5, n. 1	Posing with a giant firecracker	$40–60
1955	Tempo (pocket)	11/1/55	v. 5, n. 12	Cute in a yellow swimsuit	$40–60
1955	Tempo (pocket)	12/27/55	v. 5, n. 16	Surrounded by wrapped gifts at her feet	$40–60
1955	The American Weekly	9/25/55		In black gloves and fur; newspaper section	$100–200

Year	Title	Date	Vol./No.	Description	Value
1955	*The Marilyn Monroe Story* (pocket)		n. 3	Entire issue is devoted to her; MM in red	$50–100
1955	*The National Police Gazette*	2/55	v. 160, n. 9	With skirt blowing up from *Itcb*	$50–75
1955	*True Romance*	10/55	v. 61, n. 2	A young Marilyn in a yellow sweater	$100–150
1955	*TV Today* (digest)	8/27/55		Detroit-based television guide	$100–125
1955	*US Camera*	7/55	v. XVIII, n. 7	Reclining in a leather chair from *Itcb*	$50–75
1955	*Vue* (digest)	1/55	v. 6, n. 6	Wearing a tight red gown	$60–80

Guns, July 1956

Marilyn by Sidney Skolsky, 1954

Year	Title	Date	Vol./No.	Description	Value
1955	Who's Who in Hollywood	1955	v. 1, n. 10	A large laughing portrait from *Itch*	$60–85
1956	Films In Review (digest)	10/56	v. VII, n. 8	A cover from *Bus Stop*	$40–60
1956	Film Life	6/56	v. 1, n. 5	A lovely pose in a white strap dress	$75–125
1956	Guns	7/56	v. 2, n. 7–19	Being taught how to shoot a gun	$75–125
1956	Look	5/29/56	v. 20, n. 11	Curled up in bed with a sheet	$50–80
1956	Modern Man	6/56	v. V, n. 12–60	At a table wearing a red velvet dress	$75–100
1956	Modern Screen	11/56	v. 50, n. 11	Wearing a black fur and a serious face	$75–100
1956	Movie Life	4/56	v. 19, n. 5	In a black dress decorated with beads	$75–100
1956	Movie Stars Parade	2/56	v. 16, n. 3	A close-up, smiling	$75–100
1956	Photoplay	10/56	v. 50, n. 4	Several images in her *Bus Stop* costume	$75–100
1956	Picture Digest (digest)	2/56	v. 29, n. 4	Warming by a fireplace in long johns	$60–80
1956	Picture Week (pocket)	6/5/56	v. 2, n. 8	A red-haired MM in a black fur	$40–60
1956	Rave	8/56	v. 11, n. 5	Glamour image; 28 pages on her	$60–80
1956	Screen Stars	7/56	v. 14, n. 4	Wearing a tight red dress	$75–125
1956	Sir!	10/56	v. 13, n. 10	The famous image in the gold lamé dress	$75–125
1956	Tab (digest)	12/56	v. 6, n. 5	Sitting in a two-piece yellow suit	$60–80
1956	The Male Point of View (pocket)	2/56	v. 2, n. 4	Reclining in a skimpy yellow bikini	$40–60
1956	The National Police Gazette	3/56	v. 161, n. 3	In a button-decorated bikini top	$75–100
1956	The Press Photographer	1956		An *Itch* cover	$100–200

Year	Title	Date	Vol./No.	Description	Value
1956	*Time*	5/14/56	v. LXVII, n. 20	An absolutely lovely artwork portrait	$75–125
1957	*Filmland*	12/57	v. 7, n. 6	In the tiger dress from *Itch*	$75–125
1957	*Hollywood Screen Parade*	3/57		Showing off a diamond necklace	$50–75
1957	*Man to Man Annual*	Spring		Wearing a white terry bathrobe	$75–125
1957	*Movieland*	4/57	v. 15, n. 4	A pretty close-up from *Millionaire*	$75–125
1957	*Movie Screen Yearbook*	1957	n. 3	With bangs and big earrings	$60–90
1957	*Screen Stories*	7/57	v. 56, n. 7	A pretty, soft-looking image in stripes	$60–90
1957	*Sunday Mirror* (N.Y.)	6/22/57		Newspaper section, in a black-sequined gown	$100–200
1957	*The National Police Gazette*	10/57	v. CLXII, n. 10	A typical glamorous photograph	$50–85
1957	*True Romance*	1/57	v. 63, n. 5	In a red sweater and scarf	$75–125
1957	*True Strange*	8/57		Several artwork images	$50–75
1958	*Detective Cases*	7/58	v. 3, n. 4	Hugging a white pillar	$40–80
1958	*Inside Story*	4/58	v. 4, n. 4	Wearing a sexy lacy negligee	$40–65
1958	*Loco*	10/58		An artist's interpretation	$40–65
1958	*Movie Mirror*	5/58	v. 2, n. 7	Glamorous with her eyes half closed	$50–75
1958	*Parade*	12/7/58		Newspaper section; candid from *Some Like It Hot*	$75–100
1958	*Sunbathing Review*	Fall 1958		Nudist spiral-bound sepia cover; young MM	$75–125
1959	*Chicago Tribune Magazine*	11/17/59		Newspaper section; several images in a dress	$100–175

Year	Title	Date	Vol./No.	Description	Value
1959	Cosmopolitan	3/59	v. 146, n. 3	An illustration by John Whitcomb; all in white	$75–100
1959	Family Weekly	2/22/59		Newspaper section; posing in front of Niagara Falls	$100–150
1959	Inside Story	5/59		In her elephant-riding costume	$50–80
1959	Life	4/20/59	v. 46, n. 16	Playfully biting on diamonds	$40–60
1959	Life	11/9/59	v. 47, n. 19	Jumping in a black-sequined spangle dress	$40–60
1959	The National Enquirer	3/15–21/59	v. 33, n. 28	A b/w image on this early scandal issue	$75–100
1959	Pictorial and TV View	3/15/59		The subject of an artwork cover	$65–90
1959	The National Police Gazette	1/59	v. 164, n. 1	Looking over her shoulder and smiling	$50–75
1960	American Weekly	12/11/60		Newspaper section; with Clark Gable	$60–90
1960	Cosmopolitan	12/60	v. 149, n. 6	With Gable in *The Misfits*	$75–100
1960	Films in Review (digest)	10/60	v. XI, n. 8	In a scene from *Let's Make Love*	$30–40
1960	Inside Story	7/60	v. 6, n. 5	A revealing overhead cleavage photo	$30–55
1960	Life	8/15/60	v. 49, n. 7	A close-up with Yves Montand	$30–50
1960	Modern Screen	12/60	v. 54, n. 12	A tight close-up, wearing dark gloves	$45–60
1960	The Californian	8/19/60		A *Love* costume shot	$75–100
1960	The National Police Gazette	1/60	v. 165, n. 1	At the *Hot* premiere	$50–80
1960	This Week	8/20/60		From newspaper; with Yves Montand	$50–80

Year	Title	Date	Vol./No.	Description	Value
1960	This Week	12/11/60		From newspaper; wearing a red sweater	$50–80
1960	TV Life	10/60		Half cover in a black dress and gloves	$35–50
1960	TV and Movie Screen	9/60		In a white halter dress	$35–50
1961	Blast	1/61	v. 7, n. 10	A publicity photo from *Love*	$40–60
1961	Esquire	3/61	v. LV, n. 3	A painting of her in a *Misfits* costume	$40–60
1961	Family Weekly	2/26/61		From newspaper; from *The Misfits*	$50–80
1961	Hollywood Tattler	11/61		A sad-looking close-up portrait	$40–60
1961	Infinity	5/61		Costume fitting for riding the elephant	$75–125
1961	Modern Screen	10/61	v. 55, n. 10	On the floor with a tiger rug	$50–75
1961	Screen Stories	2/61	v. 60, n. 2	Wearing a bright orange blouse	$40–60
1961	Screen Stories	5/61	v. 60, n. 5	Wearing a black hair net in *The Misfits*	$40–60
1961	The National Police Gazette	5/61	v. 166, n. 5	A pretty close-up, wearing hoop earrings	$50–75
1962	Films in Review (digest)	10/62	v,. XIII, n. 8	A glamour image on this tribute cover	$25–45
1962	Life	6/22/62	v. 52, n. 25	In a blue terry bathrobe from *Something's Got to Give*	$40–60
1962	Life	8/17/62	v. 53, n. 7	A farewell in a beige fur hat from *Give*	$40–60
1962	Marilyn Monroe— Her Last Untold Secrets			Entire issue on her life and death	$75–125
1962	Marilyn Monroe— Her Tragic Life			Entire issue on her life and death	$75–125

Year	Title	Date	Vol./No.	Description	Value
1962	Marilyn's Life Story (by Dell)			Entire issue on her life and death	$75–125
1962	MM—The Complete Story of Her Life, Her Loves, and Her Death			Entire issue on her life and death	$75–125
1962	Modern Screen	11/62	v. 56, n. 50	A sad, downcast face from Give	$40–60
1962	Movieland and TV Time	11/62	v. 20, n. 5	In sequins at the 1961 Golden Globes	$50–75

Marilyn—Her
Tragic Life, 1962

Screen Stars, July
1956

Year	Title	Date	Vol./No.	Description	Value
1962	Silver Screen	12/62	v. 28, n. 8	A sad-looking memorial shot from *Love*	$40–60
1962	The National Police Gazette	10/62	v. 167, n. 9	Looking happy at the premiere of *Hot*	$40–60
1963	Films in Review (digest)	6–7/63	v. XIV, n. 6	A wardrobe shot from *Give*	$20–40
1963	Photoplay	1/63	v. 63, n. 6	Holding up a striped see-through scarf	$30–50
1964	Life	8/7/63	v. 57, n. 6	A head-and-shoulders portrait	$35–45
1964	This Week Magazine	4/12/63		Newspaper section; half-cover in hat	$35–45
1965	Fact	5–6/65		A smiling b/w portrait by Bert Stern	$35–45
1965	Ladies' Home Companion	1/65	v. 3, n. 2	A sad-looking face on this digest	$30–45
1965	Screen Legends	8/65	v. 1, n. 2	Marilyn and Paul Newman by an artist	$40–50
1966	Coronet (digest)	1/66	v. 4, n. 1	In a red costume from *Blondes*	$30–45
1968	Avant Garde	3/68	n. 2	An artsy Stern shot in sepia tones	$30–50
1968	Modern Photography	9/68		Biting a strand of pearls	$30–50
1969	The Blade Sunday Magazine	11/2/69		Newspaper section; half-cover in a fur	$30–40
1969	Detroit News Sunday Magazine	6/22/69		Newspaper section; *The Misfits* portrait	$40–60
1970	Hollywood Studio Magazine	9/70	v. 5, n. 5	Being fitted for a costume by Travilla	$25–35
1971	Pageant (digest)	3/71	v. 26, n. 9	A young Norma Jean in the wind	$30–50
1971	Screen Stories	9/71	v. 70, n. 10	The famous image in the white fur	$30–45
1972	Life	9/8/72	v. 73, n. 10	Reclining on pillows in a fancy slip	$30–40
1972	Ms	8/72	v. 1, n. 2	A glamorous Monroe face in a circle	$20–35

Year	Title	Date	Vol./No.	Description	Value
1972	Newsweek	10/16/72	v. LXXX, n. 16	A joyous MM in black sequins	$20–35
1973	Film Comment	5–6/73		The cast of *The Misfits* is featured	$20–30
1973	Hollywood Studio Magazine	8/73	v. 4	Holding up an eight ball	$25–35
1973	Interview	1973	n. 19	Wearing a white fluffy fur	$20–35
1973	Ladies Home Journal	7/73	v. XC, n. 7	A lovely portrait taken by Stern	$25–40
1973	Liberty	Fall 1973	v. 1, n. 10	Many images of her on an artwork cover	$25–35
1973	Parade	8/5/73		Newspaper section; in a beige fur hat	$25–45
1973	The Atlantic Monthly	8/73	v. 232, n. 2	A b/w photo by Milton Greene	$25–40
1973	Time	7/16/73	v. 102, n. 3	A created image of MM and Norman Mailer	$20–35
1973	Where It's At		v. 2, n. 8	A b/w pose from *Hot*	$25–40
1974	Sleazy Scandals		comic	An X-rated comic; art of *Golden Dreams*	$20–40
1975	Chicago Sun–Times Magazine—Midwest	8/17/75		Newspaper section; white dress blow-ing up	$20–30
1975	Films in Review (digest)	6–7/75	v. XXVI, n. 6	A publicity photo from *Eve*	$20–30
1975	Motion Picture	11/75	v. 64, n. 777	On the end of a sofa corner	$20–30
1975	Photoplay	9/75	v. 88, n. 3	Holding up a mink, surrounded by presents	$25–35
1976	Chicago Tribune Magazine	11/14/76		Newspaper section; in the gold lamé dress	$25–35
1976	Hollywood Studio Magazine	2/76		Nude in the *New Wrinkle* pose	$25–40
1976	In the Know	3/76	v. 2, n. 3	A beautiful portrait from *Give*	$20–30

Year	Title	Date	Vol./No.	Description	Value
1976	*The Velvet Light Trap*	Fall 1976	n. 16	A b/w profile in a glamorous lamé gown	$20–30
1977	*American Classic Screen*	11–12/77	v. 2, n. 2	An unflattering artist's rendition	$15–25
1977	*Film Collectors World*	9/1/77	n. 22	Tinted cover in a one-piece swimsuit	$15–20
1979	*Films In Review*	3/79	v. XXX, n. 3	A soft, pretty portrait from *Give*	$15–30
1979	*Marilyn Monroe* (by Bonomo)		n. 78	A tiny grocery store check-out issue	$15–25
1979	*The National Enquirer*	5/79		As the main subject on cover	$15–20
1979	*San Francisco Datebook*	2/11/79		Newspaper section; white skirt from *Itch*	$20–30
1980	*Celebrity Skin*			Artwork cover; cross-eyed in gold lamé	$15–25
1980	*San Francisco Datebook*	11/9–15/80		Newspaper section; *Niagara* portrait	$20–30
1980	*Screen Greats—Monroe*	1980	v. 2	Entire issue on her; in a corset from *River*	$20–30
1981	*After Dark*	9/81	v. 14, n. 3–4	A romantic windswept image in sequins	$20–30
1981	*San Francisco Datebook*	11/1/81		Newspaper section; MM on half the cover	$20–30
1981	*Hollywood Studio Magazine*	12/81	v.15, n. 4	With Jane Rusell in *Blondes*	$15–25
1981	*Life*	10/81	v. 4, n. 10	Leaning back in a turquoise swimsuit	$20–30
1981	*Sunday Life*	3/15/81		In a tinted glamour pose	$20–30
1982	*Collectibles Illustrated*	11–12/82	v. 1, n. 4	Leaning back in a turquoise swimsuit	$20–30
1982	*Film Comment*	9–10/82	v. 18, n. 5	Sultry in a black lacy dress	$20–30

Year	Title	Date	Vol./No.	Description	Value
1982	*Life*	8/82	v. 5, n. 8	A lovely 1962 portrait by Stern	$20–30
1982	*Sunday News Magazine* (N.Y.)	8/1/82		Newspaper section; holding a mirror	$20–30
1982	*The Globe*	11/23/82		Main star on this far-fetched issue	$15–20
1982	*The Newsday Magazine*	8/1/82		Newspaper section; artwork portrait	$15–20
1983	*Butterick Sewing World*	Winter	v. 15, n. 4	In a pretty ruffled off-the-shoulder top	$20–30
1983	*Entertainment N.Y.*	2/83		A typical glamour pose	$20–30
1983	*Human Digest* (digest)	1983		Wearing the one-strap *Millionaire* dress	$30–40
1983	*Films in Review* (digest)	8–9/83	v. XXXV, n. 7	A scene from *The Misfits* is featured.	$20–30
1984	*American Photographer*	7/84	v. XIII, n. 1	On a bicycle, portraying Lillian Russell	$20–30
1984	*San Francisco Datebook*	2/12/84		Newspaper section; white dress blowing up	$20–30
1985	*Crossfire* (comic)	6/85	n. 12	A fantasy artwork image of MM in bed	$20–30
1985	*Hollywood Studio Magazine*	8/85	v. 18, n. 8	A pretty portrait from *Millionaire*	$15–25
1985	*Hollywood Then & Now*	12/85	v. 18, n. 12	The common image in the white fur	$15–25
1985	*Horoscope*	3/85		A candid image in a white fur and a smile	$20–30
1985	*Picture Week*	10/14/85		A 1962 portrait taken by Stern	$15–25
1986	*Esquire*	3/86	v. 105, n. 3	In pearl-drop earrings and a white fur	$10–20

Year	Title	Date	Vol./No.	Description	Value
1986	Films in Review (digest)	5/86	v. XXXVII, n. 5	A scene from *Don't Bother to Knock*	$10–20
1986	Filthy Funnies (comic)	8/86		Appropriate artwork considering the title	$10–15
1986	National Examiner	3/25/86		A tabloid cover appearance	$10–15
1986	Nevada	12/86		A portrait of *The Misfits* cast, 1961	$15–20
1986	Picture Week	9/1/86		A young portrait of Norma Jean	$10–20
1986	The Sharper Image Catalog	7/86		A beautiful airbrush work of Norma Jean	$15–20
1987	Celebrity Focus	8/87	v. 1, n. 8	A sad-looking portrait from 1962	$10–20
1987	Gallery	9/87		Wearing the very well-known gold lamé	$10–20
1987	Hollywood Then & Now	8/87	v. 20, n. 8	A *Niagara* shot is on this tribute issue.	$10–20
1987	Michael's Thing Weekly	8/24/87	v. 17, n. 34	In a black spaghetti-strap dress	$15–20
1987	Newsweek—The Fifties	1987		A typical glamour image of the star	$10–20
1987	Palm Springs Life	8/87	v. XXIX, n. 12	Wearing a sexy black lace dress	$15–25
1987	Parleé	7/87	v. 13, n. 2	Sitting on rocks in a light blue suit	$20–40
1987	People Extra Weekly	Spring		This issue had to be purchased through the mail.	$10–20
1987	Screen Greats Presents Marilyn	1987		Extra-thick issue with photos	$15–20
1988	American Movie Classics	8/88	n. 3	A close-up portrait wearing the gold lamé	$10–15

Year	Title	Date	Vol./No.	Description	Value
1988	Fibrearts		v. 15, n. 2	A psychedelic colorized image	$10–15
1988	Hollywood Studio Magazine	10/88	v. 21, n. 10	Sharing the cover in a glamour pose	$10–15
1988	L.A. Style	2/88	v. 111, n. 9	Extra large b/w cover in NYC, 1955	$20–40
1988	The Sun Sign Astrologer	8/88		Cute photo holding jewelry	$10–20
1989	American Heritage	2/89	v. 40, n. 1	A wistful look in a white sweater	$10–20
1989	Art & Auction	9/89	v. XII, n. 2	A colorful artwork cover	$10–15
1989	Condé Nast Traveler	8/89		On the beach filming *Hot*	$10–15
1989	Facets	3/89	v. 10, n. 15	A public TV guide in Alabama; art cover	$10–15
1989	National Examiner	11/7/89		Another cover to help boost sales	$10–15
1990	American Movie Classics	12/90	v. 3, n. 12	Looking out the window in *Itch*	$10–15
1990	Fortunoff Jewelry Catalog	1990		A publicity shot from *Asphalt Jungle*	$10–20
1990	Screen Greats Hollywood Nostalgia		n. 1	A typical Marilyn in a black fur	$10–15
1990	Sports Collectors Digest	4/20/90	v. 17, n. 16	A colorized photo, holding a baseball bat	$10–20
1990	Sun	9/11/90	v. 8, n. 37	A glamour picture included on the cover	$10–15
1990	Weekly World News	12/18/90		Yet another exciting tabloid appearance	$10–15
1991	Hollywood Then & Now	10/91	v. 24, n. 10	In a green velvet dress from *River*	$10–15

Year	Title	Date	Vol./No.	Description	Value
1991	In Vermont	8/91		A sexy and glamorous photograph	$10–20
1991	Personality Classics—Marilyn Monroe			By Revolutionary Comics	$10–15
1991	The Sharper Image Catalog		v. 2, n.3	Looking like a ballerina for Greene	$10–15
1991	Woman's World	12/17/91	v. XII, n. 51	Smiling and joyful in a white fur	$10–15
1992	Hollywood Then & Now	6–7/92	v. 25, n. 5	On half the cover in a director's chair	$10–15
1992	Hollywood Then & Now	8/92	v. 25, n. 6	A glamorous photograph	$10–15
1992	Hot Air	10–11/92		B/w glamour pose on this airline issue	$15–25
1992	Hot Spots	7–8/92	Summer	Looking sultry and sexy in the gold lamé	$10–20
1992	McCall's	7/92	v. CXIX, n. 10	A cute portrait in a black turtleneck	$10–15
1992	National Examiner	10/6/92		Another appearance on a scandal issue	$10–15
1992	People Weekly	8/10/92	v. 38, n. 6	A 1962 sad portrait taken by Stern	$10–15
1992	The Sharper Image Catalog	6/92		A stunning young Norma Jean by a net	$15–20
1992	Weekly World News	9/29/92		Continuing to appear on tabloids	$10–15
1993	Autograph Collector	4/93	v. 2, n. 4	A full-body profile in the gold lamé gown	$10–15
1993	Movie Collectors World	4/23/93	n. 419	With Jane Russell in Blondes	$10–20
1993	Marilyn (by Revolutionary Comics)			Devoted to her life and death theories	$10–15
1993	Tailwinds Catalog			In Korea, standing on top of a plane	$25–40
1993	Visions Magazine	Spring	n. 9	A Sam Shaw photo, holding her hair	$10–15

Year	Title	Date	Vol./No.	Description	Value
1994	Camera & Darkroom	7/94	v. 16, n. 7	An Eve Arnold photo from *The Misfits*	$10–15
1994	Collect!	6/94		In a ruffled blouse, with longer hair	$10–15
1994	Premiere Telecard Magazine	2/94	v. 2, n. 2	A young Norma Jean on the beach in pink	$10–20
1994	Remember	8–9/94		A blue-tinted image of MM and Joe DiMaggio	$10–15
1994	Marilyn (by Starlog Group)			Entire issue on her; optical 3D cover image	$10–20
1994	Who	5/2/94	n. 114	A b/w sexy glamour photograph	$10–15
1995	American Movie Classics	2/95	v. 8, n. 2	A b/w smiling Monroe in the black lace dress	$10–15
1995	American Photo	3–4/95		An Eve Arnold portrait in a car from *The Misfits*	$10–15
1995	Collecting	4/95	v. 1, n. 1	Throwing her head back, laughing	$10–15
1995	Digital Hollywood Awards Catalog	2/22/95		In a white lamé gown	$10–20
1995	Image Laserdisc Preview	1/95	n. 12	A color publicity still from *River*	$10–20
1995	The Sciences	11–12/95	v. 35, n. 6	A pop-art–oriented artwork cover	$10–15
1995	Stamps	5–6/95		A well-done artwork cover	$10–15
1996	Dance & The Arts	7–8/96	v. 14, n. 1	A rare candid shot in a black mink and gown	$10–15
1996	Entertainment Weekly	Fall		A 1962 profile holding beads by Stern	$10–15
1997	American Photo	6–7/97	v. VIII, n. 3	A portrait from 1962 by Stern	$10–15
1997	Cable TV	12/97	v. 1, n. 1	A smiling b/w glamour photo	$10–15
1997	Collect	12/97		A common publicity glamour photo	$10–15
1997	Doll Collector	1/97		Franklin Mint's $500 MM doll	$10–15

Year	Title	Date	Vol./No.	Description	Value
1997	Drive-In Cinema	2/97	n. 2	A glamorous, sultry Monroe	$10–15
1997	Ocean Drive	10/97		A less common white fur frontal shot	$10–15
1997	Playboy	1/97	v. 44, n. 1	Wrapped up in a black sweater	$10–20
1997	The Red Diaries (comic)		n. 1	Art of Marilyn and the Kennedys	$10–15
1997	Worth	10/97	v. 6, n. 10	A full-body profile in a blue swimsuit	$10–15

Below is a list of issues in which Marilyn appears on only a part of the cover. Those listed are only a sampling of her partial cover appearances, and their values are much less than those of a full-cover appearance. Each collector has to decide for himself how much he is willing to pay for these shared partial covers. These titles serve only as an example of what has been published. They are generally worth in the thirty- to fifty-dollar range.

Movie Teen 9/51
Look 10/23/51
Look 6/3/52
The Spartan 12/52
Colliers 8/53
Confidential 8/53
Colliers 7/54
Confidential 5/54
Pic 2/54
Sensation 1/54
Stateside 2/54
Suppressed 9/54
Confidential 9/55
Lowdown 4/55
Sir! 8/55
Playboy 9/55
Police Dragnet 9/55
Private Lives 5/55

True Police Cases 1/55
TV 9/55
Bunk 2/56
Confidential 5/56
Confidential 11/56
Colliers 8/56
Husb-Husb 8/56
Inside Story 10/56
Movie World 2/56
Sir! 5/56
Bachelor 1/57
Confidential 5/57
Tip-Off 8/57
Whisper 4/57
Top Secret 4/59
Cavalier 3/60
Husb-Husb 9/60
Inside Hollywood 5/60

Cavalier 8/61
On The QT 7/61
Uncensored 2/62
On The QT 1/63
The Lowdown 1/63

FOREIGN COVER APPEARANCES

Country Codes

ARG—Argentina	CNA—China	GRE—Greece	MEX—Mexico	SPA—Spain
ATA—Austria	CUB—Cuba	HOL—Holland	NZ—New Zealand	SWE—Sweden
AUS—Australia	DEN—Denmark	IND—India	POL—Poland	SWI—Switzerland
BEL—Belgium	ENG—England	INT—International	PR—Puerto Rico	TUR—Turkey
BRA—Brazil	FIN—Finland	ITA—Italy	RUS—Russia	URU—Uruguay
CAN—Canada	FRA—France	JAP—Japan	S.AF—South Africa	VEN—Venezuela
CHI—Chile	GER—Germany	KUW—Kuwait	S.AM—South America	

Year	Title	Date	Vol. #	Description	Country	Value
1946	Leader	4/13/46		First foreign cover; playing in leaves	ENG	$400–600
1946	Votre Amie	9/46		Colorized, playing in leaves	FRA	$300–500
1947	Intimitá	8/1/47	n. 75	Standing in a floral bikini	ITA	$200–400
1947	Picture Post	12/13/47	v. 37, n. 11	Wearing a sweater, arm up	ENG	$200–350
1947	Puerto Rico Illustrado	3/22/47		Wearing checkered pants	PR	$200–350
1948	Hela Varlden	7/48	n. 27	At a ship's wheel in a striped shirt	SWE	$200–350
1948	Intimitá	8/6/48	n. 128	Norma Jean sitting in a floral bikini	ITA	$200–400
1948	New Screen News	5/28/48		Cheesecake pose in a striped bikini	AUS	$250–400
1948	Prins Reporter	8/14–28/48	n. 17	Young Norma Jean on the beach	HOL	$200–350
1948	V	2/8/48	n. 175	In dress from Ladies of the Chorus	FRA	$200–275
1949	Kroniek Van De Week	3/12/49	n. 24	Dressed as a farmgirl holding a goat	HOL	$200–300
1949	Opden Uitijk	6/49	n. 9	A rare de Dienes photo by a barn door	HOL	$300–400

Year	Title	Date	Vol. #	Description	Country	Value
1949	Picture Post	3/26/49	v. 42, n. 13	A b/w Norma Jean in the wind and sun	ENG	$200–300
1949	Picture Post	8/13/49	v. 44, n. 7	Squatting in a bikini on the beach	ENG	$200–300
1949	V	10/31/49	n. 265	Colorized Norma Jean as a sailor	FRA	$200–300
1949	Votre Sante	2/15/49	n. 35	In a tailored suit	FRA	$200–250
1949	Wereld Kroniek	1/9/49	n. 2	An early portrait of Norma Jean waving	HOL	$200–300
1950	Das Magazin	1950	n. 13	In a red one-piece swimsuit on beach	GER	$200–300
1950	Paris Hollywood	1950		A colorized cheesecake photograph	FRA	$200–300
1950	Paris Tout Bas	1950	n. 1	An early Norma Jean portrait	FRA	$200–300
1950	Piccolo	10/29/50	n. 26	A pretty Eve portrait	HOL	$125–175
1950	Revue	5/27/50	n. 21	Wearing a print blouse by de Dienes	GER	$200–300
1950	Roman Magisinet	c. 1950	n. 1	An Eve publicity still	DEN	$100–175
1951	Billed Bladet	6/26/51	n. 26	In the grass with a dandelion	DEN	$100–175
1951	Cinemonde	1951	n. 870	In a bathing suit on half the cover	FRA	$75–100
1951	Confidenze	6/17/51	v. VI	Wearing a turtleneck reclining in a lawn chair	ITA	$150–200
1951	Cuentame	12/5/51	v. 5, n. 214	In a yellow sweater with hair blowing	ARG	$150–200
1951	Hela Varlden	1951	n. 25	Holding a bouquet of roses for Eve	SWE	$100–175
1951	Le Soir Illustré	9/20/51	n. 10004	Smiling with her hair blowing in the wind	FRA	$100–175
1951	Novell Magisinet (digest)	1951	n. 15	An Eve publicity still	SWE	$75–100

Cuentame, Dec. 5, 1951

Hela Varlden, 1951

Year	Title	Date	Vol. #	Description	Country	Value
1951	Pix	8/11/51		Glamorous in a red velvet dress	AUS	$100–200
1951	Resimli Romans	13 Aralik 1951	v. 26, n. 25	With bobbed hair in a yellow turtleneck	TUR	$100–150
1951	Wereld Kroniek	6/2/51	n. 22	A de Dienes, playing on the beach	HOL	$100–200
1951	Zondagsvriend	9/27/51		Playing on the ground in a leaf pile	HOL	$200–300
1952	Billed Bladet	11/4/52		Reclining in a lamé dress with arms up	SWE	$100–175
1952	Bolero Film	7/27/52	n. 271	Smiling with a bouquet of red roses	ITA	$100–175

Year	Title	Date	Vol. #	Description	Country	Value
1952	Chic	1952		A de Dienes photo of Norma Jean	CUB	$100–175
1952	Cine Mundo	9/27/52	v. 1, n. 28	Smiling in a b/w glamour image	SPA	$100–175
1952	Cine Revue	10/3/52	v. 32, n. 40	Showing Cary Grant her leg	FRA	$100–125
1952	Dien Gluck	1952	n. 7	An early studio publicity photo	SWI	$100–150
1952	Die Trube Mar-jetta (digest)	c. 1952		An early glamorous artwork image	SWI	$40–60
1952	Ecran	11/5/52	n. 1098	Holding up a white cat	CHI	$50–75
1952	8 Otto	3/2/52	n. 9	Posing within a big heart	ITA	$100–125
1952	8 Otto	4/6/52	n. 14	Testing the water in a pool with her toe	ITA	$100–125
1952	Estampa	4/14/52	v. XIV, n. 708	The Asphalt Jungle colorized photo in suit	ARG	$100–150
1952	Film Journalen	5/25/52	n. 21	Having her photo taken by a ladder	SWE	$100–150
1952	Film Magazin	1 Jng. 1952	n. 20	Hugging a white cat	SWI	$100–150
1952	Fotographia Artistica	3/52	v. 3, n. 7	Sitting in the snow in a hat	SPA	$100–150
1952	Fotogramas	11/28/52		A glamorous photo with a hand to her chin	SPA	$100–150
1952	Fotogramas	12/12/52		Embracing Keith Andes	SPA	$100–125
1952	Funk Illustrierte	4/13/52		A glamorous publicity photo	GER	$100–150
1952	Il Lavoro Illustrato	9/7/52	n. 36	Smiling, holding a white cat	ITA	$100–125
1952	Kavalkad	1952	v. 5, n. 16	Sitting in director's chair	SWE	$100–140
1952	La Settimana Incom Illustrada	8/9/52	v. V, n. 32	Holding an envelope with a look of surprise	ITA	$100–125
1952	Novellmagisinet (digest)	1952	n. 11	A photo from The Asphalt Jungle	SWE	$75–100

Year	Title	Date	Vol. #	Description	Country	Value
1952	Mein Film	1952	n. 49	Embracing Richard Widmark	ATA	$80–120
1952	Movie Pictorial	6/52	v. 17, n. 6	A gorgeous back cover in a potato sack	JAP	$50–75
1952	Mundo Uruguayo	6/5/52	v. XXXIV, n. 1728	With Keith Andes in a romantic pose	URU	$100–125
1952	Noir Et Blanc	7/16/52	n. 386	Dancing on the beach in a swimsuit	FRA	$125–175
1952	Paris Frou Frou	1952		An early glamorous publicity still	FRA	$125–150
1952	Photoplay	11/52	v. 3, n. 2	A lovely shot, reclining with a brown mink	ENG	$100–150
1952	Picturegoer	8/9/52	v. 24, n. 901	Sitting in a director's chair at the studio	ENG	$100–125
1952	Se	11/20–26/52	v. 15, n. 47	In a sultry pose, reclining in a lamé dress	SWE	$100–125
1952	Tele Cine	1952	n. 29	A classic glamorous Marilyn	FRA	$100–150
1952	The Photoplayer	10/4/52	v. XXX, n. 23	In a swimsuit, holding on to a palm tree	AUS	$125–175
1952	True Story	5/52		With bobbed hair in a yellow turtleneck	JAP	$125–200
1952	Voir	11/23/52	n. 425	Looking over her shoulder in a skirt	FRA	$125–175
1952	Weekend Picture Magazine	8/9/52	v. 2, n. 32	Newspaper section; candid pose in dress	CAN	$125–200
1952	Zondagsvriend	3/20/52	n. 12	As a farmgirl holding a baby lamb	HOL	$125–200
1953	Acena Muda	10/21/53	n. 43	A glamour shot for Niagara	BRA	$100–150
1953	A.M. Australian Magazine	4/24/53		With Betty Grable and Lauren Bacall	AUS	$125–150

Year	Title	Date	Vol. #	Description	Country	Value
1953	*Amour Film*	9/1/53	n. 9	Getting cozy with Richard Widmark	FRA	$75–100
1953	*Antena*	2/17/53		A glamorous MM with diamond jewelry	ARG	$75–125
1953	*Antena*	10/53		The common shot with the white fur	ARG	$75–125
1953	*Beauty Book*	9/53		Norma Jean in a white robe on the beach	JAP	$200–300
1953	*Billed Bladet*	11/24/53	n. 47	In a black dress decorated with jewels	DEN	$80–125
1953	*Cabiers Du Cinema*	6/53	n. 24	With her costars from *Millionaire*	FRA	$80–125
1953	*Capriccio* (digest)	1953	n. 9	An early glamour publicity pose	GER	$80–125
1953	*Cinelandia*	6/53	v. 11, n. 15	Wearing the racy black negligee	BRA	$80–125
1953	*Cinelandia*	11/53	v. 2, n. 25	All three girls in *Millionaire*	BRA	$75–115
1953	*Cinema*	9/30/53	n. 118	With Jane Russell on a ladder	ITA	$75–125
1953	*Cinemin*	12/53	n. 27	Wearing a gold bow necklace	ARG	$75–125
1953	*Cine-Miroir*	2/53	n. 952	At the Ray Anthony party in a red dress	FRA	$100–150
1953	*Cine Radio Actualdad*	12/53		By a Christmas tree	BRA	$75–125
1953	*Cine Revue*	2/27/53	v. 33, n. 9	With Jane Russell in wedding dresses	FRA	$75–135
1953	*Cine Revue*	11/13/53	v. 33, n. 46	With Bacall and Grable in *Millionaire*	FRA	$75–115
1953	*Confessioni*	11/19/53	v. V, n. 269	Wearing a gold lamé gown	ITA	$75–125
1953	*De Post*	5/53		In *Don't Bother to Knock*	BEL	$80–115

Year	Title	Date	Vol. #	Description	Country	Value
1953	*Der Spiegel*	9/30/53	v. VII, n. 40	An unretouched glamour photo	GER	$80–125
1953	*Deutsche Illustrierte*	9/19/53	n. 38	Holding a Greek column	GER	$80–125
1953	*Ecran*	6/16/53	n. 1169	A *Niàgara* glamour pose	CHI	$50–75
1953	*Ecran*	9/29/53	n. 1184	A glamorous publicity still	CHI	$50–75
1953	*Ecran*	12/22/53	n. 1196	Looking sexy on the Christmas issue	CHI	$50–75

Regal, 1953

Movie Pictorial, 1952

Year	Title	Date	Vol. #	Description	Country	Value
1953	Eiga No Tomo	10/53	n. 249	The well-known white fur pose	JAP	$100–135
1953	Epoca	6/14/53	n. 141	A close-up in the black lace dress	ITA	$100–150
1953	Fick Journalen (digest)	4/16/53	n. 16	Norma Jean climbing steep rocks	SWE	$75–125
1953	Film Complet	1953	n. 402	Kissing Richard Allen in *Niagara*	FRA	$50–75
1953	Film en Toneel	10/53	n. 4	In a blue satin halter top	HOL	$75–100
1953	Film Journalen	10/4/53	n. 40–41	On a wire table in a yellow suit	SWE	$75–125
1953	Film Magazin	2, Jhg. 1953	n. 19	Black-gloved hands touching her face	SWI	$80–125
1953	Film Strip (digest)	11/24/53		Full figure from *The Asphalt Jungle*	RUS	$100–150
1953	Follie!	3/53	v. VI, n. 3	A young Norma Jean under an umbrella	ITA	$100–200
1953	Follie!	9–10/53	n. 9	With Jane Russell in top hats	ITA	$100–175
1953	Garbo	10/3/53	v. 1, n. 29	Color-tinted with short bobbed hair	SPA	$75–100
1953	Glamor	11/24/53	n. 44	Early publicity shot with bobbed hair	ENG	$80–125
1953	Gondel	1953	n. 54	A typical sexy shot	GER	$75–125
1953	Grand Hotel	2/28/53	n. 349	An artwork cover in a red dress	ITA	$75–100
1953	Ibz/Berliner Illustrierte	4/10/53	n. 44	The common white fur for publicity pose	GER	$75–125
1953	Illustrated	1/31/53	v. XIV, n. 49	In a lacy dress with red hair	ENG	$80–125
1953	Illustrated	8/8/53	v. XV, n. 24	The three girls in *Millionaire*	ENG	$75–100
1953	Illustrierte Post	11/4/53	n. 15	A glamorous studio publicity pose	GER	$80–125
1953	Imagenes	4/53	n. 20	Reclining in a lamé gown	SPA	$100–200
1953	Intimita	10/15/53	n. 399	In the red *Niagara* dress with arm up	ITA	$75–100

Year	Title	Date	Vol. #	Description	Country	Value
1953	La Domenica Della Donna	6/7/53	n. 23	With Richard Widmark	ITA	$75–125
1953	La Domenica Della Donna	12/18/53	n. 50	Holding 500-year-old diamond	ITA	$75–125
1953	Le Film Complet	34rd trimestr 53	n. 402	A glamorous studio photo	FRA	$75–100
1953	Le Ore	8/1/53	v. 1, n. 12	Colorized, holding an umbrella	ITA	$100–125
1953	Le Ore	8/29/53	v. 1, n. 16	Looking over her shoulder in jeans	ITA	$100–125
1953	Le Ore	11/21/53	v. 1, n. 28	Halsman photo, in scrunch dress	ITA	$100–125
1953	Mein Film	1/23/53	n. 52	In the black dress with white collar	ATA	$75–100
1953	Me Naiset	1953	n. 5	A young Norma Jean in a pink sweater	FIN	$175–300
1953	Mignon	1/1/53	n. 1	A pretty glamour pose	ITA	$75–100
1953	Movie Marquee	1/53	v. 1, n. 8	Striking a sultry pose	CAN	$100–150
1953	Mujer	5/53	n. 191	Sultry in the Niagara dress with arm up	SPA	$100–125
1953	Munchner Illustrierte	1/17/53	n. 3	With Jane Russell in top hats	GER	$125–150
1953	Munchner Illustrierte	9/12/53	n. 37	Halsman photo, in scrunch dress	GER	$125–150
1953	Mundo Uruguay	11/5/53	v. XXXV, n. 1802	In black dress with jewels on straps	URU	$100–150
1953	Motion Picture Times	7/53	n. 67	With her hair up for Eve	JAP	$125–175
1953	Neue Illustrierte	7/25/53	v. 8, n. 30	With her arm up from Millionaire	GER	$100–150
1953	New Liberty	3/53	v. 30, n. 1	A double-image mirror reflection	CAN	$100–150

Year	Title	Date	Vol. #	Description	Country	Value
1953	New Screen News	1/16/53		A tinted studio portrait	AUS	$60–80
1953	Noir Et Blanc	2/25/53	n. 418	A long-haired MM coming out of a pool	FRA	$75–125
1953	Noir Et Blanc	7/20/53	v. 9, n. 438	Two side-by-side full-length photos	FRA	$75–125
1953	Novella	1/4/53	n. 1	A studio publicity photograph	ITA	$75–125
1953	Novella	11/1/53	v. XXXIV, n. 44	A picture from *Niagara*	ITA	$75–125
1953	Novelle Film	1/17/53	n. 265	Embracing Richard Widmark	ITA	$75–100
1953	Novelle Film	7/25/53	n. 292	With Richard Allen in *Niagara*	ITA	$75–100
1953	Otto Volante	3/16–31/53	v. II, n. 6	Intently reading a script on a set	ITA	$75–100
1953	Paris Frou Frou	c. 1953	n. 1	A coy look in the black lace negligee	FRA	$100–175
1953	Paris Frou Frou	c. 1953	n. 11	With Charles Laughton and Jane Russell	FRA	$100–175
1953–54	Paris Hollywood (digest)	Dec. 53/Jan. 54	v. 2, n. 22	Standing by a snowman	SWE	$80–120
1953	Paris Match	7/25/53	n. 226	Hugging a white pillar	FRA	$75–125
1953	Photoplay	8/53		Wearing a top hat	ENG	$75–125
1953	Photoplay	5/53		In a black dress with jewel-studded straps	AUS	$100–175
1953	Photoplay	10/53		Wearing a gold halter dress	AUS	$100–175
1953	Piccolo	1/18/53	v. 29, n. 2	Standing in front of Niagara Falls	HOL	$75–125
1953	Piccolo	12/27/53		Posing with big sticks of dynamite	HOL	$75–125
1953	Picturegoer	5/9/53	v. 25, n. 940	Looking sexy in a black lace negligee	ENG	$75–100

Year	Title	Date	Vol. #	Description	Country	Value
1953	Picture Post	8/15/53	v. 60, n. 7	With Charles Laughton and Jane Russell	ENG	$75–125
1953	Pin-Up	9/2/53		Digest-sized colorized shot by a pier	SWE	$80–100
1953	Pix	5/9/53	v. 29, n. 10	A cute pose in a jewel-decorated dress	AUS	$100–150
1953	Radio Revue	9/27–10/3/53	n. 39	Posing in a glamorous fashion	GER	$75–125
1953	Radio Revue	10/3–9/53	n. 40	With Jane Russell in Blondes	GER	$75–125
1953	Regal (digest)	5/53	n. 44	A cheesecake image in a yellow bikini	FRA	$80–100
1953	Regal (digest)	6/53	n. 45	A cheesecake image in a striped bikini	FRA	$80–100
1953	Regards	6/53	n. 45	A close-up in dangling earrings	FRA	$125–150
1953	Screen	6/53		Leaning back over green satin	JAP	$125–175
1953	Screen Parade	9/53		The three girls in Millionaire	AUS	$75–100
1953	Stag	9/53		In a negligee	NZ	$100–150
1953	Tempo	4/18/53	v. XV, n. 16	Holding roses in her arms from All About Eve	ITA	$100–150
1953	Tempo	11/26/53	v. XV, n. 48	A close-up with a cigarette by Greene	ITA	$100–150
1953	Tempo	12/17/53	v. XV, n. 51	The three girls in Millionaire	ITA	$100–150
1953	Triunfo	2/25/53	n. 367	A sexy glamour pose	SPA	$60–80
1953	Triunfo	9/30/53	n. 398	A sexy glamour pose in a dress	SPA	$60–80
1953	20th Century Fox	4 & 5/53	n. 7	With Jane Russell wearing top hats	ITA	$100–150
1953	20th Century Fox	12/31/53	n. 24	Posing with a snowman	ITA	$100–150

Year	Title	Date	Vol. #	Description	Country	Value
1953	Uge Revyen	6/30/53	v. II, n. 26	A tinted digest, wearing the red *Niagara* dress	DEN	$50–75
1953	Uge Revyen	9/29/53	v. II, n. 39	A tinted digest with the *Millionaire* girls	DEN	$60–80
1953	Une Semaine De Paris	9/15/53	n. 356	A sultry publicity pose	FRA	$75–125
1953	Vea	9/19/53	n. 462	In a swimsuit holding white pillar	MEX	$100–150
1953	Vea	10/10/53	n. 465	Sitting in a one-piece swimsuit	MEX	$100–150
1953	Vision	7/24/53	v. 5, n. 6	At the *Niagara* party in the red dress	CHI	$75–125
1953	Weiner Bilderwoche	11/14/53	n. 46	Black dress with jewel straps	ATA	$100–150
1953	What's On In London?	5/8/53		A publicity pose in a tight dress	ENG	$75–100
1954	Amor Film	9/15/54	n. 34	With Jane Russell in *Blondes*	FRA	$75–100
1954	Antologia Otto Volante	8/54	n. 4	Holding a polka-dot scarf	ITA	$75–125
1954	Australasian Post	3/25/54		In a green velvet dress from *River*	AUS	$100–150
1954	Australasian Post	5/27/54		On steps undoing swimsuit strap	AUS	$100–150
1954	Capriccio Journal	1954		Digest with a diamond necklace	GER	$100–150
1954	Chi é Marilyn Monroe Collana Biographica	6/1/54	n. 7	Entire issue on her; going up a ladder	ITA	$200–300
1954	Cinelandia	2/54	v. 3, n. 30	Glamour pose in a white fur	BRA	$80–125
1954	Cinelandia	9/54	v. IV, n. 45	A sultry portrait	BRA	$80–125
1954	Cinemonde	4/16/54		In the gold lamé gown	FRA	$60–80

Cinelândia, Sept.
1954

Movie Life,
March 1, 1954

Year	Title	Date	Vol. #	Description	Country	Value
1954	*Cinema Nuovo*	12/10/54	v. 3, n. 48	A typical studio photograph	ITA	$75–125
1954	*Cinemin*	6/54	n. 33	Full length, holding white pillar	ARG	$100–140
1954	*Cine Radio Actualdad*	9/24/54	v. XIX, n. 950	With Gina Lollobrigida	URU	$75–125
1954	*Cineromanzo*	10/28/54	n. 11	A sexy glamour picture	ITA	$100–130
1954	*Clubman*	Summer 1954	n. 43	In a costume from *River*	ENG	$75–125

Year	Title	Date	Vol. #	Description	Country	Value
1954	Cronache Della Politica E Del Costume	12/10/54	n. 22	A studio portrait	ITA	$75–125
1954	Der Stern	1/31/54		Wearing the famous gold lamé gown	GER	$100–150
1954	Ecran	6/29/54	n. 1221	A pretty glamour portrait	CHI	$40–75
1954	Ecran	8/3/54	n. 1226	The three girls from Millionaire	CHI	$40–75
1954	Ecran	12/28/54	n. 1249	Showing off a diamond necklace	CHI	$40–75
1954	Eiga No Tomo	3/54	n. 254	In a fur with a striped background	JAP	$100–150
1954	Epoca	1/17/54	v. V, n. 172	Hanging out a car window in Canada	ITA	$100–150
1954	Epoca	3/21/54	v. V, n. 161	The classic image in the white fur	ITA	$100–150
1954	Epoca	8/15/54	n. 202	Leaning forward and laughing	ITA	$100–150
1954	Estudio	5/54		A studio publicity pose	SPA	$100–140
1954	Festival	2/24/54	n. 243	On the back cover as well	FRA	$75–125
1954	Frau Im Spiegel	10/16/54	v. 9, n. 42	Tinted photo from River	GER	$75–125
1954	Intimita	3/18/54	n. 421	Smiling in the white fur	ITA	$75–125
1954	Joulu Iso Kalle	12/5–20/54	n. 23	Wearing a black negligee	FIN	$100–150
1954	La Cinemato-graphie Francaise	12/4/54	n. 1595	A cute publicity photograph	FRA	$75–125
1954	Le Film Complet	11/25/54	n. 488	A 20th Century Fox publicity shot	FRA	$75–100
1954	Le Ore	1/2/54	n. 34	Hugging a white Greek column	ITA	$100–150
1954	Le Ore	4/3/54	v. II, n. 47	Putting her hands in cement at Mann's Chinese Theatre	ITA	$100–150
1954	Le Ore	7/10/54	v. II, n. 61	Leaning back against green satin	ITA	$100–150

Year	Title	Date	Vol. #	Description	Country	Value
1954	Le Ore	10/9/54	v. II, n. 74	Full-length pose hugging the white pole	ITA	$100–150
1954	Marilyn (by Skolsky)	1954		South American version of the American issue	ARG	$100–150
1954	Mexico Día	8/10/54		A studio publicity image	MEX	$100–150
1954	Min Melodi	5/7/54	n. 19	Three paintings of Marilyn poses	SWE	$50–80
1954	Min Melodi	6/4/54	n. 23	On a rock in River	SWE	$70–90
1954	Movie Life	3/1/54	v. VIII, n. 9	In a yellow dress, hugging a white cat	AUS	$100–140
1954	Movie Life	10/54		Three different images on cover	AUS	$100–140
1954	Movie Stars Parade	9/54		A glamorous and sexy pose	AUS	$80–125
1954	Münchener Illustrierte	2/27/54	n. 9	With Jane Russell in costumes	GER	$100–150
1954	New Screen News	2/12/54		Wearing a red one-piece swimsuit	AUS	$75–100
1954	New Screen News	3/12/54		Holding the white Greek column	AUS	$75–100
1954	Notte E Giorno	11/8/54	n. 7	In front of Niagara Falls	ITA	$100–150
1954	Novella	9/26/54	n. 39	A typical smiling and glamorous MM	ITA	$80–125
1954	Oggi	1/28/54	v. X, n. 4	With Joe DiMaggio on their wedding day	ITA	$80–125
1954	Oggi	3/18/54	v. X, n. 11	Posing with the troops in Korea in 1954	ITA	$80–125
1954	Oggi	10/21/54	v. X, n. 42	With Billy Wilder on the Itcb set	ITA	$80–125
1954	Paris Frou Frou	1954	n. 40	A common glamorous photo	FRA	$100–150
1954	Paris Hollywood	9/54	v. 3, n. 17	Publicity still for River	SWE	$80–110

Year	Title	Date	Vol. #	Description	Country	Value
1954	*Paris Hollywood*	7/54	v. 3, n. 14	In a red bathing suit holding umbrella	SWE	$80–110
1954	*Paris Hollywood*	11/54	v. 3, n. 21	Publicity still for *River*	SWE	$80–110
1954	*Parisia*	3/54	n. 4	A typical glamour image	FRA	$75–125
1954	*Photoplay*	3/54	v. 5, n. 12	On a wire table in a yellow bathing suit	ENG	$80–125
1954	*Photoplay*	12/54	v. 5, n. 12	In a green velvet dress from *River*	ENG	$80–125
1954	*Photoplay*	4/54		A profile shot in the gold lamé gown	AUS	$80–125
1954	*Photoplay*	7/54		In a white fur with a striped background	AUS	$80–125
1954	*Picturegoer*	1/16/54	v. 27, n. 976	Tinted cover, holding a diamond necklace	ENG	$60–95
1954	*Picturegoer*	10/23/54	v. 28, n. 1016	Tinted with her white dress blowing up	ENG	$60–95
1954	*Picture Post*	4/24/54		Her hands behind her in the gold lamé	ENG	$75–125
1954	*Picture Show*	9/25/54	v. 63, n. 1643	With Robert Mitchum in *River*	ENG	$60–95
1954	*Piff* (digest)	9/54	n. 10	In a colorful corset and headdress from *River*	ENG	$75–100
1954	*Quic*	c. 1954	v. 1, n. 1	A pose from *Millionaire*; also on back cover	ITA	$100–140
1954	*Reves*	8/12/54	n. 424	A studio publicity pose	FRA	$75–125
1954	*Revue*	5/29/54	n. 22	Showing off a 500-year-old diamond	GER	$100–140
1954	*Rosso E Nero*	1/31–2/28/54	v. 2, n. 1	A color shot from *The Asphalt Jungle*	ITA	$100–150
1954	*Rosso E Nero*	11/54	n. 8	In a yellow bathing suit on rocks	ITA	$100–150

Year	Title	Date	Vol. #	Description	Country	Value
1954	Screen Stars	4 & 5/54	v. 1, n. 2	Posing with an umbrella in a bathing suit	AUS	$80–125
1954	Se	1/28–2/4/54	v. 17, n. 5	With Joe DiMaggio on ¾ of the cover	SWE	$60–100
1954	Se	10/17/54		In the white dress from *Itch*	SWE	$75–125
1954	Seduction	2/54	v. 1, n. 2	A profile in the red *Niagara* dress	ITA	$100–175
1954	Semaine Du Monde	1/29/54	n. 64	Wearing the white fur and a smile	FRA	$100–125
1954	Semaine Du Nord Magazine	10/28/54	n. 31	An early glamour photo, smiling in gloves	FRA	$100–140
1954	Serena	1/28/54	n. 50	In a red suit holding the white pillar	ITA	$100–140
1954	Settimo Giorno	12/23/54	v. VII, n. 51	Looking over her shoulder in a dress	ITA	$100–150
1954	Sight and Sound	1–3/54	v. 23, n. 3	With Lauren Bacall and Betty Grable in *Millionaire*	ENG	$60–80
1954	Star	5/54		Wearing a fur and a serious face	JAP	$125–175
1954	Tabarin	3/54	n. 3	A double-image cheesecake shot in a suit	ITA	$100–150
1954	The Eiga Story	9/54		A younger Marilyn, with wide eyes	JAP	$125–175
1954	True Confessions	2/54		In the red *Niagara* dress and gold hoops	ENG	$125–175
1954	TV Sorrisi E Canzoni	7/11/54	n. 28	Tinted cover with Robert Mitchum	ITA	$100–130
1954	20th Century Fox	2/28/54	v. IX, n. 3–4	Sitting in a lacy red negligee and heels	ITA	$100–150
1954	20th Century Fox	12/17/54	n. 23	Cutting a cake in the white *Itch* dress	ITA	$100–150

Year	Title	Date	Vol. #	Description	Country	Value
1954	*Une Semaine De Paris*	4/28/54	n. 388	A classic glamorous Monroe	FRA	$75-125
1954	*Une Semaine De Paris*	9/27/54	n. 406	A studio released publicity still	FRA	$75-125
1954	*Visto*	7/10/54	n. 28	A dreamy image, sitting with a guitar	ITA	$80-125
1954	*Visto*	9/25/54	v. III, n. 39	The common, white-fur image	ITA	$80-125
1954	*Voila Europe Magazine*	2/21/54	n. 472	Marilyn glamour at its best	FRA	$100-150
1954	*Wiener Film Revue*	1954		A publicity photograph	ATA	$125-150
1955	*A.M. Australian Magazine*	4/5/55	n. 6	In a white satin dress by a bookcase	AUS	$150-200
1955	*A.M. Australian Magazine*	7/5/55		Full-length profile in a red negligee	AUS	$150-200
1955	*Amor Film*	3/16/55	n. 56	A studio publicity pose	FRA	$60-95
1955	*Amor Film Hebdo*	5/25/55	n. 66	Posing with Donald O'Connor	FRA	$60-95
1955	*Amor Film*	12/28/55	n. 97	Full length in the tiger-stripe dress	FRA	$60-95
1955	*Bild Journalen*	4/55	n. 13	Tinted image with her makeup man, Whitey	SWE	$100-140
1955	*Cabiers Du Cinema*	Noel 55	n. 54	In blowing white *Itch* dress	FRA	$80-125
1955	*Cine Aventuras*	2-3/55	v. IV, n. 74	In a red-and-white-striped blouse	ARG	$100-140
1955	*Cinelandia*	12/55	v. XIV, n. 155	Two pictures in a white terry robe	BRA	$80-125
1955	*Cinema*	11/25/55		A publicity pose from *Itch*	ITA	$80-125
1955	*Cine-Revelation*	5/12/55	n. 58	Sitting, in a photo by Halsman	FRA	$100-150

A.M. The Australian Magazine, April 5, 1955

The Showgirl, circa 1955

Year	Title	Date	Vol. #	Description	Country	Value
1955	Cine Revue	7/15/55	v. 35, n. 28	With Tom Ewell in *Itch*	FRA	$80–125
1955	Cine Revue	11/18/55	v. 35	Wrapped in deep red with a choker	FRA	$100–150
1955	Der Stern	10/4/55	n. 15	Sitting near mirrors and reflections	GER	$100–140
1955	Ecran	6/21/55	n. 1274	With Joe DiMaggio at the *Itch* premiere	CHI	$50–80

Year	Title	Date	Vol. #	Description	Country	Value
1955	Eiga No Tomo	9/55	n. 272	Sitting in a director's chair in a jeweled gown	JAP	$125–175
1955	Epoca	7/24/55	v. VI, n. 251	Coyly looking over her shoulder	ITA	$100–150
1955	Filmlandia	9/55	n. 10	Sitting in a director's chair in a jeweled gown	ARG	$75–125
1955	Film Magazin	1/4/55	n. 52	Tinted cover in director's chair	SWI	$75–125
1955	Flix	c. 1955	n. 4	Wearing high heels and a potato sack	ENG	$100–140
1955	Flix	c. 1955	n. 5	From *Itch* by a staircase	ENG	$100–140
1955	Flix	c. 1955	v. 1, n. 8	International edition; with Tom Ewell	ENG	$100–140
1955	Fotogramas	1955	v. X, n. 319	A tinted glamour cover from *Niagara*	SPA	$100–140
1955	Garbo	9/17/55	v. III, n. 131	Joe DiMaggio escorting MM to the *Itch* premiere	SPA	$50–75
1955	Grand Hotel	7/2/55	n. 471	An artwork cover	ITA	$75–125
1955	Hemmets Veckotidning	7/2/55	v. 27, n. 27	Young Norma Jean on the beach in pants	SWE	$125–200
1955	Illustrierte Alm Bubne	1955	n. 2755	In a white costume from *Business*	GER	$100–140
1955	Junior Women's Weekly	8/22/55		A digest insert with Tom Ewell	AUS	$50–75
1955	Jours De France	3/24–31/55	n. 20	With a surprised look and a flower choker	FRA	$100–150
1955	L'Europeo	12/4/55	n. 49	A standard movie-star glamour face	ITA	$100–150
1955	Le Ore	6/4/55	v. III, n. 108	A close-up in a striped turtleneck	ITA	$100–150
1955	Le Ore	11/19/55	v. III, n. 132	Standing in the striped turtleneck	ITA	$100–150
1955	Liberty	7/55	v. 32, n. 5	Wearing the one-strap *Millionaire* dress	CAN	$100–150

Year	Title	Date	Vol. #	Description	Country	Value
1955	Marilyn	c. 1955	v. 1, n. 1	A comic about Marilyn with an art cover	ARG	$100–140
1955	Marilyn	c. 1955	v. 1, n. 2	A comic about Marilyn with an art cover	ARG	$100–140
1955	Marilyn Monroe (pocket)	1955		Entire issue is dedicated to her	SPA	$75–100
1955	Mein Film	1/55		With Rory Calhoun in River	ATA	$75–90
1955	Mimosa (digest)	1/55	n. 23	The three girls from Millionaire	ITA	$60–85
1955	Movie Life	11/55		Holding the 500-year-old diamond	AUS	$100–150
1955	New Screen News	11/1/55		With Tom Ewell in Itch	AUS	$60–85
1955	Photoplay	7/55	v. 6, n. 7	In a black swimsuit on steps	ENG	$100–140
1955	Photoplayer	2/19/55		On the couch from Itch	AUS	$100–150
1955	Piccolo	4/3/55	v. 31, n. 12	With Donald O'Connor	HOL	$100–130
1955	Radio Revue	5/22–28/55	n. 21	A typical glamour image	GER	$100–130
1955	Radio Revue	9/18/55	n. 38	A studio publicity pose	GER	$100–130
1955	Revue	8/6/55	n. 32	Wearing the gold lamé gown on ¾ of the cover	GER	$100–130
1955	Rhythme	4/15/55		A studio publicity pose	HOL	$80–100
1955	Ricu Ritas	c. 1955	v. II, n. 49	Sitting on Tom Ewell's lap	ARG	$100–130
1955	Rosso E Nero	1/55	n. 11	Blowing a kiss to the camera	ITA	$100–140
1955	Seura	11/9/55	n. 45	Dancing barefoot in a red skirt	FIN	$125–175
1955	Show (digest)	c. 1955	n. 4	Sitting in a swimsuit and lace-up sandals	ENG	$75–100
1955	Sixty-six(66) (pocket)	c. 1955	n. 2	Entire issue is on her; in the tiger-stripe dress	ENG	$100–130
1955	Stars & Sterne	1955	n. 8	In a suit with a polka-dot scarf	GER	$100–130

Year	Title	Date	Vol. #	Description	Country	Value
1955	*Tempo*	11/14/55	n. 47	A semiprofile in the gold lamé gown	ITA	$100–150
1955	*The Showgirl* (pocket)	c. 1955	n. 21	Wearing a blue satin halter dress	ENG	$80–100
1955	*Visioni*	5/14/55	n. 18	The white *Itch* dress blowing up	ITA	$100–140
1955	*Visto*	8/27/55	v. IV, n. 35	A large portrait from *Itch*	ITA	$100–130
1955	*Wiener Film Revue*	1955	n. 12	In the red dress, posed with Lassie	ATA	$125–175
1956	*ABC*	7/7/56		Seated at the *Bus Stop* press conference	BEL	$100–130
1956	*Bella*	9/24–10/7/56		A glamour shot with the white fur	GER	$100–130
1956	*Billed Bladet*	7/10/56		Next to Arthur Miller	SWE	$100–130
1956	*Blighty*	10/6/56	n. 884	In a purple off-the-shoulder dress	ENG	$125–175
1956	*Bolero Film*	7/15/56	n. 479	In the red *Niagara* dress	ITA	$100–130
1956	*Bravo*	8/26/56	n. 1	A studio glamour pose	GER	$100–130
1956	*Cahiers Du Cinema*	11/56	n. 64	Onstage during *Bus Stop*	ENG	$60–95
1956	*Cine Revelation*	1/5/56	n. 92	In a blue dress decorated with jewels	FRA	$100–130
1956	*Cine Revelation*	7/19/56	n. 120	With her arm up, from *Niagara*	FRA	$100–130
1956	*Cine Revue*	7/20/56	v. 36, n. 29	Standing in front of a house	FRA	$75–125
1956	*Cine Universal*	c. 1956		Holding her arm in the black lace dress	MEX	$150–200
1956	*Das Schweizer Magazin* (digest)		n. 156	In a blouse, sitting on rocks	SWI	$100–130
1956	*Eiga No Tomo*	12/56	n. 287	In a black spaghetti-strap dress	JAP	$125–150

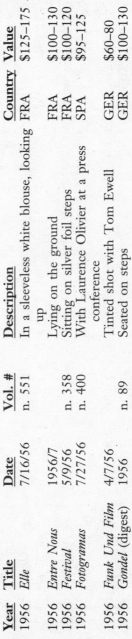

Wiener Film Revue, 1955

Visioni, May 14, 1955

Year	Title	Date	Vol. #	Description	Country	Value
1956	*Elle*	7/16/56	n. 551	In a sleeveless white blouse, looking up	FRA	$125–175
1956	*Entre Nous*	1956/7		Lying on the ground	FRA	$100–130
1956	*Festival*	5/9/56	n. 358	Sitting on silver foil steps	FRA	$100–120
1956	*Fotogramas*	7/27/56	n. 400	With Laurence Olivier at a press conference	SPA	$95–125
1956	*Funk Und Film*	4/7/56		Tinted shot with Tom Ewell	GER	$60–80
1956	*Gondel* (digest)	1956	n. 89	Seated on steps	GER	$100–130

Year	Title	Date	Vol. #	Description	Country	Value
1956	Grand Hotel	10/6/56	n. 537	Marilyn is portrayed on this artwork cover	ITA	$75–125
1956	Hayat	5/4/56	n. 5	Sitting on large rocks in a pantsuit	TUR	$100–150
1956	Hjemmet	11/6/56	v. 59, n. 45	In the red dress in front of Niagara Falls	DEN	$100–150
1956	Hola!	7/22/56		On half the cover	SPA	$50–75
1956	Hollywood Festival	9/1/56	v. XII, n. 164	A double-mirror-reflected image	ITA	$125–175
1956	Illustrated	7/14/56	v. XVIII, n. 21	Lying back against green satin	ENG	$100–150
1956	Il Travaso	7/1/56	n. 27	Marilyn is portrayed on this art cover.	ITA	$35–65
1956	La Cinemato-graphie Francaise	2/1/56	n. 1698	A typical studio glamour image	FRA	$75–125
1956	La Cinemato-graphie Francaise	10/3/56	n. 1885	A studio glamour portrait	FRA	$75–125
1956	La Vida Escando-losa De M. Monroe	8/56	n. 1	Entire issue on her; a candid photo cover	ARG	$150–200
1956	Le Film Complet	5/4/56	n. 566	A studio publicity pose	FRA	$75–100
1956	Le Ore	3/3/56	v. IV, n. 147	In a lacy black negligee with clouds behind	ITA	$100–150

Blighty, Oct. 6, 1956

Stage and Cinema, Nov. 15, 1957

Year	Title	Date	Vol. #	Description	Country	Value
1956	*Le Ore*	5/5/56	v. IV, n. 156	Holding a guitar in a corset	ITA	$100–150
1956	*Le Ore*	9/22/56	v. IV, n. 176	Profile in the red *Niagara* dress	ITA	$100–150
1956	*L'Europeo*	7/8/56	n. 28	Wearing the black lace negligee	ITA	$100–150
1956	*Mandens Blad*	10/56		On half the cover	DEN	$50–75
1956	*Mascotte*	3/28/56	v. 3, n. 44	*Golden Dreams* nude with a blue bikini	ITA	$100–130

Year	Title	Date	Vol. #	Description	Country	Value
1956	Men Only	8/56		An artist's cartoonlike rendering of MM	ENG	$75–95
1956	Munchner Illustrierte	3/17/56	n. 11	Wearing a black-and-white-striped turtleneck	GER	$100–130
1956	Novella	7/1/56	n. 27	Marilyn's glamour at its height	ITA	$80–125
1956	Novella	8/5/56	n. 32	A studio glamour shot	ITA	$80–125
1956	Oggi	11/8/56	n. 45	Meeting Queen Elizabeth	ITA	$80–125
1956	Parade	10/56	n. 2	In the detailed gold lamé gown	ITA	$100–130
1956	Paris Frou Frou	1956	n. 40	In a skirt, sitting on a suitcase	FRA	$85–120
1956	Paris Hollywood (digest)		v. 5, n. 24	An image from Bus Stop	DEN	$80–125
1956	Paris Match	7/7/56	n. 378	With husband Arthur Miller	FRA	$100–125
1956	People	7/25/56	v. 7, n. 11	Wrapped in white sheets	AUS	$125–150
1956	Photoplay	8/56	v. 7, n. 8	Standing in a tight, detailed dress	ENG	$100–150
1956	Picturegoer	11/17/56		In a red velvet dress at a dinner table	ENG	$60–90
1956	Picture Show	10/13/56	v. 67, n. 1750	With Don Murray in Bus Stop	ENG	$60–90
1956	Picture Post	7/14/56	v. 71, n. 15	In a khaki shirt, sitting in front of a rock	ENG	$100–130
1956	Picture Post	10/22/56	v. 73, n. 3	A tight portrait from Bus Stop	ENG	$100–130
1956	Pin Up	7/56	v. 12, n. 17	Leaning against a tipped over table	SWE	$80–100
1956	Point De Vue Images Du Monde	7/7/56	n. 421	Close-up in the striped turtleneck	FRA	$125–175

Year	Title	Date	Vol. #	Description	Country	Value
1956	Radio Cinema Television	11/18/56	n. 357	In a white costume from Business	FRA	$100–130
1956	RCA Victor Cancionero			Monroe is featured on this digest.	S.AM	$75–110
1956	Realta Illustrata	12/5/56	n. 47/48	In the gold lamé gown	ITA	$100–130
1956	Revelation	c. 1956	n. 3	A close-up in a long-sleeved, lace dress	FRA	$100–150
1956	Revue	10/27/56	n. 43	The common image in the white fur	GER	$100–130
1956	Settimo Giorno	7/7/56	v. IX, n. 28	In a white fur sitting in a chair	ITA	$100–150
1956	Tempo	9/13/56	v. XVII, n. 37	In a long-sleeved lace dress	ITA	$100–140
1956	The Australian Woman's Weekly	7/25/56	v. 24, n. 8	A bluebird is perched on her finger.	AUS	$100–140
1956	Vea	1956	n. 899	In the white Itch dress on half the cover	CHI	$50–70
1956	Vie Nuove	7/21/56	v. XI, n. 30	Arm in arm with Arthur Miller	ITA	$75–125
1957	ABC	1/5/57	n. 1	A large, tinted portrait	BEL	$100–125
1957	ABC	6/22/57		In a dress on a soccer field	BEL	$100–125
1957	ABC Film Review	10/57	v. 7, n. 10	In a white dress from Showgirl	ENG	$100–130
1957	Amour Film	9/1/57	n. 149	A pretty, studio-released photograph	FRA	$60–95
1957	Billed Bladet	2/12/57	v. 20, n. 7	Eyes closed, holding a little bird	DEN	$80–125
1957	Billed Bladet	10/11/57	v. 20, n. 42	Hanging out the window from Itch	DEN	$80–125
1957	Bild Journalen	11/16–23/57	n. 46	A tinted dreamy image with blowing hair	SWE	$80–125

Year	Title	Date	Vol. #	Description	Country	Value
1957	Cinemonde	10/10/57	v. 25, n. 1209	An extra-large full-face photo from *Itch*	FRA	$100–125
1957	Cine Revelation	9/5/57	n. 179	Wearing a flame-colored dress with spangles	FRA	$100–130
1957	Cine Revue	4/12/57	v. 35, n. 15	Posing with the white fur	FRA	$75–110
1957	Deutsche Illustrierte	9/14/57	n. 37	A romantic image by Jack Cardiff	GER	$100–130
1957	Din Tidning	11/25/57	n. 22	In black sequins and a fur by Richard Avedon	SWE	$100–130
1957	Ecran	7/23/57	n. 1383	A standard, studio-released photograph	CHI	$40–60
1957	Film D'Oggi	10/19/57	n. 42	Hanging out a window from *Showgirl*	ITA	$75–100
1957	Films and Filming	7/57		With Laurence Olivier in *Showgirl*	ENG	$50–70
1957	Garbo	9/28/57	v. V, n. 237	Cheek to cheek with Laurence Olivier	SPA	$40–70
1957	Hjemmet	1/29/57	v. 60, n. 5	With Don Murray in *Bus Stop*	DEN	$85–110
1957	Il Travaso	5/26/57	n. 21	An artwork cover	ITA	$75–100
1957	Kavalkad	11/7/57		A cover from *Bus Stop*	DEN	$75–125
1957	Le Film Complet	4/18/57	n. 613	In a skirt, sitting on a suitcase in *Bus Stop*	FRA	$75–100
1957	Life (International)	7/8/57	v. 23, n. 1	Seated with Laurence Olivier in *Showgirl*	INT.	$200–275
1957	Mon Film	12/4/57	n. 589	In a ruffled dress from *Showgirl*	FRA	$75–100
1957	Neue Illustrierte	11/16/57	v. 12, n. 46	In a dress, in a photo by Cardiff	GER	$100–140
1957	Paseo	5/4/57		Wearing a long green satin gown	MEX	$75–125

Year	Title	Date	Vol. #	Description	Country	Value
1957	Picture Show	7/4/57		With Laurence Olivier in *Showgirl*	ENG	$50–70
1957	Rotosei	10/25/57	v. 1, n. 32	By Avedon, dreamy in a black-sequined dress	ITA	$100–130
1957	Screen	11/57		Wrapped in a fur in black sequins	JAP	$100–150
1957	Se	10/11–18/57	v. 20, n. 41	Lying on the floor in a flowing dress	SWE	$75–125
1957	Settimo Giorno	5/25/57	v. X, n. 21	A profilelike shot in the gold lamé dress	ITA	$100–140
1957	Sight and Sound	Summer 1957	v. 27, n. 1	A scene in a dress from *Showgirl*	ENG	$60–80
1957	Stage & Cinema	11/15/57	v. 44, n. 10	Glamorous in a gold halter-style dress	S.AFR	$100–130
1957	Svensk Damtidning	9/12/57		With Laurence Olivier	SWE	$75–125
1957	Tele Magazine	10/57	n. 6	A pretty, glamorous Monroe	FRA	$100–120
1957	The New Fiesta	7/57	v. 2, n. 6	Digest with a romantic ruffle-clad Marilyn	ENG	$100–120
1957	Tova	1957		In a flowing dress on the floor; by Greene	JAP	$100–120
1957	Vecko Revyn	9/27/57	n. 39	Wearing the long black-sequined gown	SWE	$75–125
1957	Visto	10/19/57	v. VI, n. 42	In a blue blouse; a Greene photo	ITA	$75–120
1957	Weekend	10/5/57	v. 4, n. 7	In a black dress with a white collar	AUS	$80–130
1958	Antena	5/13/58	v. XXVII, n. 1409	In a *Bus Stop* costume	ARG	$100–120
1958	Grand Hotel	2/13/58	n. 608	An artwork rendering	ITA	$75–125
1958	Idolos (digest)	7/17/58	v. 1, n. 5	All on her; wearing a white coat and gloves	SPA	$50–75

Year	Title	Date	Vol. #	Description	Country	Value
1958	Lectures d'Aujord'hui	5/3/58	n. 296	A candid, smiling Marilyn in a white terry robe	BEL	$100–140
1958	Le Ore	6/21/58	v. V, n. 267	A close-up, hugging the white pole	ITA	$100–140
1958	L'Europeo	4/13/58	n. 15	Wearing the famous gold lamé gown	ITA	$100–140
1958	New Screen News	1/10/58		Embracing Laurence Olivier	AUS	$75–100
1958	Novella	11/23/58	v. XXXIX, n. 47	Candid, with her eyes closed, smiling	ITA	$100–140
1958	Oggi	9/25/58	v. XIV, n. 39	With her hair blowing around her face	ITA	$75–125
1958	Settimo Giorno	1/4/58	v. XI, n. 1	A close-up with her eyes shut, by Avedon	ITA	$100–140
1958	Settimo Giorno	5/22/58	v. XI, n. 21	A hazy profile in an oversized hat	ITA	$100–140
1958	Settimo Giorno	10/9/58	n. 41	In a black dress and white gloves	ITA	$100–140
1958	Star Weekly	11/22/58		Newspaper section; in a red dress	CAN	$100–140
1958	Tempo	11/4/58	v. XX, n. 45	In the fuschia one-strap dress with a hand to her face	ITA	$100–150
1959	Bild Journalen	6/10/59	n. 24	Tinted in a robe by a bathtub	SWE	$75–125
1959	Cocktail	4/25/59		In a black jewel-decorated dress, laughing	ENG	$75–125
1959	De Post	2/15/59	v. 11, n. 7	At the *Bus Stop* press conference in a suit	BEL	$80–125
1959	Deutsche Illustrierte	2/14/59	n. 7	With Jane Russell in *Blondes*	GER	$50–65
1959	Epoca	3/8/59	v. X, n. 440	A half cover, by Avedon	ITA	$50–70
1959	Epoca	6/7/59	n. 453	A partial cover	ITA	$50–70

Year	Title	Date	Vol. #	Description	Country	Value
1959	Fan's Star Library—Monroe	1959	n. 18	Entire issue is on her; a glamour cover	ENG	$125–175
1959	Films and Filming	6/59	v. 5, n. 9	With Tony Curtis and Jack Lemmon	ENG	$75–100
1959	Gran Via	1959	n. 109	Wearing a black jeweled-strap dress	SPA	$75–100
1959	Hollywood Festival	8/22/59	n. 167	In a bandanna skirt with her arm up	ITA	$125–175
1959	Il Musichiere	4/30/59	v. 1, n. 17	Portrayed by an artist	ITA	$75–125
1959	Jours De France	6/13/59	n. 239	Biting a strand of pearls	FRA	$100–140
1959	La Settimo Incom Illustrata	11/7/59	v. XII, n. 45	A picture from Niagara	ITA	$100–140
1959	L'Europeo	7/19/59	n. 29	Playing on the beach in a swimsuit	ITA	$100–125
1959	Liberty	3/59		Wearing the white fur on ¾ of the cover	CAN	$50–65
1959	Lunes	7/6/59	n. 59	In a black negligee from Hot	URU	$100–120
1959	Marie Claire	9/59		A very tight close-up from Hot	FRA	$100–140
1959	Mundo Argentino	5/13/59	n. 2515	A tinted cover with her hand to her cheek	ARG	$100–120
1959	Neue Illustrierte	12/12/59	v. 14, n. 50	Jumping, in a dress	GER	$100–140
1959	Noi Donne	5/3/59	v. XIV, n. 18	In the red Niagara dress and hoops	ITA	$80–120
1959	Oggi	4/19/59	v. XV, n. 16	Sitting in a chair, wearing triple pearls	ITA	$80–100
1959	Oggi	10/8/59	v. XV, n. 41	In a black dress, biting a strand of pearls	ITA	$80–100
1959	Paris Match	2/28/59	n. 516	A close-up from Bus Stop	FRA	$100–125

Year	Title	Date	Vol. #	Description	Country	Value
1959	*Picture Show*	12/26/59		A portrait decorated by Christmas ornaments	ENG	$50–75
1959	*Pix*	4/11/59		In a cocktail dress, wearing a lot of jewelry	AUS	$100–140
1959	*Platea*	12/4/59	v. 1, n. 5	In a beaded gown, holding an earring	ARG	$80–120
1959	*Regards*	11/59		A close-up from *River*, in earrings	FRA	$100–120
1959	*Revue*	2/21/59	n. 8	In a white dress with gold drapes behind her	GER	$150–200
1959	*Se*	12/17/59	v. 22, n. 51	Two images of Marilyn jumping, by Halsman	SWE	$75–100
1959	*Se Og Hor*	2/13/59	v. 20, n. 7	Sitting with Karen Blixen	DEN	$80–110
1959	*Sissi*	1959	v. 2, n. 76	Holding the 500-year-old diamond	SPA	$60–80
1959	*Sissi*	1959	v. 2, n. 77	With shorter hair and black gloves	SPA	$60–80
1959	*Sissi*	8/24/59	v. 2, n. 78	With Arthur Miller	SPA	$60–80
1959	*Sissi*	1959	v. 2, n. 79	A younger glamour portrait with hand up	SPA	$60–80
1959	*Star Revue*	11/59		A standard studio-released photo	GER	$100–140
1959	*Star Weekly*	10/3/59	n. 24	Marilyn on top in sequins; Arthur Miller on bottom	CAN	$40–60
1959	*The Australian Woman's Weekly*	4/8/59		In the black-sequined dress, a profile by Avedon	AUS	$100–140
1959	*The Queen*	3/17/59		A photo showing Marilyn at her best	ENG	$75–125
1959	*TV Cine Actualite*	6/14/59	n. 272	A glamorous publicity photo	FRA	$75–120
1959	*Vie Nuove*	10/3/59	n. 39	In a black negligee in *Hot*	ITA	$80–120

Year	Title	Date	Vol. #	Description	Country	Value
1959	Weekend	10/21–25/59	n. 2852	Biting playfully on a strand of pearls	ENG	$85–110
1959	Zondagsvriend	12/31/59	n. 53	Jumping up with Halsman	HOL	$80–120
1960	Bild Journalen	5/11/60		In the famous gold lamé halter dress	SWE	$75–120
1960	Bonnes Soirees	4/10/60	n. 1991	Displaying "the Marilyn Look"	FRA	$75–120
1960	Bravo	7/17–23/60	n. 29	In a glamorous gown	GER	$80–110
1960	Capri	5/60	n. 18	A studio publicity pose	FRA	$80–110
1960	Cinemonde	5/10/60	v. 28, n. 1344	A less common white fur pose	FRA	$80–120
1960	De Post	10/9/60	v. 12, n. 41	In a black dress and a sad face	BEL	$80–120
1960	Ecran	12/16/60	n. 1638	A serious face in a white fur	CHI	$40–60
1960	Elite	10/29/60		In the plunging gold lamé gown	VEN	$75–100
1960	Elokuwa Aitta	1960	n. 12	A tinted glamour photo	FIN	$50–70
1960	Epoca	2/14/60	v. XI, n. 489	In a beige dress, holding a champagne glass	ITA	$75–110
1960	Frau Im Spiegel	2/20/60	v. 15	A glamorous portrait	SWI	$75–110
1960	Funk Und Film	9/24/60	n. 39	A standard studio photograph	GER	$75–110
1960	Gaceta Illustrada	5/21/60	n. 189	Sitting on the floor throwing money in the air	SPA	$125–175
1960	Gente	1/29/60	n. 5	A typical glamour studio shot	ITA	$80–110
1960	Jours De France	8/6/60	n. 299	Being embraced by Yves Montand	FRA	$80–110
1960	Jours De France	11/26/60	n. 315	A close-up from The Misfits, with bangs	FRA	$80–110
1960	La Cinematographie Francaise	10/1/60	n. 1885	A studio glamour photograph	FRA	$75–125

Year	Title	Date	Vol. #	Description	Country	Value
1960	La Settimana Incom Illustrata	11/24/60	n. 47	In a silver lamé gown	ITA	$80–120
1960	L'Ecran Lorrain	11/60	n. 161	A studio publicity photo	FRA	$75–100
1960	Lecturas	9/1/60		A studio glamour image	SPA	$80–120
1960	Le Films Pour Vous	6/20/60	n. 184	Marilyn at her best	FRA	$75–125
1960	Le Films Pour Vous	9/12/60	n. 196	In a glamorous dress	FRA	$75–125
1960	Le Ore	4/6/60	n. 363	Jumping up in a black-sequined dress	ITA	$100–120
1960	Le Ore	9/6/60	v. VIII, n. 382	Dancing in a purple sweater, from Love	ITA	$100–120
1960	Le Ore	12/13/60	v. VIII, n. 396	Throwing money into the air	ITA	$125–160
1960	L'Europeo	4/10/60	n. 15	A glamour shot in a chair from Love	ITA	$80–110
1960	L'Europeo	9/18/60	v. XVI, n. 38	Doing the Charleston in a black dress	ITA	$80–110
1960	L'Europeo	11/20/60	v. XVI, n. 47	Sitting on a table looking at diamonds	ITA	$80–110
1960	Liberty	10/60	v. 37, n. 7	¾ cover with a reflection from a mirror	CAN	$50–75
1960	L'Officiel Des Spectacles	10/12/60	n. 726	A glamour photograph	FRA	$75–95
1960	Manana	7/9/60	n. 880	In a red spaghetti-strap dress	MEX	$125–175
1960	Me Naiset	12/6/60	n. 18	With Yves Montand in director's chairs	FIN	$80–120

Year	Title	Date	Vol. #	Description	Country	Value
1960	*Meridiano*	1/10/60	n. 2	A large b/w candid portrait	ITA	$80–100
1960	*Munchner Illustrierte*	9/30/60	n. 36	A publicity shot with Montand	GER	$100–130
1960	*Neue Illustrierte*	10/22/60	v, 15, n. 43	A portrait by Avedon	GER	$100–130
1960	*Noir Et Blanc*	1/29/60	n. 778	With Yves Montand	FRA	$75–100
1960	*Noir Et Blanc*	11/16/60	n. 820	A candid with husband Arthur Miller	FRA	$75–100
1960	*Paris Match*	2/13/60	n. 566	Embracing Yves Montand	FRA	$75–100
1960	*Photo Roman*	6/15/60	n. 10	A tinted cover, being held by Keith Andes	FRA	$125–150
1960	*Piccolo*	11/60		A glamorous face shot	HOL	$50–75
1960	*Picture Show*	10/15/60		In a leotard from *Love*	ENG	$65–95
1960	*Popular Hi-Fi*	10/60		In a negligee by a bookcase	ENG	$100–130
1960	*Revue*	3/26/60	n. 13	Dancing in a black sheath dress	GER	$100–130
1960	*Revue*	12/17/60	n. 51	An unretouched portrait from *Misfits*	GER	$100–130
1960	*Roman Bladet*	9/1/60	n. 314	In a gold halter dress looking glamorous	DEN	$100–120
1960	*Romanschatz*	1960	n. 204	A pose with Tony Curtis	GER	$65–85
1960	*Settimo Giorno*	11/27/60	v. XIII, n. 49	With Yves Montand	ITA	$100–130
1960	*Sight and Sound*	Autumn 1960	v. 29, n. 4	A shot from *Love*	ENG	$60–80
1960	*Stage And Cinema*	4/1/60	v. 55, n. 2	A glamorous Marilyn	S.AFR	$100–120
1960	*Star Revue*	5/60	n. 10	A close-up by Avedon	GER	$90–120

Year	Title	Date	Vol. #	Description	Country	Value
1960	Star Weekly	9/24/60		Newspaper section; holding pole from Love	CAN	$90–110
1960	Stern	6/18/60	v. 13, n.25	Surrounded by men in a number from Love	GER	$100–130
1960	Stern	9/17/60	v. 13, n. 38	With Yves Montand	GER	$100–130
1960	Stern	12/17/60	v. 13, n. 51	A cute photo, looking at diamonds	GER	$80–110
1960	Tempo	8/27/60	v. XXII, n. 35	Hair blowing in the black-sequined dress	ITA	$80–100
1960	The Australian Woman's Weekly	12/7/60		A less common shot in white gloves	AUS	$90–110
1960	Today	10/1/60	n. 37	With Yves Montand	ENG	$90–110
1960	Vecko Revyen	9/60		Onstage with men from Love	SWE	$80–110
1960	Visto	10/6/60	n. 41	A candid shot in a suit with a bouquet of roses	ITA	$80–100
1960	Weekend	4/9/60	v. 6, n. 34	A candid with Arthur Miller	AUS	$100–120
1960	Weekend	30 Mar.–3 Apr. 1960	n. 2875	With Frankie Vaughn	ENG	$100–120
1960	Weekend	9/7–11/60		Onstage with men from Love	ENG	$100–120
1961	ABC Met TV Gids	4/15/61		With her idol, Clark Gable	BEL	$75–100
1961	Bild Journalen	5/24/61		In a chair, by photographer Arnold	SWE	$60–80
1961	Cinelandia	4/61	v. X, n. 203	In a bright orange blouse	BRA	$85–110
1961	Cinelandia	6/61	v. X, n. 207	In a black hair net from The Misfits	BRA	$85–110
1961	Cinemonde	2/21/61	v. 28, n. 1385	In a black dress with white gloves	FRA	$100–120

Year	Title	Date	Vol. #	Description	Country	Value
1961	*Cine Universal*	7/1/61	n. 119	Embracing Clark Gable	MEX	$100–125
1961	*Epoca*	2/5/61	v. XII, n. 540	On the floor in a white terry robe	ITA	$80–110
1961	*Filmski Svet*	10/10/61	n. 345	A typical glamour shot	POL	$100–110
1961	*Funk Und Film*	4/8/61		A studio-released publicity still	GER	$80–110
1961	*Hayat*	5/18/61	n. 21	Three different tinted portraits of her	TUR	$100–140
1961	*Hayat*	8/24/61	n. 35	In a bikini in a director's chair on *The Misfits* set	TUR	$100–140
1961	*Hebdo Roman*	1/25/61	n. 4	A glamorous photograph	FRA	$80–110
1961	*Jours De France*	2/18/61	n. 327	A close-up by Arnold	FRA	$75–120
1961	*Kristall*	1961		A b/w image by Greene, in a top hat	GER	$75–100
1961	*Le Monde Et La Vie*	9/61	n. 100	Smiling in the black-sequined dress	FRA	$100–120
1961	*Lecturas*	1961	n. 511	A portrait from *Love*	SPA	$80–100
1961	*L'Espresso Mese*	3/61	n. 3	A photo by Arnold in a car	ITA	$80–110
1961	*L'Europeo*	3/12/61	v. XVII, n. 11	From *Misfits* in a black polka-dot hair net	ITA	$80–120
1961	*L'Europeo*	6/25/61	v. XVII, n. 26	In a black fur and black leather gloves	ITA	$100–120
1961	*L'Europeo*	12/17/61	v. XVII, n. 51	In a black strapless dress decorated with beadwork	ITA	$100–120
1961	*Manana*	7/1/61	n. 931	Reflection from *Misfits* in a car mirror	MEX	$100–150
1961	*Mi Vida*	8/24/61	n. 176	A tinted glamour photo in a dress	CHI	$75–110
1961	*Radio*	11/1/61	n. 130	A typical glamour photograph	SPA	$60–80

Year	Title	Date	Vol. #	Description	Country	Value
1961	Star Weekly	9/16/61		A candid from the set of Hot	CAN	$80–100
1961	Tempo	4/11/61	n. 15	Tinted shot with Clark Gable and Montgomery Clift	DEN	$80–110
1961	The Eiga Geijutsu	1961		A shot from Love on a chair	JAP	$80–120
1961	Today	2/4/61	v. 3, n. 50	Standing with husband Arthur Miller	ENG	$80–110
1961	Visto	2/16/61	n. 7	A sexy studio photograph	ITA	$75–100
1961	Weekend	3/1–5/61	n. 2923	A cute glamour portrait	ENG	$75–100
1962	ABC	8/12/62	n. 33	A b/w Greene photo	ITA	$90–110
1962	Antena TV	9/4/62		In a costume from Love	ARG	$80–110
1962	Avondlectur	3/23/62		In the cherry-print dress from The Misfits	HOL	$80–110
1962	Billed Bladet	8/10/62	v. 25, n. 32	With a surprised look from Hot	DEN	$80–110
1962	Bunte Illustrierte	8/22/62	n. 34	In the black-sequined dress by Avedon	GER	$100–130
1962	Celuloid	9/62		A glamour image on this death issue	SPA	$80–100
1962	Cine Avance	8/62	n. 1	A close-up in gold hoop earrings and a smile	MEX	$125–175
1962	Cine Monde	8/14/62	n. 1462	In a dark pink halter dress on this tribute	FRA	$100–150
1962	Cine Tele-Revue	8/8/62	n. 33	Entire issue devoted to her; two images on cover	FRA	$100–175
1962	Cineuniversal	9/1/62		A candid photo from her last trip to Mexico	MEX	$100–200
1962	Contre Champ	10/62	n. 4	A glamour photograph on another memorial	FRA	$80–100
1962	Ecran	6/15/62	n. 1560	A photo from Love	CHI	$40–60

Year	Title	Date	Vol. #	Description	Country	Value
1962	Ecran	8/10/62	n. 1646	Another image from *Love*	CHI	$40–60
1962	El Aventuras	8/8/62		Entire issue is on her; a profile in the gold lamé	MEX	$125–200
1962	Epoca	8/12/62	v. XIII, n. 620	At her last Golden Globes Awards	ITA	$100–150
1962	Everybody's	9/19/62		In a blue terry robe from *Give*	AUS	$100–150
1962	Everybody's	9/26/62		In a chair, wearing the cherry dress from *Misfits*	AUS	$100–150
1962	Fatos & Fotos	8/18/62		Typical Marilyn on this memorial-oriented cover	SPA	$100–120
1962	Festival Film Special	1962		Entire issue is on her; in the white fur	FRA	$175–225
1962	Fotogramas	3/16/62	v. XVII, n. 694	A studio publicity still	SPA	$80–120
1962	Fotogramas	6/8/62	v. XVII, n. 706	Tinted, in the flower dress from *Give*	SPA	$80–120
1962	Frau Im Spiegel	8/25/62	v. 17, n. 34	Face shot at an awards show in Hollywood	SWI	$80–110
1962	Gaceta Illustrada	8/11/62	v. VII, n. 305	A still from *Love*	SPA	$80–110
1962	Gente	8/17/62	n. 33	With Yves Montand	ITA	$80–100
1962	Hemmets Journal	12/27/62	v. 42, n. 52	In a beige fur hat from *Give*	SWE	$85–120
1962	Idilio	10/16/62		In a white dress from *Love*	ARG	$80–120
1962	Intervalo De Cine Presenta—MM	1962		Entire issue is dedicated to her life and death.	ARG	$150–200

Year	Title	Date	Vol. #	Description	Country	Value
1962	Kavalkad (digest)	4/62	v. 14, n. 9	A young Norma Jean holding ski poles	SWE	$80–110
1962	La Grande Tra-gedia—MM	1962		Entire issue on her, looking over her shoulder	ARG	$150–200
1962	Le Soir Illustre	8/9/62	n. 1572	Classic Monroe in a white-collared dress	FRA	$100–140
1962	L'Europeo	3/25/62	n. 12	Three pictures from the Golden Globe Awards	ITA	$80–120
1962	L'Europeo	6/18/62	n. 24	In a swimming pool from Give	ITA	$80–120
1962	L'Europeo	8/12/62	n. 32	In a black fur and black gloves on this tribute issue	ITA	$80–120
1962	Luxembourg Selection	11/62	n. 8	In the black negligee from publicity stills	FRA	$80–110
1962	Manchet	8/62		Another publication says good-bye to Monroe	MEX	$100–125
1962	Maschere	8/62		A glamorous Marilyn in a publicity still	ITA	$80–120
1962	Mi Vida	8/30/62	n. 229	In a red dress standing next to a green chair	CHI	$100–150
1962	Mujer	2/62		A Greene photo, lying on the floor	SPA	$90–125
1962	Neue Illustrierte	8/12/62	v. 17, n. 32	In a beige fur hat, biting her tongue	GER	$100–130
1962	Noir Et Blanc	8/10/62	n. 910	A glamour shot in a necklace and earrings	FRA	$100–125
1962	Oggi	8/12/62	v. XVIII, n. 33	A moment with her hair up from Love	ITA	$100–140

Year	Title	Date	Vol. #	Description	Country	Value
1962	Oggi	9/20/62	v. XVIII, n. 38	With her eyes closed in a pink shirt	ITA	$100–140
1962	Paris Match	6/23/62	n. 689	Laying her head on her arm	FRA	$100–120
1962	Paris Match	8/18/62	n. 697	A close-up portrait from 1962	FRA	$100–120
1962	Piccolo	9/2/62	n. 704	Wearing a jean jacket on *The Misfits* set	HOL	$80–110
1962	Point De Vue Images Du Monde	8/10/62	v. 18, n. 739	In a blue gown with jewels	FRA	$100–130
1962	Positif	10/62	n. 48	A b/w image with her hair up	FRA	$75–100
1962	Radio Film	9/30/62		A publicity still from *Love*	ARG	$100–120
1962	Sabado Grafico	8/11/62	n. 306	At a press conference	SPA	$100–120
1962	Se	6/28/62	v. 25, n. 26	Almost naked, seated by the pooi in *Give*	SWE	$80–100
1962	Se	8/9/62	v. 25, n. 32	With her eyes shut in the black-sequined dress	SWE	$80–100
1962	Se Apago La Estrella—MM	1962		Entire issue is on her life and death.	ARG	$150–200
1962	Se Og Hor	6/29/62	v. 23, n. 27	In the swimming pool during the filming of *Give*	DEN	$80–100
1962	Stop	8/62	n. 16	In the gold lamé gown	FRA	$70–95
1962	Svensk Dam Tidning	8/22/62	n. 34	A portrait from *Love*	SWE	$75–110
1962	Tempo	8/18/62	v. XXIV, n. 33	Seated on a sofa in the black-sequined dress	ITA	$100–150
1962	Todo	8/16/62	n. 1349	A glamorous Marilyn in a dress	MEX	$125–175

Year	Title	Date	Vol. #	Description	Country	Value
1962	*Town*	11/62		A portrait by George Barris during her last summer	ENG	$100–150
1962	*TV France*	8/18–24/62	n. 20	Smiling in a white terry robe from *Itch*	FRA	$90–120
1962	*Vie Nuove*	8/9/62	v. XVII, n. 32	A close-up portrait on this tribute issue	ITA	$90–110
1962	*Wereld Kroniek*	8/62		A ¾ cover with a large face shot	HOL	$85–100
1962	*Woman's Day*	3/19/62	n. 274	A pretty portrait from *Love*	AUS	$95–115
1962	*Cine Monde*	7/30/62	v. 31, n. 1512	In the beige fur hat, biting her tongue	FRA	$100–130
1962	*Crapouillot*	1/63	n. 59	By the swimming pool in *Give*	FRA	$75–90
1963	*Cine Hoy*	11–12/63		A close-up	ARG	$80–110
1963	*Epoca*	8/11/63	v. XIV, n. 672	A semiprofile in the gold lamé gown	ITA	$80–110
1963	*Frissons Films*	6/63	n. 3	A studio publicity still	FRA	$75–100
1963	*Movie TV & Show Times*	1963		Holding a pole from *Love*	JAP	$90–120
1963	*Se*	5/9/63	n. 19	A tinted Stern shot with a scarf	SWE	$75–100
1963	*Successo*	5/63	n. 5	An artwork cover of Marilyn dancing	ITA	$60–80
1963	*Towa*	1963		Sitting by the swimming pool in *Give*	JAP	$80–110
1964	*Idun Vecko Journalen*	11/6/64	n. 45	A portrait in the blue terry robe from *Give*	SWE	$75–100
1964	*Le Ore*	3/2/64	n. 13	Curled up in a bed with a red carnation on it	ITA	$75–100

Year	Title	Date	Vol. #	Description	Country	Value
1964	L'Europeo	2/9/64	v. XX, n. 6	A portrait in the blue terry robe from *Give*	ITA	$75–100
1964	Listener	8/28/64	v. 51, n. 1300	Posing for a picture	NZ	$75–100
1964	Panorama	10/64	v. 2, n.25	Wearing the gold lamé gown	ITA	$70–100
1964	Tidens Kvinder	10/6/64		A pretty portrait in the beige fur-trimmed hat	SWE	$75–110
1964	Vecko Revyen	11/4/64		Wrapped in a fur wearing the black-sequined dress	SWE	$75–100
1965	Film Ideal	8/1/65		With a stand-in during a scene in *Blondes*	SPA	$60–90
1965	Marie Claire	1/18/65	n. 128	A joyful face in the black-sequined dress	FRA	$80–110
1965	7 Dias	10/65		A sad face, holding up a tinted scarf over her torso	CHI	$75–95
1965	Tele Derniere	10/20/65	n. 186	A portrait from her last summer	FRA	$75–95
1966	Cine Tele Revue	4/28/66		In the flame-colored dress from *Blondes*	FRA	$60–80
1966	Gente	8/31/66	v. X, n. 35	In a black spaghetti-strap dress	ITA	$75–100
1966	Interview	8/66	n. 6	A classic glamour photograph	FRA	$75–95
1966	Kristall	9/23/66		In a sweater in the mid-1950s	GER	$75–100
1966	La Storia Del Cinema	3/30/66	n. 1	Jumping in a Halsman picture	ITA	$75–95
1966	Mi Vida	11/66	v. VIII, n. 442	Sitting in the flame-colored gown from *Blondes*	CHI	$75–110
1966	Mujeres Celebras	1966		A glamour still by the studio	SPA	$70–100

Year	Title	Date	Vol. #	Description	Country	Value
1966	Secretos	1/8/66		An Arnold portrait on *The Misfits* set	ARG	$75–100
1966	Stern	8/7/66	n. 32	In the blue terry robe by the pool from *Give*	GER	$75–120
1967	La Storia Del Cinema	2/1/67	n. 44	With Laurence Olivier on the set of *Showgirl*	ITA	$50–75
1967	Noir Et Blanc	12/6/67	v. 22, n. 1187	A candid shot with her hand on her chin	FRA	$50–80
1968	Cine Avance	8/10/68		A close-up portrait in the gold lamé gown	MEX	$75–100
1968	Historia Hors Serie	1968	n. 10	The typical Monroe glamour image	FRA	$40–60
1968	Observer	7/14/68		A sad portrait taken by Stern	ENG	$45–60
1969	Buenbogar	1969		The overused photo in the white fur	SWE	$40–60
1969	Gente	1/22/69	n. 4	A half cover close-up from *Love*	ITA	$40–60
1969	Se	12/23/69		Sitting in a director's chair for *Love*	SWE	$40–60
1971	Fotogramas	2/12/71	v. XXVI, n. 1165	A romantic glamour photograph	SPA	$30–40
1971	Headlines	12/71		Various newspaper clippings	ENG	$30–50
1971	Stop	7/17/71	n. 1189	With John Kennedy	ITA	$30–40
1971	Tele 7 Jours	8/7/71	n. 589	A classic Marilyn at her best	FRA	$30–40
1972	Cine Revue	12/21/72	v. 52, n. 51	A Barris photo by the ocean	FRA	$30–40
1972	Grand Hotel	10/12/72	v. XXVII, n. 1371	An artwork cover depicting Monroe	ITA	$30–40

Year	Title	Date	Vol. #	Description	Country	Value
1972	*Hitweek*	9/22/72		A reproduction of the 1952 *Life* cover	HOL	$30–40
1972	*Oggi*	10/3/72	n. 40	On most of the cover, in an orange shirt	ITA	$30–40
1972	*Skema*	11/72	n. 11	Dancing with a large ostrich plume	ITA	$30–40
1972	*Vogue*	12/71–1/72	n. 522	A glamour portrait	FRA	$30–40
1973	*Film Index*	1973	n. 15	With Richard Widmark	AUS	$20–30
1973	*Film Index*	1973	n. 16	With Cary Grant and Charles Coburn	AUS	$20–30
1973	*HP*	8/11/73	v. 60, n. 32	In the blue terry robe from *Give*	HOL	$25–40
1973	*Q-Quick*	9/6/73		Lying on the floor by Greene	GER	$25–40
1973	*The Sunday Times Magazine*	9/16/73		A young Norma Jean holding a ball	ENG	$25–40
1973	*Thursday*	11/22/63		A Barris photo from her final summer	AUS	$25–40
1973	*Vecko Journalen*	8/8/73	n. 32	A classic glamour image	SWE	$25–40
1973	*Women's Weekly*	10/17/73		Holding a champagne glass	AUS	$25–40
1974	*Domenica Del Corriere*	7/7/74	n. 27	An Avedon photo in a glamorous dress	ITA	$25–35
1974	*Historia*	3/74	n. 328	Partially featured on the cover	FRA	$20–30
1974	*La Fiera Letteraria*	1/20/74	n. 3	A glamour photograph	ITA	$25–35
1974	*Le Grand Journal Illustre*	7/20/74		Monroe at her best	FRA	$25–35
1974	*L'Express*	10/21/74	n. 1215	A studio-released publicity photo	FRA	$25–35
1974	*L'Express*	10/28/74	n. 1216	Another publicity still	FRA	$25–35

Year	Title	Date	Vol. #	Description	Country	Value
1974	Miroir De L'Historie	1974	n. B 280	Looking seductive in a black negligee	FRA	$25–35
1974	Movie	1974	part 1	A classic glamour image	ENG	$25–35
1974	Movie	1974	part 2	Another glamour photo	ENG	$25–35
1974	Photo	11/74	n. 86	Dressed as a ballerina in white	FRA	$25–35
1974	Samedi Teleguide	7/27/74	n. 2196	An image from her final summer	BEL	$25–35
1974	Telerama	10/30/74	n. 1294	The majority of the cover is an image by Stern	FRA	$25–35
1975	Le Nouvel Observateur	7/21/75	n. 558	Holding a mirror in an Arnold shot	FRA	$25–35
1975	Positif	1/75	n. 165	A sexy and glamorous Marilyn	FRA	$25–35
1975	Tele Magazine	7/19/75	n. 1028	A standard studio photograph	FRA	$25–35
1975	Tele 7 Jours	1/25/75	n. 767	Another studio publicity still	FRA	$25–35
1976	Guida TV	10/1/76	n. 29	Wearing a tight dress and a smile	ITA	$20–30
1976	Le Vedettes Internationales	6/26/76		Looking glamorous in a studio photo	FRA	$20–30
1976	Panorama	11/26/76		A studio-produced photograph	ITA	$20–30
1976	Top Tele	12/22/76	n. 15	In a low-cut sexy gown	FRA	$20–30
1977	Comment	8/77	n. 5	An overused publicity still	FRA	$20–30
1977	Revue	5 & 6/77	n. 79	Another 20th Century-Fox still	FRA	$20–30
1977	Settimana TV	8/21/77	n. 35	A smiling Marilyn at her finest	ITA	$20–30
1978	Encyclopedia Alpha Du Cinema	9/20/78	v. 1, n. 1	A pretty portrait from her final summer	FRA	$20–30
1978	Figure	5/78	v. 1, n. 2	Artwork by artist Tempest	ITA	$20–30
1978	Film Portraits	3 & 4/78	n. 2	A portrait by Arnold	FRA	$20–30
1978	Le Soir Illustre	8/24/78		Wearing the beige fur hat from Give	FRA	$25–30

Year	Title	Date	Vol. #	Description	Country	Value
1978	*Metal Hurlant*	12/78	n. 36	Artwork of MM and a lion head	FRA	$20–30
1978	*Panorama*	7/14/78		A typical glamour image	ITA	$20–30
1979	*Bravo*	4/5/79		A standard glamour portrait	GER	$20–30
1979	*Bravo*	11/15/79		Another glamour photograph	GER	$20–30
1979	*Confidences*	5/79	n. 1638	Smiling, in a sexy dress	FRA	$20–30
1979	*Epoca*	7/7/79	n. 1500	A smiling glamorous Monroe	ITA	$20–30
1979	*Golboy*	1/79	n. 81	A studio still	FRA	$20–30
1979	*Golboy*	10/79	n. 89	Another studio portrait	FRA	$20–30
1979	*Grafiti*	7/79		A smiling portrait	FRA	$20–30
1979	*Titbits*	8/25/79		A sexy Monroe pose	ENG	$20–30
1980	*Bravo*	5/29/80		In a low-cut dress	GER	$20–30
1980	*Cahiers Du Cinema*	4/80	n. 310	A studio publicity pose	FRA	$20–30
1980	*Confidences*	6/80	n. 1696	A classic glamorous Marilyn	SPA	$20–30
1980	*Encyclopedie Alpha Du Cinema*	7/2/80	n. 93	A sexy-looking Monroe	FRA	$20–30
1980	*Encyclopedie Alpha Du Cinema*	8/30/80	n. 132	An overused publicity still	FRA	$20–30
1980	*Dizionario Del Film*	1980	n. 10	Monroe glamour	ITA	$20–30
1980	*Guida TV*	9/21/80	n. 38	A studio-released photo	ITA	$20–30
1980	*I Grandi Fatti*	1980		A pretty, soft portrait	ITA	$20–30
1980	*Mikro Gids*	7/12–18/80		A studio photograph	ITA	$20–30
1980	*Movies Chap*	1980		A glamour image in a dress	ENG	$20–30
1980	*Oggi*	9/10/80	n. 37	A flattering portrait	ITA	$20–30
1980	*Paris Liosirs*	9/80	n. 9	A typical Marilyn pose	FRA	$20–30

Year	Title	Date	Vol. #	Description	Country	Value
1980	*Ragazza*	8/20/80	n. 35	Wearing a bright orange blouse	ITA	$20-30
1980	*Se*	5/80	n. 20	Wearing an expensive silk slip	SWE	$20-30
1980	*Tele Cine Video*	12/80	n. 2	A studio-released publicity still	FRA	$20-30
1980	*Tele Guide*	11/12/80	n. 189	A smiling, vibrant Marilyn	FRA	$20-30
1980	*Telerama*	7/2/80	n. 1590	A glamorous photo	FRA	$20-30
1980	*Tele Sette*	5/1/80	n. 18	Posing with the white fur	ITA	$20-30
1980	*Tele Star*	8/5/80	n. 201	In the velvet green dress from *River*	FRA	$20-30
1980	*Vara Gids*	7/12/80	v. 51, n. 28	In a white bikini top with a sky background	HOL	$20-30
1981	*Bunte*	2/7/81		A close-up portrait	GER	$20-30
1981	*Cult Movie*	12/81–1/82		Entire issue on her; in *Itch* dress	ITA	$20-30
1981	*Encyclopedie Alpha Du Cinema*	4/15/81	v. X, n. 132	In the pool from *Give*	FRA	$20-30
1981	*Fotogramas*	3/4/81	v. 32, n. 647	Wrapped in a towel on the beach	SPA	$20-30
1981	*Grand Hotel*	7/20/81	n. 30	In the train from *Hot*	ITA	$20-30
1981	*La Recherche*	12/81	n. 128	A studio publicity still	FRA	$20-30
1981	*Metal Hurlant*	7/81	n. 64	In a sexy pose	FRA	$20-30
1981	*Photo*	3/81	n. 162	Wrapped in white sheets, by Douglas Kirkland	FRA	$20-30
1981	*Pilote*	3/81	n. 82	A studio publicity pose	FRA	$20-30
1981	*Pilote*	5/81	n. 84	Another studio publicity pose	FRA	$20-30
1981	*Popular Video*	10/81		A studio publicity photo	ENG	$20-30
1981	*Presse*	12/26/81	n. 4	A studio glamour shot	FRA	$20-30
1981	*Q-Quick*	1/81		A studio publicity photo	GER	$20-30
1981	*Q-Quick*	10/81		A smiling glamour image	GER	$20-30

Year	Title	Date	Vol. #	Description	Country	Value
1981	Star Club	1981		Entire issue on her; in black lace	GER	$20–30
1981	Telerama	5/23/81	n. 1636	A studio glamour photograph	FRA	$20–30
1981	Video News	3 & 4/81	n. 2	A classic Monroe image	FRA	$20–30
1982	Amica	6/22/82	n. 25	Majority of issue is on her; in the gold lamé	ITA	$25–35
1982	Bravo	8/3/82	n. 66	A peekaboo nude by Stern	CHI	$20–30
1982	Cinema & Cinema	10–12/82	n. 33	In the sheets, by Kirkland	ITA	$20–30
1982	Cosmos	3/82		A pretty portrait	VEN	$20–30
1982	El Cine Enciclopedia Salvat	1982		A close-up from her final summer	SPA	$20–30
1982	Emma	6/82		In the scrunch dress by Halsman	GER	$20–30
1982	France Soir Magazine	5/2/82	n. 11746	A typical glamour image by Stern	FRA	$20–30
1982	Il Cinema	1982	n. 59	A studio-released photograph	ITA	$20–30
1982	Intimidades	1982		In the gold lamé gown	SPA	$20–30
1982	Le Cinema	1982	n. 1–2	A classic glamour photo	FRA	$20–30
1982	Lecturas	8/82		A smiling glamour-clad Monroe	SPA	$20–30
1982	Le Nouveau F	7 & 8/82	n. 6/6	A tight close-up from River	FRA	$20–30
1982	Metal Extra	4/82	n. 1	An artwork cover of Marilyn	ITA	$20–30
1982	Piejk	8/82		A pretty, flattering portrait	JAP	$20–30
1982	Q-Quick	8/82	n. 32	A glamour pose by Greene	GER	$20–30
1982	Ragazza In	4/82	n. 16	A studio glamour publicity still	ITA	$20–30
1982	Salut	9/1/82	n. 181	A glamour photograph	FRA	$20–30
1982	Star Retro	6/82	n. 2	A classic and famous Monroe shot	FRA	$20–30

Year	Title	Date	Vol. #	Description	Country	Value
1982	Star System	9/82	n. 10	Entire issue on her; in a dress from *Blondes*	FRA	$25–35
1982	Stern	8/5/82	n. 32	A close-up portrait by Stern	GER	$20–30
1982	Sunday	1982	n. 31	A young Marilyn demonstrates many exercises.	ENG	$20–30
1982	Super Tele	11/13/82	n. 184	A classic glamour photograph	FRA	$20–30
1982	Tele Guide	2/2/82	n. 253	Another glamour shot	FRA	$20–30
1982	Tele Guide Jeux	1/82	n. 9	A smiling, vibrant Monroe	FRA	$20–30
1982	Tele Poche	3/27/82	n. 116	A sexy, smiling Marilyn	FRA	$20–30
1982	Telerama	7/28/82	n. 1698	A studio-released pose	FRA	$20–30
1982	Tele 7 Jours	7/31/82	n. 1157	A pretty studio portrait	FRA	$20–30
1982	Titbits	9/25/82	n. 5020	Drinking a glass of champagne, by Stern	ENG	$20–30
1982	TV Radio Corriere	8/1/82	n. 31	A flattering photograph by the studio	ITA	$20–30
1982	TV Sorrisi E Canzoni	8/8/82	n. 32	A typical sexy Monroe	ITA	$20–30
1982	Video	7 & 8/82	n. 12	A classic well-known photograph	FRA	$20–30
1982	Video TV Jaquettes	5/1/82	n. 1	Wearing a sexy dress and a big smile	FRA	$20–30
1983	Christiane	1/83	n. 390	A glamour photo, often used	FRA	$20–30
1983	Grandi Temi Della Fotografia		n. 6	A studio glamour still	ITA	$20–30
1983	Histoire De L'Art	2/83	n. 154	A common photograph	FRA	$20–30
1983	Le Cinema	1983	n. 59	Wearing a tight, sexy dress	FRA	$20–30
1983	Positif	7 & 8/83	n. 269/70	A smiling, glamorous Monroe	FRA	$20–30

Year	Title	Date	Vol. #	Description	Country	Value
1983	*Psychologies*	9/83	n. 3	An often-seen studio still	FRA	$20–30
1983	*Q-Quick*	7/7/83	v. 7, n. 28	Four different photos of MM	GER	$20–30
1983	*Q-Quick*	10/83		In the well-known white *Itcb* dress	GER	$20–30
1983	*Retro Revue*	1/83	n. 2	On this nostalgia-oriented issue	FRA	$20–30
1983	*Salut*	12/21/83		A studio-released publicity still	FRA	$20–30
1983	*Screen*	2/25/83	n. 215	Holding a striped scarf over her torso	JAP	$20–30
1983	*Skoop*	11/83		Another common publicity pose	HOL	$20–30
1983	*Tele Cine Video*	2/83	n. 26	A studio-released publicity still	FRA	$20–30
1983	*Tele De Aaz*	7/9/83	n. 43	Wearing a sexy, tight dress	FRA	$20–30
1983	*Tele K-7*	9/17/83	n. 1	A well-known photograph	FRA	$20–30
1983	*Telerama*	8/17/83	n. 1753	Smiling and looking vibrant	FRA	$20–30
1983	*Telerama*	12/10/83	n. 1759	Another shot of the ultimate star	FRA	$20–30
1983	*Tele Star*	3/1/83	n. 335	In a glamorous gown	FRA	$20–30
1983	*TV Couleur*	7/9/83	n. 8	Another common studio shot	FRA	$20–30
1983	*Video Actualite*	2/83	n. 26	A common publicity pose	FRA	$20–30
1984	*Cine Revue*	6/28/84	v. 64, n. 26	A studio publicity photograph	FRA	$20–30
1984	*L'Ebdo Des Savanes*	11/2/84	n. 3	In a glamorous gown	FRA	$20–30
1984	*Le Cinema*	1984	v. 1, n. 2	In the black-sequined gown and fur	FRA	$20–30
1984	*Novella 2000*	11/6/84	n. 45	A common familiar photo	FRA	$20–30
1984	*Observer*	5/6/84		A young Norma Jean in shorts	ENG	$20–30
1984	*Rev'Ameriques*	Ete 1984		A familiar, often-used photo	FRA	$20–30
1984	*Revista Veronica*	3/10/84	n. 34	Looking glamorous for the camera	CHI	$20–30
1984	*Tele Cine Video*	7 & 8/84	n. 42	An often-used still	FRA	$20–30
1984	*Tele Star*	1/31/84	n. 383	In the white fur	FRA	$20–30

Year	Title	Date	Vol. #	Description	Country	Value
1984	Telegraph Sunday Magazine	7/22/84	n. 404	Norma Jean posing for artist Earl Moran	ENG	$20–30
1984	Tele Magazine	4/7/84	n. 1483	A common publicity still	FRA	$20–30
1984	The Movie	1984	v. 1, n. 1	In the black-sequined dress and a long fur	ENG	$20–30
1984	Unsolved	1984	v. 1, n. 3	A glamour shot with a pearl necklace	ENG	$20–30
1984	Veronica	3/10/84		Holding a striped scarf over her torso	CHI	$20–30
1985	Bolero	7/17/85	n. 28	A well-known glamour photo	ITA	$20–30
1985	Cine Revue	4/25/85	n. 17	In a costume from River	FRA	$20–30
1985	Conoscerti	1985	n. 3	A studio publicity still	ITA	$20–30
1985	Cos	11/14/85		Posing for Stern in 1962	CHI	$20–30
1985	Epoca	11/22/85	n. 1833	A common glamour photograph	ITA	$20–30
1985	Grandeur Nature	1985	n. 4	Another publicity shot	FRA	$20–30
1985	Just Seventeen	10/2/85	n. 68	In the gold lamé gown	ENG	$20–30
1985	La Lettre Du Livre	12/85	n. 3	A typical Marilyn glamour image	FRA	$20–30
1985	Orient Express	2/85	n. 29	An artwork cover	ITA	$20–30
1985	Prima Stripblad	9/85		A comic book cover	HOL	$20–30
1985	Rev'Ameriques	85–86		Continues to fascinate France	FRA	$20–30
1985	Silence On Tourne	5/85	n. 5	A well-used publicity photo	FRA	$20–30
1985	Speciale Derniere	9/21/85	n. 1201	Wearing a smile and a dress	FRA	$20–30
1985	Super Tele	4/27/85	n. 312	A common publicity shot	FRA	$20–30
1985	Telerama	7/3/85	n. 1851	Looking as glamorous as possible	FRA	$20–30
1985	Tele Star	4/2/85	n. 447	A common studio-released still	FRA	$20–30

Year	Title	Date	Vol. #	Description	Country	Value
1985	TV Couleur	4/27/85	n. 102	A common studio portrait	FRA	$20–30
1985	Vous Et Votre Avenir	6/85	n. 25	A close-up portrait from *River*	FRA	$20–30
1986	Bunte	3/20/86		With her eyes closed, from *Bus Stop*	GER	$20–30
1986	Cirnoc	1986	n. 6	Nude artwork by Gonzalez	SPA	$20–30
1986	Clic Photos	4/86	n. 61	A common studio portrait	FRA	$20–30
1986	Gente Mese	8/86	n. 8	Looking sexy for the camera	ITA	$20–30
1986	Le Grand Alpha De La Peinture		n. 89	Looking like the biggest movie star	FRA	$20–30
1986	Le Nouvel Absolu	11/86	n. 10	A classic Monroe pose	FRA	$20–30
1986	Perfection	12/86	n. 2	In a white-collared dress, with earrings	FRA	$20–30
1986	Playboy	1986		Art cover, in a fur	JAP	$20–30
1986	Primer Plano	9/86		In the detailed gold lamé gown	FRA	$20–30
1986	Rev'Ameriques	86–87		A common publicity photograph	FRA	$20–30
1986	Selection Du Readers Digest	1/86		A common studio portrait	FRA	$20–30
1986	Super Flash	6/86	v. XVIII, n. 216	A pretty pose in a gown, by Avedon	ITA	$20–30
1986	You	3/23/86		Norma Jean kneeling down with a lamb	ENG	$20–30
1987	Cahiers Du Cinema	8/87	n. 398	Lying down, reading a book	FRA	$20–30
1987	Cine Tele Revue	7/23/87		In the one-piece yellow swimsuit	FRA	$20–30
1987	Circus-Hors Serie 106	2 & 3/87	n. 30	A classic photo	FRA	$20–30

Year	Title	Date	Vol. #	Description	Country	Value
1987	Confidences Magazine	6/87		Entire issue on her; in the white fur	FRA	$20–30
1987	Eclipse Comics	6/87		Marilyn appears on this comic book.	FRA	$20–30
1987	Esquire	Autumn 1987	v. 1, n. 3	Jumping in the red dress, by Halsman	JAP	$20–30
1987	Rev'Ameriques	1987–88		A classic glamour pose	FRA	$20–30
1987	Fantastik	10/87	n. 31	A studio publicity still	FRA	$20–30
1987	Funk Uhr	8/31/87		A young Norma Jean wearing a sailor hat	GER	$20–30
1987	Gente Mese	1/87	n. 13	Wrapped in the white fur boa	ITA	$20–30
1987	Gente Mese	7/87	v. 2. n. 19	In the gold lamé gown	ITA	$20–30
1987	Gente	8/7/87	n. 31	A common glamour publicity still	ITA	$20–30
1987	Icones	10 & 11/87	n. 9	A sexy, glamour-oriented image	FRA	$20–30
1987	Jours de France	10/1/87	n. 1976	A studio publicity photograph	FRA	$20–30
1987	La Epoca	3/22/87	n. 1	A young Norma Jean by a fence in jeans	CHI	$20–30
1987	La Tribuna Illustrata	5/87	n. 5	A glamorous, studio-released image	ITA	$20–30
1987	Librum–Pistas Sensitivas Por Marilyn	11/87		Art cover	SPA	$20–30
1987	Observer	8/2/87		Norma Jean holding a camera, in a red sweater	ENG	$20–30
1987	Okapi	5/10/87	n. 371	A still taken by the studio	FRA	$20–30
1987	Onda TV	8/8/87	n. 32	A common glamour photograph	ITA	$20–30
1987	Playboy	1987		Young Norma Jean posing for Moran	GRE	$40–85

Year	Title	Date	Vol. #	Description	Country	Value
1987	*Promenades Americaines*		TWA	A well-used glamour shot	FRA	$20–30
1987	*Psychologies*	10/87	n. 47	An overused publicity photograph	FRA	$20–30
1987	*Seven*	11/14/87		In a white bikini with a sky background	ITA	$20–30
1987	*7 Corriere Della Sera*	11/14/87		A common publicity photograph	ITA	$20–30
1987	*Subway*	7 & 8/87		Wearing a sexy, tight dress	ITA	$20–30
1987	*Spotlight*	87–88	n. 5	Looking coyly at the camera	FRA	$20–30
1987	*Tele Star*	8/1/87	n. 565	Posing in a smile and a dress	FRA	$20–30
1987	*Titanic*	1987	n. 31	An artwork image	HOL	$20–30
1987	*You*	7/26/87		A sad portrait from her last summer	ENG	$20–30
1987	*Vrig*	8/1/87		Wrapped in white bed sheets, by Kirkland	HOL	$20–30
1988	*BD Magazine*	6/2/88		An overused publicity photo	FRA	$20–30
1988	*Bologna In Anterrima*	1/9/88	n. 2	A cool-looking glamour photo	ITA	$20–30
1988	*Canal + Magazine*	12/88	n. 15	Another common still	FRA	$20–30
1988	*Cine Tele Revue*	8/18/88	n. 33	An airbrushed artwork cover	BEL	$20–30
1988	*Cine Tele Revue*	8/18/88	n. 33	Wearing the white robe at a window	FRA	$20–30
1988	*Elle*	4/11/88	n. 2205	Looking like a ballerina in a chair	FRA	$20–30
1988	*Emois*	7 & 8/88	n. 13	An often-used common still	FRA	$20–30
1988	*Foto Music*	8/88	n. 29	Smiling sweetly for the camera	FRA	$20–30

Year	Title	Date	Vol. #	Description	Country	Value
1988	Il Venerdi Di Republica	2/19/88	n. 17	In a car from *The Misfits* set	ITA	$20-30
1988	La Recherche	2/88	n. 196	Wearing a tight dress and a smile	FRA	$20-30
1988	Network Pictorial	10/88		Curled up in bedsheets, by Kirkland	IND	$20-30
1988	Paris Match	9/2/88	n. 2049	Wearing a long black sweater for Greene	FRA	$20-30
1988	Rev' Ameriques	Ete 1988		Posing in a tight dress for the camera	FRA	$20-30
1988	Tele Cine Fiches	12/17/88	n. 4	A common glamour photo	FRA	$20-30
1988	Tele K 7	4/4/88	n. 239	A studio-released publicity still	FRA	$20-30
1988	TV France Soir Magazine	4/11/88	n. 13581	One of the more common shots	FRA	$20-30
1988	TV Hebdo La Voix Du Norde	4/1/88	n. 13602	Wearing one of the common gowns	FRA	$20-30
1988	Video 7	7 & 8/88	n. 80	The typical movie-star pose	FRA	$20-30
1988	Woman	8/6/88		In the scrunch dress, by Halsman	AUS	$20-30
1989	Art Dossier	6/89	n. 36	An artwork cover	ITA	$15-25
1989	Beaux Arts	2/89	n. 65	A common publicity pose	FRA	$15-25
1989	Breve Storia Del Cinema	11/24/89		Wearing a tight, sexy dress	ITA	$15-25
1989	Business Art	12/89-1/90	n. 1	A nice artwork cover	ITA	$15-25
1989	Ca M'Interesse	9/89	n. 103	A typical Marilyn pose	FRA	$15-25
1989	Contact Fnac	4/89	n. 267	A studio publicity still	FRA	$15-25
1989	Errol's	12/89	v. 1, n. 1	An artsy image from *Niagara*	CHI	$15-25
1989	Idoles Magazine	10/89	n. 1	The common shot in the white fur	FRA	$15-25

Year	Title	Date	Vol. #	Description	Country	Value
1989	La Gazette De L'Hotel Drout	3/24/89	n. 12	Haming it up for the camera	FRA	$15–25
1989	New Idea	6/10/89		Two shots: MM and Norma Jean	AUS	$15–25
1989	Riza Psicosomatica	6/89	n. 100	An artwork cover	ITA	$15–25
1989	Spotlight	3rd Trimes-ter '89	n. 27	An overused publicity still	FRA	$15–25
1989	The Sunday Telegraph	11/19–25/89		Norma Jean sitting on the beach in pants	ENG	$15–25
1989	Tele Coulisses	1/7/89	n. 29	Wearing a smile and a glamorous dress	FRA	$15–25
1989	Tele Loisirs	7/31–8/6/89	n. 179	In the white fur and long earrings	FRA	$15–25
1989	Tele 7 Video	7/1/89	n. 16	A common publicity still	FRA	$15–25
1989	Tele Video	1/7/89	n. 5	Posing as only Marilyn can	FRA	$15–25
1989	TV Magazine Le Figaro	7/29/89	n. 13972	A studio-released portrait	FRA	$15–25
1989	Vocable	10/89	n. 112	A commonly used studio portrait	FRA	$15–25
1989	Voici	5/13/89	n. 79	Wearing the gold lamé gown	FRA	$15–25
1989	Zoom	3/89	n. 88	In a blue swimsuit holding a rope	ITA	$15–25
1990	Arri Yadab Wa'Shabab	5/15–22/90	n. 474	In a bright orange blouse	KUW	$15–25
1990	Blitz	2/2/90	n. 3	A studio publicity still	ITA	$15–25
1990	Chip Chats	3–4/90	v. 37, n. 2	A Monroe statue by artist Chris Rees	CAN	$15–20
1990	Flash Art	12/89–1/90	n. 153	Another piece of Monroe artwork	ITA	$15–20
1990	Il Venerdi Di Republica	3/16/90	n. 110	A portrait in a car, by Arnold	ITA	$15–20

Year	Title	Date	Vol. #	Description	Country	Value
1990	L'Amateur De L'Art	6/90	n. 768	A common studio shot	FRA	$15–20
1990	L'Arte Moderna	1990	n. 10	An artwork cover	ITA	$15–20
1990	Memorie & Ricordi	3/90	n. 3	Smiling sweetly for the camera	ITA	$15–20
1990	Mimuti Menardni	4/90	v. XIV, n. 244	Artwork by Andy Warhol	ITA	$15–25
1990	Non Solo Poster	11/90	n. 4	A studio publicity still	ITA	$15–20
1990	Paris Match Hors Serie	1990		A classic Marilyn pose	FRA	$15–20
1990	Raro!	1 & 2/90	n. 7	Holding a guitar from River	ITA	$15–20
1990	Saturday Night	3/90	v. 105, n. 3	In the bedsheets, posing for Kirkland	CAN	$15–20
1990	Sound & Vision	11–12/90	n. 17/18	An artwork cover	ITA	$15–20
1990	Speak-Up	8/90	n. 65	A common publicity pose	ITA	$15–20
1990	Speak-Up	11/90	v. VI, n. 63	In a red bathing suit	SPA	$15–20
1990	Speciale Derniere	7/28/90	n. 2356	Wearing a sexy, tight dress	FRA	$15–20
1990	Studio Magazine	9/90	n. 41	Another classic glamour image	FRA	$15–20
1990	Tele Video Scope	5/12/90	n. 7	Posing coyly for the camera	FRA	$15–20
1990	The Paris Free Voice	7/90	n. 6	A classic glamour photograph	FRA	$15–20
1990	The Sun Pictorial Daily	8/30/90		A candid at a press conference	JAP	$20–30
1990	TV Cable Hebdo	10/13/90	n. 23	An appearance on a television guide	FRA	$15–20
1990	TV Cable Hebdo	12/1/90	n. 30	A common glamour photo	FRA	$15–20
1990	TYNAIKA	1990		Norma Jean posing on the beach	GRE	$15–20
1990	Zoom	12/90		Wearing a bulky coat in the mid-50s	HOL	$15–20

Year	Title	Date	Vol. #	Description	Country	Value
1991	Al Marxed	8/24/91	n. 1470	A close-up face shot in color	KUW	$15–20
1991	Chat	6/1/91		In a jewel-studded-strap dress	ENG	$15–20
1991	Cine Fiches	4/15/91		Wearing the gold lamé gown	FRA	$15–20
1991	Cineteca TV	6/14/91	n. 14	A glamorous studio photograph	ITA	$15–20
1991	Diagonal	3/91	v. V, n. 20	Artwork by Warhol	SPA	$15–20
1991	El Pais Seminal	1991		An often-seen studio shot	FRA	$15–20
1991	Emma	8/91	n. 8	Marilyn blowing her fans a kiss	GER	$15–20
1991	Flix	5/91	v. 12	A glamour picture with hoop earrings	JAP	$25–40
1991	Focus	10/91		Holding fabric flowers over her breasts	HOL	$15–20
1991	Globe.	7 & 8/91	n. 59	A studio glamour pose	FRA	$15–20
1991	Grazia	12/15/91	n. 2650	A common studio photograph	ITA	$15–20
1991	L'Autre Journal	6/91	n. 13	Sleeping in a chair	FRA	$15–20
1991	L'Evenement Du Jeudi	5/30/91	n. 343	A glamorous studio photograph	FRA	$15–20
1991	Le Nouvel Observateur	10/91	n. 7	Marilyn continues to fascinate.	FRA	$15–20
1991	Max	12/91		An airbrushed artwork	GER	$15–20
1991	Observer	1991		A common studio photograph	ENG	$15–20
1991	Psy Autrement	1991	n. 2	Wearing a tight dress and a smile	FRA	$15–20
1991	7A Paris	6/19–25/91		Embracing Tom Ewell	FRA	$15–20
1991	Raccolta Skorpio	9/3/91	n. 188	An artwork cover	ITA	$15–20
1991	Speak Up	2/91	n. 46	A common studio photo	FRA	$15–20
1991	Studio Magazine	7 & 8/91	n. 52	A sad portrait by Greene	FRA	$15–20
1991	Sunday	5/5/91		A young Marilyn in a white robe	ENG	$15–20

Year	Title	Date	Vol. #	Description	Country	Value
1991	Sunday Sun	5/26/91	v. 18, n. 35	Posing in Canada during *Niagara*	CAN	$15–20
1991	Super TV	11/2–8/91	n. 44	In the gold lamé dress	GER	$15–20
1991	Tele K7	8/19/91	n. 415	Looking glamorous as always	FRA	$15–20
1991	Touch It	5 & 6/91	n. 1	Living on in more artwork	ITA	$15–20
1991	TV Movie	1991	n. 26	In a black dress with jewel-studded straps	GER	$15–20
1991	Tele Poche	8/19/91	n. 1332	A common publicity still	FRA	$15–20
1991	Zoom	3/91	n. 108	A studio publicity still	ITA	$15–20
1992	Anteprima	8/28/92		With Jane Russell in *Blondes*	ITA	$15–20
1992	Auf Einen Blick	7/30/92	n. 32	With fellow legend James Dean	GER	$15–20
1992	Blanco Negro	1992		An artsy photo of Marilyn posing	SPA	$15–20
1992	Bolero	8/92	n. 8	A common publicity still for *Niagara*	SWI	$15–20
1992	Ciak	8/8/92	v. 8, n. 8	A glamorous-looking Marilyn	ITA	$15–20
1992	Cinemazero	4/92	n. 4	Many pictures of her on the floor	ITA	$15–20
1992	Cine Revue Hors-Serie	c. 1992		Entire issue is on her; in gold lamé	BEL	$30–40
1992	Cine Tele Revue	7/30/92	n. 31	A side profile taken by Stern	FRA	$15–20
1992	Corriere Cultura	4/19/92		An often-used photograph	ITA	$15–20
1992	Enigmistika	10/92	n 3	A sexy Monroe pose	ITA	$15–20
1992	Flix	9/92	v. 27	In the white-collared dress	JAP	$30–40
1992	Foto Pratica	12/91–1/92	n. 276–7	In pink long johns, by the fire	ITA	$15–25
1992	Foto Pro	8/92	n. 53	Portrayed by an artist	ITA	$15–20
1992	Friday	1992	n. 29	A photo by Stern that MM crossed out	JAP	$15–25

Year	Title	Date	Vol. #	Description	Country	Value
1992	Funk Ubr	7/24/92		Monroe on the majority of the cover	GER	$15–20
1992	Gente	2/24/92	v. XXXVI, n. 9	On half the cover, in a fur	ITA	$10–15
1992	Gente Mese	8/92	v. VII, n. 8	In a costume from *Blondes*	ITA	$15–25
1992	Good Weekend	9/1/92		Wearing a blue robe by a pool	AUS	$15–20
1992	Hp De Tijd	7/3/92		A common publicity still	HOL	$15–20
1992	Il Venerdì Di Republica	7/31/92	n. 233	A nice artwork cover	ITA	$15–20
1992	Intimita "Vita Vera De M. Monroe"	8/20/92	n. 2424	A special tribute; in the gold lamé	ITA	$15–25
1992	I Maestri Del Colore	1992	n. 50	An attractive artwork cover	ITA	$15–20
1992	Impacto	8/20/92	n. 2216	Sitting on steps, holding a purse by Greene	SPA	$15–20
1992	Kai	5/92	n. 32	Young Norma Jean combing her hair	GRE	$15–25
1992	Le CoQ Gourmand	1992	n. 14	A common publicity pose, often seen	FRA	$15–20
1992	L'Express	1992	n. 1	A full-length profile in the black-sequined dress	FRA	$15–20
1992	Life Stories	1992	n. 3	Entire issue is devoted to her; in the white fur	FIN	$15–20
1992	Madame Jours De France	8/3/92		Another issue exploring 30 years since her passing	FRA	$15–20

Year	Title	Date	Vol. #	Description	Country	Value
1992	Marilyn—Super Star	1992		All on her; an art cover in white sheets	SPA	$25–35
1992	Marilyn—The Complete Story	1992		All on her; in the white-collared dress	SPA	$25–35
1992	Paralleli	8/92	n. 8	A common photo	ITA	$15–20
1992	Pin's Collection	6/15/92	n. 20	A well-known publicity photo	FRA	$15–20
1992	Popcorn	4/92	n. 4	A photo on the rocks, by Greene	ITA	$15–20
1992	Premiere "Movie Extra"	9/92	n. 9	Sitting in a director's chair in a blue dress	JAP	$15–20
1992	Premiere	9/92	n. 9	Looking out a window, by Sam Shaw	JAP	$15–25
1992	Prisma	8/92	n. 32	In a black dress with jewel-decorated straps	SWI	$15–20
1992	Ragazza	1992		With hands clasped at her breast	ITA	$15–20
1992	SAT-TV International	8/92		In a black lacy negligee	GER	$15–20
1992	Serai	1992	v. 5, n. 21	In a bubble bath from Itch	JAP	$15–25
1992	7 Corriere Della Sera	7/11/92	n. 27	Several 1952 photos by Halsman	ITA	$15–20
1992	Sorrisi E Canzoni TV	8/2–8/92	n. 31	A Stern photo with a bead necklace	ITA	$15–20
1992	Stern	8/6/92	n. 33	Lying facedown and naked on a bed, by Stern	GER	$15–20
1992	Stop	8/8/92	n. 2289	Entire issue on her; in the gold lamé gown	ITA	$25–35
1992	Sunday Express Magazine	7/19/92		A gorgeous, smiling portrait from 1962	ENG	$15–20

Year	Title	Date	Vol. #	Description	Country	Value
1992	Super!	7/16/92		In the gold lamé gown and a shot from her autopsy	GER	$15–20
1992	Super TV	8/8–14/92	n. 32	In the white-collared black low-cut dress	GER	$15–20
1992	Tele Cable	8/1/92	n. 109	A common publicity photo	FRA	$15–20
1992	Tele Cable	10/14/92	n. 121	Another photo used too often	FRA	$15–20
1992	Tele K-7	7/27/92	n. 464	In a white bikini on orange cushions	FRA	$15–20
1992	Tele Loisirs	7/27–8/2/92	n. 335	Wearing the white fur	FRA	$15–20
1992	Tele Moustique	7/30/92	n. 3470	A publicity still from River	BEL	$15–20
1992	Tele Poche (digest)	7/27/92	n. 1381	A portrait in the jewel-studded-strap dress	FRA	$15–20
1992	Television Programmes	1992	n. 32	In a white ruffled dress, looking beautiful	FRA	$15–20
1992	Tele 7 Jours	8/29/92	n. 1683	A common publicity still	FRA	$15–20
1992	The Record's Thursday Entertainment Guide	7/30/92		With a glamour face, in a newspaper section	CAN	$15–20
1992	Timbroloisirs	2/15/92	n. 35	A studio publicity still	FRA	$15–20
1992	Time Out	7/8–15/92	n. 1145	In a sleeveless shirt, reading a book	ENG	$15–20
1992	Tip Berlin	8/13–26/92	v. 21, n. 17	A shot from Love	GER	$15–20
1992	TV Cable Hebdo Magazine	7/6/92	n. 114	A common publicity photograph	FRA	$15–20
1992	TV France Soir Magazine	8/1/92	n. 14923	One of the more common studio shots	FRA	$15–20

Year	Title	Date	Vol. #	Description	Country	Value
1992	TV Magazine Centre France	8/2/92	n. 1157	The typical Monroe allure	FRA	$15–20
1992	TV Magazine Corse Matin	8/92	n. 10227	A studio publicity photo	FRA	$15–20
1992	TV Magazine Le Figaro	8/1/92	n. 14912	Looking glamorous and sexy	FRA	$15–20
1992	TV France Soir Magazine	8/1/92	n. 14923	One of the often-used pictures	FRA	$15–20
1992	TV Movie	7/25–8/7/92		A lovely, soft portrait	GER	$15–20
1992	TV Sorrisi E. Canzoni	8/2/92	n. 31	A portrait by Stern from 1962	ITA	$15–20
1992	TV Studio	7/10/92	n. 27	In the dress with the white collar	HOL	$15–20
1992	Veronica	7/10/92		In the dress with the white collar	HOL	$15–20
1992	Video Magazine	8/92		On the majority of the cover, in a dress	GER	$15–20
1992	Vita Vera	8/13/92	n. 2424	Entire issue on her; in the gold lamé gown	ITA	$25–35
1992	Weekend	8/1/92		A news supplement with a tinted glamour pic	ENG	$15–20
1992	World Report	12/92	issn 09424520	A portrait from 1962 by Stern	GER	$15–20
1993	Flight Jacket Museum Catalog	1993		In Korea with a U.S. pilot during the war	JAP	$25–40
1993	Globe Hebdo	8/14/93	n. 28	In bed holding a flower to her chest	FRA	$15–20
1993	Grandes Ciclos TV	1993		A glamour photograph, seldom used	SPA	$10–20
1993	Le Cable Video	8/23/93	n. 83	A studio still for publicity	FRA	$10–20

Year	Title	Date	Vol. #	Description	Country	Value
1993	Le Nouvel Observateur	7/15/93	n. 1497	A lovely portrait of Monroe's beauty	FRA	$10–20
1993	Les Beaux Films D'Hollywood	1/93		A classic publicity photo of the queen	FRA	$10–20
1993	Pins Collection	2/15/93	n. 26	An often-used portrait	FRA	$10–20
1993	Positif	7/93		A photo of the band from Hot	FRA	$10–20
1993	Stern	4/1/93	n. 1	A tinted glamour pose with half-closed eyes	GER	$10–20
1993	TV Cable Hebdo	8/23/93	n. 173	A photo taken by the studio for promotion	FRA	$10–20
1993	Vogue Hommes	11/93	n. 164	A sad b/w portrait taken by Avedon	FRA	$15–25
1994	El Caso Extra	1994		All on her; sitting on steps with a purse	SPA	$25–35
1994	Foto Revista	11/94	v. XII, n. 43	Three pics in the black dress, by Avedon	SPA	$10–20
1994	Gong	7/23–29/94	n. 29	Tinted cover in the jewel-studded-strap dress	GER	$10–20
1994	Playboy	12/94		In the black dress with the white collar	GER	$20–30
1994	TV Times	3/12–18/94		A digest with a portrait by Greene	AUS	$10–20
1994	Weekend	6/4/94		A young Norma Jean and her sister on the beach	ENG	$10–20
1995	Airbrush	10–12/95		An airbrushed art image	HOL	$10–15
1995	Brief Marken Spiegel	6/95	v. 35, n. 6	The United States Monroe postal stamp art	GER	$10–15
1995	Cinema	2/95	n. 201	Curled up in bedsheets with hand on head	GER	$15–20

Year	Title	Date	Vol. #	Description	Country	Value
1995	Filmihullu	5/95		A tinted glamour pose, in a dress	FIN	$10–15
1995	Sette Corriere Della Sera	2/23/95	n. 8	On the beach with an umbrella	ITA	$10–15
1995	The Australian Magazine	5/27–8/95		Jumping in the black spangle dress	AUS	$10–15
1995	Trova Roma	11/95		The *Golden Dreams* nude pose	ITA	$10–15
1995	TV Krant	1/7–13/95		An artist's portrait	HOL	$10–15
1995	UN Ospite A Roma	12/16–31/95 n. 23		A digest with the white-collared dress	ITA	$10–20
1995	Weekend	3/9/95		A newspaper section with a glamour photo	ENG	$10–15
1996	OK! Weekly	6/2/96		With the ever-present white fur	ENG	$10–15
1996	Horzu	5/25–31/96		A beautiful portrait all in white, by Greene	GER	$15–20
1996	Premiere	1/96	v. 3, n. 12	In the black-lace negligee, looking sexy	ENG	$10–15
1996	Satellite (Veronica)	5/21–31/96		A common publicity pose	HOL	$10–15
1996	Saturday Night	9/96	v. III, n. 7	Smoking a cigarette on the *Niagara* set	CAN	$10–15
1996	Specchio Della Stampa	4/27/96	n. 14	Wearing a long black knit sweater	ITA	$10–15
1996	Today's Seniors	8/96		A lovely photo from *Give* in 1962	CAN	$10–15
1997	Cine Action Performance	1997	n. 44	A frontal glamour pic in a white fur	CAN	$10–12
1997	De Puzzelaar	1997	n. 3	A classic, well-known studio photograph	HOL	$10–12

Year	Title	Date	Vol. #	Description	Country	Value
1997	Eye	5/97		The *New Wrinkle* nude pose	ENG	$10–12
1997	HP De Tijd	11/21/97		A studio publicity pose	HOL	$10–12
1997	Internet Magazine	6/97	n. 31	Smiling, holding a pile of jewels in her hands	ENG	$10–12
1997	Playboy	1/97		Holding a scarf in front of her nude torso	CAN	$40–50
1997	Playboy	2/97		In a long black sweater open on one side	FRA	$20–30
1997	Playboy	10/97		A lovely, smiling portrait from the *Niagara* set	JAP	$30–40
1997	Viva!	9/2/97	n. 13	In the white-collared dress	POL	$20–30

BOOKS

International Books on Marilyn Monroe

Marilyn Monroe is undoubtedly the most written about star ever. Hundreds of books exist on her in every language imaginable. Authors in countries around the world began writing books about Marilyn in unison with the first American books on the star.

The first, which were published in 1952 and 1953, featured a selection of studio photographs of Marilyn and chronicled her rise to stardom. The early 1960s brought a biography or two, but the greatest number of works were published after her death in 1962.

A few of the books published in the late 1960s speculated about the circumstances of Marilyn's death and the possibility that it hadn't been an accident. From the early 1970s on, just about anyone who had ever even brushed shoulders with Marilyn Monroe began writing books about her. Some of the finest publications came in the 1980s and 90s and consisted of photos taken by the world's leading photographers who had photographed Marilyn extensively and quite beautifully. These are the books most treasured by Marilyn fans. As in most cases, there are also a certain number of books that fall into the "trash" category, but they are the minority, thank goodness.

It's inevitable that the flow of books will continue on Marilyn as "lost" photos and new murder theories continue to arise and new generations "discover" the mystery and intrigue that will forever surround our all-American icon, Marilyn Monroe.

What follows is an exhaustive listing of nearly all of the books ever written on or with reference to Marilyn Monroe. They are arranged alphabetically by author's name, which is followed by the book's title; the publisher; the original price; the number of the edition; the number of the reprint, the number of pages; the International Standard Book Number; whether it is softcover, hardcover, or paperback; the year it was published; the country in which it was published, and finally, the estimated value in U.S. dollars at this writing.

Abbreviations

ed.—number of edition
re.—number of reprint
p.—number of pages
ISBN—International
   Standard Book Number

Sc—Softcover
Hc—Hardcover
Pb—Paperback

Country

ARG—Argentina
AUS—Australia
BEL—Belgium
BRA—Brazil
CAN—Canada
CAT—Cataluña
CHI—Chile

DEN—Denmark
ESP—Spain
FIN—Finland
FRA—France
GER—Germany
ITA—Italy

MEX—Mexico
SWE—Sweden
SWI—Switzerland
UK—United Kingdom
USA—United States
   of America

Books on MARILYN MONROE

Author	Title/Info	Value
Anitti ALANEN	*Marilyn. Alaston naamio. Marilyn Monoen elokuvat* Valtion painatuskeskus 218 p. ISBN-951-859-284-5 Sc/1982/FIN	$50–75
Alfanso ALCADE	*Marilyn Monroe que est'as en el cielo* inscription no. 39,948 University Ed. Sc/1972/CHI	$50–70
Jack ALLEN	*Marilyn By Moonlight* Barclay House 1 ed. 133 p. ISBN-0-935016-45-7 Hc/1996/USA	$75–125
Janice ANDERSON	*Marilyn Monroe* Crescent Books 1 ed. 192 p. ISBN-0-517-41476-7 Hc/1993/USA	$40–60
————	*Marilyn Monroe* Optimum Books 1 ed. 192 p. ISBN-0-603-03099-8 Hc/1993/UK	$40–60
————	*Marilyn Monroe* W. H. Smith 4 re. 192 p. ISBN-0-603-03125-0 Sc/1987/UK	$40–60
————	*Marilyn Monroe: Quote UnQuote* Crescent 80 p. 1 ed. ISBN-1-85813-831-0 Hc/1995/USA	$15–20
————	*Violations of the Child: Marilyn Monroe*—by her psychiatrist friend Bridgehead Books 1 ed. 159p. Hc/1962/USA	$75–125
Anonymous	*Marilyn Monroe—Collection Cinema pour tous* Anagramme (Ariel Camacho) 1 ed. 62p. ISBN-2-85199-364-X Hc/1985/FRA	$30–50
————	*Marilyn Monroe: Marilyn Monroe—Album Souvenir Cine Revue n. 1* Cine-Revue 1 ed. 78p. ISBN-000-0272395-19 Sc/1987/BEL	$30–50
————	*Marilyn Monroe: Grandes reportajes de crisis* Ed. de Crisis (Julia Constenla) 1 ed. 141p. Sc/1974/ARG]	$50–70
Serge ANTIBI	*Album photos, Marilyn Monroe* Pac 195F 1 ed. 139 p. Hc/1984/FRA	$40–60

Author	Title/Info	Value
	Marilyn Monroe: Revelations et passion Favre 110F 1 ed. 313 p. ISBN-2-8289-0364-8 Sc/1988/FRA	$40-55
Eve ARNOLD	*Marilyn Monroe: An Appreciation by Eve Arnold* Alfred A. Knopf $30 1 ed. 141p. ISBN-0-394-55672-0 Hc/1987/USA	$40-60
_____	*Marilyn Monroe: An Appreciation by Eve Arnold* Hamish Hamilton 1 ed. 141 p. ISBN-0-241-12381-X Hc/1987/UK	$40-60
_____	*Marilyn Monroe: An Appreciation by Eve Arnold* Pan Books Ltd. 9.99 1 re. 141 p. ISBN-0-330-30991-9 Sc/1987/UK	$40-60
_____	*Marilyn, For Ever* Albin Michel 1 ed. 141 p. ISBN-2-226-03021-2 Hc/1987/FRA	$40-55
_____	*Marilyn Monroe: Un homenaje de Eve Arnold* Mondadori Espana S. A. 1 ed. 141 p. ISBN-84-397-1122-0 Hc/1987/ESP	$40-55
_____	*Omaggio a Marilyn* Arnoldo Mondadori L. 45.000 143 p. ISBN-88-04-30523-1 Hc/1987/ITA	$40-55
Francoise ARNOULD & F. GERBER	*Marilyn Monroe* Pac 1 ed. 185 p. Sc/1982/FRA	$40-60
Erica AROSIO	*Marilyn Monroe* (In folding box with cassette) Multiplo Edizioni L. 35.000 170 p. Sc/1989/ITA	$40-60
Renzo BAILINI	*Marilyn Monroe: Un mistero all'americana* (Vita & Memoria N. 11) Book Editore L.19.000 1 ed. 158 p. Sc/1988/ITA	$40-60

Author	Title/Info	Value
Roger BAKER	*Marilyn Monroe United Press International/Bettmann* Portland House 1 ed. 176 p. ISBN-0-517-69326-7 Hc/1990/UK	$40–60
———	*Marilyn Monroe United Press International/Bettmann* Soline 1 ed. 176 p. ISBN-2-87677-104-7 Hc/1991/FRA	$40–60
———	*Marilyn Monroe: Eine biographische Fotodokumentation O. Verlag* Orbis Verlag DM28.80 176 p. ISBN-3-572-00508-6 Hc/1991/GER	$40–60
———	*Marilyn Monroe* Grange Books Hc/1994/UK	$20–40
George BARRIS	*Marilyn: Her Life in Her Own Words* Birch Lane 166 p. 1 ed. ISBN-1-55972-306-8 $24.95 Hc/1995/USA	$30–50
Carlo BASSI	*Che Fine Ha Fa Ho Norma Jeane?* Skema Sc/1992/ITA	$30–50
Bruno BERNARD	*Requium for Marilyn by Bernard of Hollywood* Kensal Press 12.50 1 ed. 207 p. ISBN-0-946041-52-0 Hc/1996/UK	$70–125
Susan BERNARD	*Bernard of Hollywood's Marilyn* St. Martin's $29.95 122 p. ISBN-0-312-08882-5 Hc/1993/USA	$30–50
———	*Bernard of Hollywood's Marilyn* (Ed. du collectioneur) HC/1993/FRA	$80–90
Herb BOYD	*Seductive Sayings: Marilyn Monroe* Longmeadow 1 ed. 60p ISBN-0-681-45364-8 Hc/1994/USA	$30–50
Pierre BROUSSEAU	*Marilyn et ses amants celebres: Sa vie secrete* Quebecor Inc. 1 ed. 156 p. ISBN-2-89089-197-6 Sc/1983/CAN	$40–60
Peter Harry BROWN & Patte BARNHAM	*Marilyn Monroe: The Last Take* Dutton $23.00 452 p. ISBN-0-525-93485-5 Hc/1992/USA	$25–35

Author	Title/Info	Value
	Marilyn Monroe: The Last Take	$8–12
	Signet $6.50 549 p. 1 ed. ISBN-0-451-40420-3 Pb/1993/USA	
	Marilyn Das Ende: wie es wirklich War	$30–45
	Droemer Knaur 447 p. ISBN-3-425-26567-2 Hc/1992/GER	
Richard BUSKIN	*The Films of Marilyn Monroe*	$20–40
	Publications Int'l Unlimited 96 p. ISBN-1-56173-277-X Hc/1992/USA	
Marie CAHILL	*Forever Marilyn*	$35–50
	Binson Group 1 ed. 64 p. ISBN-0-86124-819-8 Hc/1991/UK	
	Forever Marilyn	$30–45
	Smithmark 64 p. ISBN-0-8317-3470-1 Hc/1992/USA	
	Marilyn	$30–45
	ISBN-157215-0319 Hc/1994/USA	
	Stars, Mythen and Legend: Marilyn	$35–50
	Lechner 64 p. ISBN-3-85049-098-X Hc/1992/GER	
	Marilyn	$30–40
	Libsa Hc/1993/ESP	
Domenico CAMMAROTA	*Il cinema di Marilyn Monroe: Futuro saggi vol. XVII*	$40–60
	Fanucci L22.000 1 ed. 275 p. ISBN-88-347-0301-4 Sc/1988/ITA	
Francesco CAMPANESE	*Io Marilyn: No. 3*	$40–60
	D. N. Milano 1 ed. 122 p. Sc/1977/ITA	
Frank A. CAPELL	*The Strange Death of Marilyn Monroe*	$60–125
	Herald of Freedom $2.00 1 ed. 79 p. Sc/1994/USA	
Truman CAPOTE	*Marilyn Monroe: Photographies 1945-1962-Biblietheque Visuelle*	$40–60
	Schirmer/Mosel 1 ed. 119 p. ISBN-3-88814-577-5 Pb/1991/FRA	
	Marilyn Monroe: Photographien 1945–1962	$40–60
	Schirmer/Mosel 1 ed. 119 p. ISBN-3-88814-385-3 Pb/1991/GER	

Author	Title/Info	Value
———	*Marilyn Monroe Photographs 1945–1962* Norton Schirmer's Visual Library Sc/1994/UK	$20–40
Ernesto CARDENAL	*Marilyn Monroe and other poems* (with only one poem about MM) Search Press London 2 re. 136 p. ISBN-0-85532-358-2 Sc/1975/UK	$20–30
Ernesto CARDENAL & Dorothee SOLLE	*Gebet fur Marilyn Monroe: Meditationen* Jugenddienst-Verlag 1 ed. 64 p. ISBN-3-7795-7385-7 Sc/1984/GER	$30–50
George CARPOZI, Jr.	*Marilyn Monroe: Her Own Story* Belmont Books 1 ed. 222 p. Pb/1961/USA	$60–90
———	*The Agony of Marilyn Monroe* Consul Books/World D. 1 ed. 187 p. Pb/1962/UK	$80–125
———	*Marilyn Monroe: su propia historia* Ibero Mundial Ed. 1 ed. 211 p. Pb/1962/ESP	$80–125
———	*Marilyn Monroe: historia de su vida* Malinca Pocket 1 ed. 186 p. Pb/1963/ARG	$80–125
Jock CARROLL	*Falling for Marilyn* Friedman/Fairfax $25.00 101 p. ISBN-1-56799-411-3 Hc/1996/USA	$30–50
David CONOVER	*Finding Marilyn: A Romance by David Conover* Grosset & Dunlap $14.95 1 ed. 199 p. ISBN-0-448-12020-8 Hc/1981/USA	$50–75
———	*Norma Jean/Marilyn Monroe: The Discovery Photographs—1945* A Moment in Time Gallery (Brochure) ISBN-0-9695079-0-9 Sc/1990/CAN	$30–45
Michael CONWAY & Mark RICCI	*The Films of Marilyn Monroe* Bonanza & Citadel 1 ed. 160 p. Hc/1964/USA	$40–60

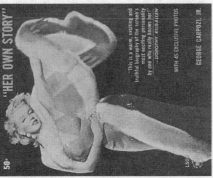

The Agony of Marilyn Monroe, 1962

Marilyn Monroe— Her Own Story, 1961

Author	Title/Info	Value
	The Films of Marilyn Monroe	
	The Citadel Press $7.95 160 p. ISBN-0-8065-0145-6 Sc/1964/USA	$40–60
	The Complete Films of Marilyn Monroe (different cover)	
	The Citadel Press $12.95 160 p. ISBN-0-8065-1016-1 Sc/1964/USA	$40–60

Author	Title/Info	Value
	The Films of Marilyn Monroe The Citadel Press (C-265) 7 re. 160 p. ISBN-0-8065-0145-6 Sc/ 1974/USA	$40–50
	The Films of Marilyn Monroe Cadillac & Citadel 9 re. 160 p. Hc/1964/USA	$40–50
	The Complete Films of Marilyn Monroe Citadel/Carol Press $14.95 1 ed. 160 p. ISBN-0-8065-1016-1 Sc/ 1990/USA	$25–35
	Todas Las Peliculas De Marilyn Monroe Odin Sc/1993/ESP	$40–50
& Enrico MAGRELLI	*Marilyn Monroe* Gremese Editore Hc/1992/ITA	$30–40
	Marilyn Monroe Henri Veyrier 160 p. ISBN-2-85199-209-0 Sc/1990/FRA	$30–50
	Marilyn Monroe Henri Veyrier 68F 160 p. ISBN-2-85199-219-8 Sc/1990/FRA	$30–50
	Marilyn Monroe Henri Veyrier 78F 160 p. ISBN-2-85199-286-4 Sc/1983/FRA	$30–50
	Marilyn Monroe Artefact 160 p. Sc/1986/FRA	$30–50
	Marilyn Monroe und ihre filme Goldmann Magnum/Citadel 174 p. ISBN-3-442-10208-1 Sc/1980/ GER	$30–50

Author	Title/Info	Value
—— & Enrico MAGRELLI	*Marilyn Monroe: Le Stelle Filanti, 10* Gremese Ed. L20.000 1 ed. 156 p. ISBN-88-7605-028-0 Hc/1981/ITA	$30-50
Lawrence CROWN	*Marilyn at Twentieth Century Fox* Comet 1 ed. 213 p. ISBN-1-85227-025-X Hc/1987/USA	$20-35
——	*Marilyn at Twentieth Century Fox* Planet Books 14.95 1 ed. 213 p. ISBN-1-85527-025-X Hc/1987/UK	$25-45
——	*Marilyn at Twentieth Century Fox* W. H. Allen/Planet 8.99 213 p. ISBN-1-855227-002-0 Sc/1987/UK	$20-40
Peter DAINTY	*Marilyn Monroe* Collins ELT 1 ed. 69 p. ISBN-0-00-370170-0 Pb/1986/UK	$20-35
——	*Marilyn Monroe* Collins ELT 5 re. 69 p. ISBN-0-00-370170-0 Pb/1991/UK	$20-35
Oliver DAZAT	*Marilyn Monroe: Les Noms duCinema 'M' Le Club des Stars* Seghers (Phillippe) 82F 1 ed. 189 p. ISBN-2-232-10190-8 Sc/1989/FRA	$40-60
Michael DEL MAR	*Marilyn Cherie* Ige Michel Lafon 100F 1 ed. 144 p. ISBN-2-902259-04-2 Hc/1982/FRA	$40-60
——	*Marilyn Cherie: Collection MA VIE No. 3* Ige Michel Lafon 49F 144 p. ISBN-2-902259-04-2 Sc/1982/FRA	$40-60
Kathy ROOKS DENES	*Marilyn* Grange 176 p. ISBN-185627-289-3 Hc/1993/UK	$30-40
Andre de DIENES	*Marilyn Mon Amour: The Private Album* St. Martin's $24.95 1 ed. 155 p. ISBN-0-312-51504-9 Hc/1985/USA	$40-60

Author	Title/Info	Value
	Marilyn Mon Amour: The Private Album	
	Sidgwick & Jackson 13.00 155 p. ISBN-0-283-99337-5 Hc/1986/UK	$40–60
	Marilyn Mon Amour: The Private Album	
	Sidgwick & Jackson 10.99 155 p. ISBN-0-283-99533-5 Sc/1989/UK	$40–60
	Marilyn Mon Amour: L'album intime	
	Filipacchi 199F 1 ed. 155 p. ISBN-2-85018-595-7 Hc/1985/FRA	$40–60
	Marilyn Mon Amour	
	Schirmer/Mosel 155 p. ISBN-3-88814-189-3 Sc/1986/GER	$40–60
	Marilyn Mon Amour	
	Bracken Sc/1993/UK	$20–30
Susan DOLL	*Marilyn: Her Life and Legend*	
	Omnibus Press 1 ed. 256 p. ISBN-0-7119-2421-X Hc/1990/GER	$40–60
	Marilyn: Her Life and Legend	
	Beekman House 256 p. ISBN-0-517-03069-1 Hc/1990/USA	$40–60
	Marilyn: vie & legende	
	Karl Muller Verlag 1 ed. 256 p. Hc/1991/GER	$40–60
	Marilyn: Leben und Legende	
	Karl Muller Verlag 1 ed. 256 p. Hc/1991/GER	$40–60
James E. DOUGHERTY	*The Secret Happiness of Marilyn Monroe*	
	Playboy Press $1.95 1 ed. 150 p. Pb/1976/USA	$35–55
	El amor secreto de Marilyn Monroe	
	Dopesa/Espectaculo, 9 1 ed. 192 p. Pb/1976/ESP	$35–55
Claude DUFFAU	*La femme poete: Un portrait de Marilyn Monroe dans son miroir*	
	Jean-Claude Simoen 1 ed. 189 p. Sc/1978/FRA	$45–55
Richard DYER	*Marilyn Monroe Star Dossier One (The Images of Marilyn Monroe)*	
	bfi education 1 ed. 46 p. Sc/1980/UK	$60–80

Author	Title/Info	Value
Ed FEINGERSH & Bob LABRASCA	*Marilyn: March 1955* Delta/Bantam $12.95 1 ed. ISBN-0-385-30119-7 Sc/1990/USA	$30-50
———	*Marilyn: Fifty-Five.* Bloomsbury 1 ed. ISBN-0-7475-0746-5 Hc/1990/UK	$30-50
———	*Marilyn* Nathan Image 1 ed. ISBN-2-09-240072-X Hc/1990/FRA	$40-50
Ed FEINGERSH & Michael OCHS	*Marilyn in New York (aus dem Michael Ochs Archives)* Schirmer/Mosel 1 ed. ISBN-3-88814-445-0 Hc/1991/GER	$40-55
Piergiorgio FIRINU	*Marilyn Monroe: Immagini di un mito* Studio 46 1 ed. 111 p. Sc/1980/ITA	$40-50
Mogens FONSS	*Marilyn Monroe: Samlerens Filmboger—2* Samlerens Forlag Kr. 5,85 1 ed. 55 p. Sc/1958/DEN	$65-125
Joe FRANKLIN & Laurie PALMER	*The Marilyn Monroe Story* Rudolph Field Company 1 ed. 63 p. Hc/1953/USA	$300-600
	The Marilyn Monroe Story: The Intimate Inside Story of . . . Rudolph Field Company 1 ed. 63 p. Sc/1953/USA	$250-350
Lluis GASCA	*Marilyn Monroe: Toda la verdad* Plaza & Janes 1 ed. 191 p. ISBN-84-0137281-X Hc/1987/ESP	$35-55
	Marilyn Monroe: La Diosa Del Deseo Mascara Pb/1994/ESP	$30-40
Ruth Esther GEIGER	*Marilyn Monroe* Rororo Pb/1995/GER	$8-12
Nicki GILES	*The Marilyn Album* Gallery Books 1 ed. 303 p. ISBN-0-8317-5743-4 Hc/1991/USA	$35-55
———	*The Marilyn Album* Binson Group 1 ed. 303 p. ISBN-0-86124-842-2 Hc/1991/UK	$35-55

The Secret Happiness of Marilyn Monroe, 1976

The Marilyn Monroe Story, 1953

Author	Title/Info	Value
Rene GILSON	*Marilyn Monroe: Anthologie du cinema n. 43–Suppl. to Avant Scene* Avant-Scene Mars/1969 1 ed. Pb/1969/FRA	$45–60
Jonio GONZALEZ	*Marilyn Monroe* Mitografias Pb/1993/ESP	$25–35
Jacky GOUPIL	*Marilyn je t'aime* Vents d'Quest 129F 1 ed. 96 p. ISBN-2-86967-016-8	$40–60

Author	Title/Info	Value
Neil GRANT	*Marilyn in Her Own Words* Crescent 1 ed. 64 p. ISBN-0-517-06103-1 Hc/1991/USA	$30–50
————	*Marilyn in Her Own Words* Hamlyn 1 ed. 64 p. ISBN-0-600-57205-6 Hc/1991/UK	$30–50
————	*Marilyn in Her Own Words* Pyramid Books 1 ed. 64 p. ISBN-1-85510-073-8 Hc/1991/UK	$30–50
————	*Marilyn par elle-meme* Grund 1 ed. 64 p. ISBN-2-7000-6610-3 Hc/1991/FRA	$30–50
GREEK BOOK	*Marilyn 1962–1982* 175 p. Sc/1982/GRE	$50–70
GREEK BOOK	*Marilyn Monroe* 124 p. Sc/1988/GRE	$50–70
Adela GREGORY & Milo SPERIGLIO	*Crypt 33* Birch Lane Press $21.95 310 p. ISBN-1-55972-125-1 Hc/1993/USA	$25–35
Fred Lawrence GUILES	*Norma Jean by Fred Lawrence Guiles* McGraw-Hill Book 1 ed. 373 p. Hc/1969/USA	$50–75
————	*Norma Jean: The Life of Marilyn Monroe* Bantam Book Aug. 1970 1 ed. 406 p. Pb/1970/USA	$40–60
————	*Norma Jean: The Life of Marilyn Monroe* Bantam Book 6 re. 406 p. Pb/1970/USA	$40–60
————	*Norma Jean: The Life of Marilyn Monroe* W. H. Allen 1 ed. 341 p. Hc/1969/UK	$50–75
————	*Norma Jean: The Tragedy of Marilyn Monroe* Mayflower .40 1 ed. 351 p. Pb/1971/UK	$40–60
————	*Norma Jean: F. L. Guiles Biography of Marilyn Monroe* Mayflower/Granada .50 1 re. 351 p. ISBN-0-583-11834-8 Pb/1973/UK	$40–60

Author	Title/Info	Value
	Norma Jean: F. L. Guiles Biography of Marilyn Monroe Mayflower/Granada .75 3 re. 351 p. ISBN-0-583-11834-8 Pb/1975/UK	$40–60
	Norma Jean: F. L. Guiles Biography of Marilyn Monroe Granada 1.95 7 re. 351 p. ISBN-0-583-11834-8 Pb/1982/UK	$20–40
	Norma Jean: F. L. Guiles Biography of Marilyn Monroe Granada/Panther 2.50 9 re. 351 p. ISBN-0-583-11834-8 Pb/1985/UK	$20–40
	Norma Jeen vida de Marilyn Monroe: Palabras en el tiempo n. 72 Lumen 1 ed. 450 p. Pb/1970/ESP	$40–60
Fred Lawrence GUILES	*Legend: The Life and Death of Marilyn Monroe* Stein & Day 1 ed. 501 p. ISBN-0-8182-2983-2 Hc/1984/USA	$30–50
	Legend: The Life and Death of Marilyn Monroe Scarborough House $16.95 1 ed. 501 p. ISBN-0-8128-8525-2 Sc/ 1991/USA	$30–50
	Norma Jeane: The Life and Death of Marilyn Monroe Granada 12.95 2 ed. 377 p. ISBN-0-246-12307-9 Hc/1985/UK	$30–50
	Norma Jeane: The Life and Death of Marilyn Monroe Grafton Books 3.95 1 re. 528 p. ISBN-0-586-06246-7 Pb/1986/UK	$30–50
	Norma Jean: The Life and Death of Marilyn Monroe Grafton Books 3.95 2 re. 528 p. ISBN-0-586-06246-7 Pb/1988/UK	$20–35
James HASPIEL	*Marilyn: The Ultimate Look at the Legend* Henry Holt $45.00 1 ed. 207 p. ISBN-0-8050-1856-5 Hc/1991/USA	$50–60
	Marilyn: The Ultimate Look at the Legend Smith Gryphon 1 ed. 207 p. ISBN-1-85685-007-2 Hc/1991/UK	$50–60
	Young Marilyn: Becoming the Legend Hyperion $34.95 168 p. ISBN-0-7868-6077-4 Hc/1994/USA	$35–45

Author	Title/Info	Value
_____	*Young Marilyn: Becoming the Legend* Smith Gryphon, Ltd. Hc/1994/UK	$35–45
Joe HEMBUS	*Marilyn: The Destruction of an American Dream* Tandem .35 1 ed. 112 p. ISBN-426-13362-5 Pb/1973/UK	$70–100
_____	*Marilyn Monroe: Glanz und Tragik eines idols* Heyne Verlag DM4.80 1 ed. 127 p. ISBN-3-453-01120-1 Pb/1973/ GER	$70–100
Iris HOWDEN	*Marilyn Monroe: Real Lives Series* Sc/1994/UK	$25–35
Edwin P. HOYT	*Marilyn: The Tragic Venus* Duel Sloan & Pierce 1 ed. 279 p. Hc/1965/USA	$70–125
_____	*Marilyn: The Tragic Venus* (New Edition) Chilton Books $6.95 279 p. ISBN-0-8019-5915-2 Hc/ 1973/USA	$60–80
_____	*Marilyn: The Tragic Venus* Robert Hale 1 ed. 256 p. Hc/1967/UK	$70–125
James A. HUDSON	*The Mysterious Death of Marilyn Monroe—Suicide? Accident? . . .* Volitant 1 ed. 112 p. Pb/1968/USA	$60–90
Tom HUTCHINSON	*The Screen Greats: Marilyn Monroe* Optimum 1 ed. 80 p. ISBN-0-600-37789-X Hc/1982/USA	$40–60
_____	*The Screen Greats: Marilyn Monroe* Gallery Press 1 ed. 80 p. ISBN-0-861-36965-3 Hc/1982/UK	$40–60
Katleen IRVING	*Les plus belles Histoires d'amour de Hollywood Marilyn Monroe* Balland 1 ed. 216 p. ISBN-2-7158-0304-4 Sc/1981/FRA	$40–60
Elton JOHN & Bernie TAUPIN	*Candle in the Wind* Hyperion 1 ed. 45 p. ISBN-0-7868-6000-6 Hc/1993/USA	$20–40

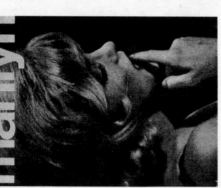

Marilyn—The Tragic Venus, 1965

	Value
	$20–40
	$20–35
	$8–12

Marilyn—The Destruction of an American Dream, 1973

Author	**Title/Info**
——————	*Candle in the Wind*
	Pavilion Hc/1993/UK
Ted JORDAN	*Norma Jean: My Secret Life with Marilyn Monroe*
	Morrow & Comp. $18.95 1 ed. 255 p. ISBN-0-688-09118-0 Hc/1989/USA
——————	*Norma Jean: My Secret Life with Marilyn Monroe*
	Signet $4.99 1 ed. 285 p. ISBN-0-451-16912-3 Pb/1991/USA

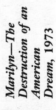

Author	Title/Info	Value
———	*Norma Jean: A Hollywood Love Story* Sigwick & Jackson 13.95 234 p. ISBN-0-28-99879-2 Hc/1989/UK	$20–35
———	*Norma Jean: A Hollywood Love Story* Pan 3.99 1 ed. 358 p. ISBN-0-330-31396-7 Pb/1990/UK	$8–15
Roger KAHN	*Joe & Marilyn: A Memory of Love* Morrow & Comp. $16.95 1 ed. 269 p. ISBN-0-688-02517-X Hc/1986/USA	$20–40
———	*Joe & Marilyn: The Hero Athlete, the Sex Goddess . . . .* Avon Books $4.95 1 ed. 295 p. ISBN-0-380-70462-5 Pb/1988/USA	$20–40
———	*Joe & Marilyn: A Memory of Love* Sidgwick & Jackson 10.95 269 p. ISBN-0-283-99427-4 Hc/1987/UK	$40–60
Clark KIDDER & Madison DANIELS	*Marilyn Monroe UnCovers* Quon Editions $19.95 160 p. 1 ed. ISBN-0-9695539-7-8 Sc/1994/CAN	$80–100
Clark KIDDER	*Marilyn Monroe: Cover to Cover* Krause Publications $24.95 1 ed. 160 p. ISBN-0-87341-740-2 Sc/1999/USA	$20–30
———	*Marilyn Monroe Collectibles: A Comprehensive Guide to the Memorabilia of an American Legend* Avon Books $15.00 1 ed. ISBN-0-380-79909-X Sc/1999/USA	$15–20
John KOBAL & David ROBINSON	*Marilyn Monroe: A Life of Film* Hamlyn 1 ed. 176 p. ISBN-0-600-36172-1 Hc/1974/UK	$40–60
———	*Marilyn Monroe: A Life of Film* Gondola/Hamlyn 4.99 1 ed. 176 p. ISBN-0-600-37310-X Sc/1983/UK	$30–50

Author	Title/Info	Value
	Marilyn Monroe: A Life of Film Hamlyn 4.99 176 p. ISBN-0-600-37310-X Sc/1987/UK	$20–40
	Marilyn Monroe Henri Veyrier 148F 1 ed. 174 p. ISBN-2-85199-319-4 Sc/1984/FRA	$30–50
	Marilyn Monroe Taco 176 p. ISBN-3-8228-0014-7 Sc/1986/GER	$30–50
	Marilyn Monroe Taco 176 p. ISBN-3-89268-092-2 Hc/1989/GER	$40–60
James KOTSILIBAS- DAVIS	*Milton's Marilyn* Schirmer/Mosel 220 p. ISBN-09646873-3-X Hc/1994/GER	$60–70
Ado KYROU	*Marilyn Monroe: Collection Etoiles* E. P. Denoel 1 ed. 239 p. Pb/1972/FRA	$50–70
Michael LACLOS	*Marilyn Monroe: Vedettes du Cinema—Col. dirigee J. P. Castelnau* Jean-Jacques Pauvert 1 ed. 41 p. Sc/1962/FRA	$50–80
Hans Jorgen LEMBOURN	*Diary of a Lover of Marilyn Monroe* Arbor House $8.95 214 p. ISBN-0-87795-216-7 Hc/1979/USA	$20–30
	Diary of a Lover of Marilyn Monroe: A Forty-Night Love Affair . . . Bantam Books $2.25 214 p. ISBN-0-553-13123-0 Pb/1979/USA	$10–15
	Forty Days with Marilyn Hutchinson 1 ed. 214 p. ISBN-0-09-139010-9 Hc/1979/UK	$20–30
	40 Days with Marilyn Arrow Books 1.25 214 p. ISBN-0-09-922690-1 Pb/1980/UK	$10–15
	Quarante jours et Marilyn Robert Laffont 240 p. ISBN-2-221-00454-X Sc/1980/FRA	$20–30
	40 dias con Marilyn: Cuarenta dias con Marilyn Brugera 1 ed. 221 p. ISBN-84-02-06190-7 Hc/1979/ESP	$20–35

Author	Title/Info	Value
	40 dage med Marilyn	$20–35
	Schonberg 1 ed. 190 p. ISBN-87-570-0960-0 Sc/1977/DEN	
	40 dage med Marilyn	$10–20
	Spaendende boger Forum 190 p. ISBN-87-553-0651-9 Pb/1977/DEN	
	40 Noites com Marilyn Monroe	$20–35
	Ricord 178 p. Sc/1979/BRA	
Lyn LIFSHIN	*Marilyn Monroe: Poems*	$15–20
	Quiet Lion Press Sc/1994/USA	
Ann LLOYD	*Marilyn: A Hollywood Life*	$40–50
	Mallard Press 1 ed. 118 p. ISBN-0-792-45088-4 Hc/1989/USA	
	Marilyn: A Hollywood Life	$40–50
	W. H. Smith 118 p. ISBN-0-86124-541-5 Hc/1989/UK	
	Marilyn: A Hollywood Life	$40–50
	Park Lane 118 p. ISBN-0-9509620-9-0 Hc/1989/UK	
	Marilyn: Une vie d'Hollywood	$40–50
	Minerva 120F 118 p. ISBN-2-8303-0079-1 Hc/1990/FRA	
Guus LUIJTERS	*Marilyn: Marilyn Monroe—A Never Ending Dream*	$40–60
	St. Martin's Press $22.95 1 ed. 171 p. ISBN-0-312-01148-2 Hc/1987/USA	
	Marilyn: Marilyn Monroe—A Never Ending Dream	$40–50
	Plexus 6.95 171 p. ISBN-0-85965-145-2 Sc/1986/UK	
	Marilyn, un Reve sans Fin	$40–50
	ArteFact 75F 171 p. ISBN-2-86697-082-9 Sc/1985/FRA	
	Marilyn Monroe: In Her Own Words	$40–50
	Omnibus Press 128 p. ISBN-0-7119-2302-7 Sc/1991/UK	
	Marilyn Monroe	$40–50
	Moewig DM16.80 112 p. ISBN-3-8118-3080-5 Sc/1991/GER	

Author	Title/Info	Value
	Marilyn Monroe: In Her Own Words Uplink 146 p. ISBN-4-309-90097-6 Sc/1992/JAP	$45-65
	Marilyn Monroe Complete Loeb 295 p. ISBN-90-6213-795-4 Sc/1988/HOL	$40-60
Kai Berg MADSEN	*En amerikansk Sukces: Historien om Marilyn Monroe* Kobenhavn 1 ed. 32 p. Sc/1953/DEN	$300-400
Christa MAERKER	*Marilyn Monroe—Arthur Miller* Rowohlt Hc/1997/GER	$20-40
Norman MAILER	*Marilyn* (Limited Signed Edition in box) Grosset & Dunlap 1 ed. 270 p. ISBN-0-448-01029-1 Hc/1973/USA	$70-120
	Marilyn: A Biography by Norman Mailer Grosset & Dunlap 1 ed. 270 p. ISBN-0-448-01029-1 Hc/1973/USA	$50-70
	Marilyn: A Biography by Norman Mailer Grosset & Dunlap 1 ed. 270 p. ISBN-0-448-11813-0 Sc/1974/USA	$50-70
	Marilyn: A Biography by Norman Mailer Warner Books $3.50 1 ed. 381 p. ISBN-0-446-96747-5 Pb/1975/USA	$20-30
	Marilyn: A Biography by Norman Mailer Warner Pub. Lib. $2.50 381 p. ISBN-0-446-71850-5 Pb/1975/USA	$20-30
	Marilyn: A Biography by Norman Mailer Holdder/Stroghton 4.95 1 ed. 270p. ISBN-0-340-18104-4 Hc/1973/UK	$50-75
	Marilyn: A Biography by Norman Mailer Coronet Books 2.50 270 p. ISBN-0-340-18828-6 Sc/1974/UK	$45-65
	Marilyn: A Biography by Norman Mailer Spring Books 8.95 1 ed. 270 p. ISBN-0-600-55726-X Hc/1988/UK	$40-60

Author	Title/Info	Value
_____	*Marilyn: A Biography by Norman Mailer* Spring Books 2 re. 270 p. ISBN-0-600-55726-X Hc/1989/UK	$40–60
_____	*Marilyn: une biographie par Norman Mailer* Stock/Albin Michel 1 ed. 270 p. Sc/1974/FRA	$45–65
_____	*Marilyn: une biographie par Norman Mailer* Ramsay/Stock Albin Michel 270p. ISBN-2-85956-437-3 Sc/1985/FRA	$35–55
_____	*Marilyn: une biographie par Norman Mailer* Ramsay/Stock Albin Michel 270p. ISBN-2-85956-437-3 Sc/1986/FRA	$35–55
_____	*Marilyn: una biografía . . .* Los mas destacados fotografos . . . Lumen 1 ed. 270 p. ISBN-84-264-2510-0 Hc/1974/ESP	$60–80
_____	*Marilyn: una biografía . . .* Los mas destacados fotografos . . . Lumen 270 p. ISBN-84-264-2510-0 Sc/1974/ESP	$45–55
_____	*Marilyn Monroe: eine Biographie von Norman Mailer* Knaur #429 DM9.80 391 p. ISBN-3-426-00424-0 Pb/1976/GER	$30–45
_____	*Marilyn: biografia di Norman Mailer* Arnoldo Mondadori L35.000 2 ed. 261 p. Hc/1982/ITA	$40–60
_____	*Marilyn: en biografi av Norman Mailer* Bonniers/Manadens Book 292 p. ISBN-91-0-038841-6 Hc/1973/SWE	$50–75
_____	*Marilyn: una biografía . . .* Los mas destacados fotografos . . . Lumen Circulo de Lectores 270 p. ISBN-84-264-2510-0 Hc/1987/ESP	$40–60
_____	*Marilyn: eine biographie* Knaur Pb/1993/GER	$10–20
_____	*Marilyn: The Classic by Norman Mailer* Galahad 271 p. ISBN-0-88365-731-7 Hc/1993/USA	$30–45
_____	*Memories imaginaires de Marilyn (Of Women & Their Elegance)* Robert Laffont 30F 1 ed. 193 p. ISBN-2-221-00812-X Sc/1982/FRA	$40–60

Marilyn Monroe, 1956

Will Acting Spoil Marilyn Monroe? 1956

Author	Title/Info	Value
MARC'O	L'impossible, et pourtant-di MARC'O con Marilyn e Federica Edizioni Nuovi Strumenti (Cavellini, Bertelli) Sc/1984/ITA	$40–60
Julie MARS	Marilyn Monroe Ariel $4.95 79p. 1 ed. ISBN-0-8362-3115-5 Hc/1995/USA	$10–15
Pete MARTIN	Will Acting Spoil Marilyn Monroe? Doubleday & Co. $2.95 1 ed. 128 p. Hc/1956/USA	$125–200
	Will Acting Spoil Marilyn Monroe? Pocket Books; Cardinal $0.35 128 p. Pb/1957/USA	$60–100

Author	Title/Info	Value
	Will Acting Spoil Marilyn Monroe? Frederick Muller, Ltd. London 110 p. Hc/1956/UK	$200–250
Dorothea KUHL MARTINE	*Marilyn an pabst Johannes* Patmos Hc/1997/GER	$20–40
Graham McCANN	*Marilyn Monroe* Rutgers University Press 1 ed. 241p. ISBN-0-8135-1302-2 Hc/1988/USA	$40–60
	Marilyn Monroe Rutgers University Press 1 ed. 241p. ISBN-0-8135-1303-0 Sc/1988/USA	$40–55
	Marilyn Monroe Polity Press 35.00 1 ed. 241 p. ISBN-0-7456-0378-5 Hc/1988/UK	$40–60
	Marilyn Monroe: The Body in the Library Polity Press 7.95 1 ed. 241 p. ISBN-0-7456-0379-3 Sc/1988/UK	$40–55
Joan MELLEN	*Marilyn Monroe: The Pictorial Treasury of Film Stars* Galahad Books $4.95 157 p. ISBN-0-88365-165-3 Hc/1973/USA	$40–60
	Marilyn Monroe: Pyramid Illustrated History of The Movies Pyramid Books $1.45 157 p. ISBN-0-515-03129-1 Pb/1973/USA	$30–40
	Marilyn Monroe: Pyramid Illustrated History of The Movies Pyramid Books $1.75 157 p. ISBN-0-515-03129-1 Pb/1976/USA	$30–40
	Marilyn Monroe: Pyramid Illustrated History of The Movies Star Book/W. Allen .70 157 p. ISBN-0-352-30059-0 Pb/1973/UK	$30–40
	Marilyn Monroe: Historia Illustrada del Cine n. 3 Iesa 1 ed. 152 p. ISBN-84-7311-017-X Pb/1977/ESP	$30–40
	Marilyn Monroe: Storia Illustrata del Cinema Milano Libri E. 1 ed. 157 p. Pb/1975/ITA	$30–40
	Marilyn Monroe: Ihre Filme-Ihr Leben Heyne Film Bibliothek Pb/1992/GER	$20–35

Author	Title/Info	Value
	Marilyn Das M. M. Kultbuch-Heyne Mini no. 33/26 W. Heyne Verlag DM3,-1 ed. 121 p. ISBN-3-453-35372-2 Pb/1986/ GER	$20–35
Gianni MERCURIO & Stephano PETRICCA	*Marilyn Monroe: La Vita Il Mito* Rizzoli L75.000 319 p. ISBN-88-17-24824-X Sc/1995/ITA	$50–65

Marilyn—The Last Months, 1975

Will Acting Spoil Marilyn Monroe? 1957

Author	Title/Info	Value
	Marilyn: The Life and Myth	$50–70
	Rizzoli $60.00 1 ed. 319p. ISBN-0-8478-1960-4 Hc/1996/USA	
Bart MILLS	*Marilyn On Location*	$40–60
	Sidgwick & Jackson 13.95 160 p. ISBN-0-283-99766-4 Hc/1989/UK	
	Marilyn On Location	$30–50
	Pan Books 9.99 160 p. ISBN-0-330-31841-1 Sc/1990/UK	
Bernice Baker MIRA-	*My Sister Marilyn*	$30–40
CLE & Mona Rae	Algonquin $19.95 238 p. 1 ed. ISBN-1-56512-070-1 Hc/1994/USA	
MIRACLE		
	Mijn zus Marilyn	$30–40
	de Kern Sc/1994/HOL	
Vincenzo MOLLICA	*Dedicato a Marilyn*	$30–40
	(boxed with two compact discs) Ed. del Grifo Sc/1990/ITA	
Marilyn MONROE	*My Story by Marilyn Monroe*	$45–60
	Stein & Day $5.95 1 ed. 143 p. ISBN-0-8128-1707-9 Hc/1974/USA	
	My Story by Marilyn Monroe	$20–40
	Stein & Day $1.75 1 ed. 143 p. ISBN-0-8128-2112-X Pb/1976/USA	
	My Story by Marilyn Monroe	$10–15
	Stein & Day $3.50 2 re. 239 p. ISBN-0-8128-8283-0 Pb/1986/USA	
	My Story by Marilyn Monroe—Never before published	$45–65
	W. H. Allen 1 ed. 143 p. ISBN-0-491-01754-5 Hc/1975/UK	
	Marilyn Monroe: Confession inacbevee	$25–45
	Robert Laffont 233 p. Pb/1974/FRA	
	Recuerdos de mi vida: Marilyn Monroe—Coll. Personae, 8—No. 565	$45–65
	Euros/Club de Vanguardia 232 p. ISBN-84-7364-041-1 Hc/1975/ESP	

Author	Title/Info	Value
	Marilyn Monroe: Meine Story Fischer cinema–3663 Fischer Taschenbucker 156 p. ISBN-3-596-23663-0 Pb/1980/GER	$15-25
	Nuorunteni Otava 1 ed. 156 p. ISBN-951-1-01972-4 Sc/1975/FIN	$45-65
Robin MOORE	*Marilyn & Joe DiMaggio* Manor Books $1.95 1 ed. 298 p. ISBN-0-532-19132-8 Pb/1977/USA	$30-50
Richard S MOORE	*Marilyn Monroe: Su vida—sus amores—su muerte* Petronio 250 Pt. 1 ed. 245 p. ISBN-84-365-0196-9 Hc/1973/ESP	$50-80
	Marilyn Monroe: Su vida—sus amores—su muerte Petronio 250 Pt. 2 re. 245 p. ISBN-84-365-0196-9 Hc/1973/ESP	$50-80
	Marilyn Monroe: Su vida—sus amores—su muerte Gaviota 700 p. 245 p. ISBN-84-7693-066-6 Sc/1987/ESP	$40-55
Eunice MURRAY & Rose SHADE	*Marilyn: The Last Months—Intimate Facts Never Before Revealed* Pyramid Books $1.75 1 ed. 157 p. ISBN-0-515-03787-7 Pb/1975/USA	$35-45
Joel OPPENHEIMER	*Marilyn Lives! By Joel Oppenheimer* Delilah Books $8.95 1 ed. 123 p. ISBN-0-933328-02-8 Sc/1981/USA	$40-60
	Marilyn Lives! By Joel Oppenheimer Pipeline Books 5.95 1 ed. 123 p. ISBN-0-933328-02-8 Sc/1981/UK	$40-60
Mary Jo PACE	*Marilyn Monroe: Una donna bruciata—I magnifici di Hollywood N. 10* Alberto L500 1 ed. 66 p. Pb/1981/ITA	$20-40
Ulises PARAMO	*Marilyn Suicidio o Asesinato?* Esamex Sc/1993/MEX	$60-80
Lena PEPITONE & William STADIEM	*Marilyn Monroe Confidential: An Intimate Personal Account* Simon & Shuster $9.95 1 ed. 251 p. ISBN-0-671-24289-X Hc/1979/USA	$20-40

Author	Title/Info	Value
___	*Marilyn Monroe Confidential: An Intimate Personal Account* Simon & Shuster (Book Club Ed.) 1 ed. 222 p. Hc/1979/USA	$30–45
___	*Marilyn Monroe Confidential* (blue cover) Pocket Books $2.50 1 ed. 223 p. ISBN-0-671-83038-4 Pb/1980/USA	$10–15
___	*Marilyn Monroe Confidential: The Whole World Knows Her* (pink cvr) Pocket Books $2.50 1 ed. 223 p. ISBN-0-671-83038-4 Pb/1980/USA	$10–15
___	*Marilyn Monroe Confidential: An Intimate Personal Account* Sidgwick & Jackson 1 ed. 251 p. ISBN-0-283-98537-2 Hc/1979/UK	$25–45
___	*Marilyn Monroe Confidential: An Intimate Personal Account* New English Libr. 1.25 1 ed. 221 p. ISBN-0-45-04765-2 Pb/1980/UK	$15–20
___	*Marilyn Monroe Secrete: Les bouleversantes revelations . . .* Pygmalion/G. Watelet 253 p. ISBN-2-85704-052-0 Sc/1979/FRA	$35–45
___	*Marilyn Monroe Secrete: Les bouleversantes revelations . . .* Pygmalion/G. Watelet 253 p. ISBN-2-85704-052-0 Sc/1979/FRA	$35–45
___	*Marilyn Secrete* Pygmalion/G. Watelet 248 p. ISBN-2-85704-206-X Sc/1986/FRA	$35–45
___	*Marilyn Monroe Intim* Heyne Verlag DM5.80 1 ed. 189 p. ISBN-3-453-01045-0 Pb/1979/GER	$15–25
___	*Marilyn Monroe Confidencial confidencialmente* Crea 2 ed. 149 p. Pb/1980/ARG	$15–25
___	*Farval Lammunge Marilyn Monroe in pa skinnet* Corona 1 ed. 180 p. ISBN-91-564-0990-7 Hc/1979/SWE	$40–60

Author	Title/Info	Value
Maurice PERISSET	*Marilyn Monroe: Sa vie, ses films et son mystere* Garanciere 48F 1 ed. 195 p. ISBN-2-7340-0087-3 Pb/1985/FRA	$15–20
Anna PRADERIO	*Marilyn Monroe: Ciakintasca No. 1* (supplement to Ciak Mag. No. 6) Silvio Berlusconi/Ciak 1 ed. 126 p. Pb/1989/ITA	$15–25
Silvain REINER	*La Tragedie de Marilyn Monroe: victime de l'usine a idoles* Presses Pocket 309 p. Pb/1966/FRA	$70–100
————	*La Tragedia de Marilyn Monroe: Coll. 'Fifuras del Cine No.2* Grigalbo 1 ed. 277 p. Pb/1972/ESP	$70–100
Tony RICHARDSON	*La vida privada de Marilyn Monroe: Coll. 'Rosa' No.1* Tarquimia 1 ed. 63 p. ISBN-84-300-2501-4 Pb/1980/ESP	$30–40
Randall RIESE & Neil HITCHENS	*The Unabridged Marilyn: Her Life from A to Z* Congdon & Weed $25.00 1 ed. 578 p. ISBN-0-86553-176-5 Hc/1987/USA	$30–40
————	*The Unabridged Marilyn: Her Life from A to Z* Congdon & Weed $14.95 578 p. ISBN-0-86553-167-6 Sc/1987/USA	$30–40
————	*The Unabridged Marilyn: Her Life from A to Z* Bonanza Books $25.00 578 p. ISBN-0-517-69619-3 Hc/1990/USA	$30–40
————	*The Unabridged Marilyn: The Definitive, Illustrated A–Z . . .* Corgi 9.95 587 p. ISBN-0-552-99308-5 Sc/1988/UK	$20–30
P. RODELLAR (Helmuth Von Soegl)	*Marilyn Monroe—Inedita* Prod. Editoriales 150Pt. 1 ed. 95 p. ISBN-84-65-0951-X Sc/1976/ESP	$40–65
Carl E. ROLLYSON, Jr.	*Marilyn Monroe: A Life of the Actress* U.M.I. Research Press $16.95 255 p. ISBN-0-8357-1771-2 Hc/1986/USA	$25–40

Author	Title/Info	Value
	Marilyn Monroe: A Life of the Actress Souvenir Press 1 ed. 255 p. ISBN-0-285-62827-5 Hc/1986/UK	$25–40
	Marilyn Monroe: A Life of the Actress New English Libr. 4.50 1 ed. 306 p. ISBN-0-450-53720-X Pb/1990/UK	$10–15
Norman ROSTEN	*Marilyn: An Untold Story*— Signet/New Amer. Lib. $1.50 1 ed. 125 p. ISBN-0-451-08880-8 Pb/1973/US	$25–40
	Marilyn: A Very Personal Story by Norm Rosten Millington 1 ed. 125 p. ISBN-0-86000-001 Hc/1974/UK	$45–65
	Marilyn: A Very Personal Story by Norm Rosten Millington 114 p. ISBN-0-86000-118-0 Pb/1980/UK	$20–30
	Marilyn un relato inedito Grijalbo 2 ed. 144 p. ISBN-84-253-0461-X Pb/1980/UK	$20–35
	Marilyn: A unica estoria nao revelada Nova Epoca 111 p. Sc/1980/BRA	$25–45
	Marilyn Monroe un autre regard—et Marilyn Monroe par elle—meme Lherminier 136F 1 ed. 189 p. ISBN-2-86244-029-9 Sc/1984/FRA	$40–50
Roger ST. PIERRE	*Marilyn Monroe: An Independent Story in Words and Pictures* Anabas Look Book Series 1 ed. 27 p. ISBN-1-85099-013-1 Sc/1985/UK	$20–35
Jeannie SAKOL & Joseph JASGUR	*The Birth of Marilyn: The Lost Photographs of Norma Jean* St. Martin's Press $25.00 1 ed. 93p. ISBN-0-312-06770-4 Hc/1991/USA	$30–40
	The Birth of Marilyn: The Lost Photographs of Norma Jean Sidgwick & Jackson 17.50 1 ed. 93 p. ISBN-0-283-99852-0 Hc/1991/UK	$30–40
Lothar SCHIRMER	*Marilyn Monroe and the Camera* (with Jane Russell & G. Belmont) Bloomsbury 40.00 1 ed. 245 p. ISBN-0-7475-0490-3 Hc/1989/UK	$50–70

Author	Title/Info	Value
________	*Marilyn Monroe et les Cameras* (with Jane Russell & G. Belmont) Schirmere/Mosel 1 ed. 248 p. ISBN-3-88814-538-4 Hc/1989/FRA	$50–70
________	*Marilyn Monroe und die Kamera* (Jane Russell & George Belmont) Schirmer/Mosel 1 ed. 248 p. ISBN-3-88814-334-9 Hc/1989/GER	$50–70
________	*Marilyn Monroe immagini di un mito* (Jane Russell & G. Belmont) RCS Rizzoli 1 ed. 248 p. ISBN-88-17-24244-6 Hc/1989/ITA	$50–70
________	*Marilyn Monroe and the Camera* (Japanese) New Art Seibu 1 ed. 245 p. ISBN-4-8457-0464-1 Hc/1989/JAP	$60–80
Tony SCIACCA	*Who Killed Marilyn? And Did the Kennedys Know?* Manor Book $1.75 1 ed. 222 p. ISBN-532-17124-175 Pb/1976/USA	$20–30
________	*Quien Mato a Marilyn? y . . . Lo sabian los Kennedy?* Novarro 1 ed. 182 p. Sc/1977/MEX	$25–35
Esther SELSDON	*They Died Too Young: Marilyn Monroe* Parragon Mini Book Hc/1995/UK	$15–25
Sam SHAW	*Marilyn Monroe as The Girl (based on The Seven-Year Itch)* Ballantine Books $0.35 1 ed. 123 p. Pb/1955/USA	$60–100
________	*The Joy of Marilyn: In the Camera Eye* Exeter Books 1 ed. 160 p. ISBN-0-89673-030-1 Hc/1979/USA	$45–60
________	*Marilyn: In the Camera Eye* Hamlyn 4.95 1 ed. 160 p. ISBN-0-600-34156-9 Hc/1979/UK	$45–60
________	*Marilyn: Dans l'objectif* L. Champs-Elysees 1 ed. 160 p. ISBN-2-7024-0972-5 Hc/1979/FRA	$45–60

Author	Title/Info	Value
Sam SHAW & Norm ROSTEN	*Marilyn among Friends* Henry Holt 1 ed. 192 p. ISBN-0-8050-0843-8 Hc/1987/USA	$40–60
	Marilyn among Friends Bloomsbury 14.95 1 ed. 192 p. ISBN-0-7475-0012-6 Hc/1987/UK	$40–60
	Marilyn among Friends Bloomsbury 9.95 192 p. ISBN-0-7475-0172-6- Sc/1988/UK	$40–60
	Marilyn among Friends Bloomsbury 6.99 2 re. 192 p. ISBN-0-7475-0629-9 Sc/1989/UK	$40–60
	Marilyn et ses amis Ramsay 250F 1 ed. 192 p. ISBN-2-85956-678-3 Hc/1988/FRA	$40–60
	Marilyn ganz privat Heyne Verlag 1 ed. 192 p. ISBN-3-453-02498-2 Hc/1987/GER	$40–60
	Marilyn fra i suoi amice A. Vallardi L50.000 1 ed. 192 p. ISBN-88-11-95291-3 Hc/1988/ITA	$40–60
	Marilyn among Friends (Japanese book) Bungeishunju 1 ed. 192 p. ISBN-4-16-380310-6 Hc/1989/JAP	$60–80
Sandra SHEVEY	*The Marilyn Scandal: Her True Life Revealed By Those Who Knew* W. Morrow & Co. $18.95 1 ed. 326 p. ISBN-0-688-08219-X Hc/1988/USA	$20–35
	The Marilyn Scandal: Her True Life Revealed By Those Who Knew Jove Book $4.95 341 p. ISBN-0-515-10238-5 Pb/1990/USA	$10–15
	The Marilyn Scandal: Her True Life Revealed By Those Who Knew Sidgwick & Jackson 12.95 326 p. ISBN-0-283-99456-8 Hc/1987/UK	$20–35
	The Marilyn Scandal: The True Story Arrow 3.99 434 p. ISBN-0-09-960760-3 Pb/1989/UK	$10–15

Author	Title/Info	Value
————	*Le scandale Marilyn* Press Renaissance 120F 342 p. ISBN-2-85616-526-5 Sc/1989/FRA	$20–35
Neil SINYARD	*Marilyn* Gallery Books 1 ed. 109 p. ISBN-0-8317-5753-1 Hc/1989/USA	$20–35
————	*Marilyn* Magna Books 1 ed. 109 p. ISBN-1-85422-020-9 Hc/1989/UK	$20–35
Robert F. SLATZER	*The Life and Curious Death of Marilyn Monroe* Pinnacle House 1 ed. 348 p. ISBN-0-8467-001-8 Hc/1974/USA	$50–65
————	*The Life and Curious Death of Marilyn Monroe* Pinnacle House 2 ed. 348 p. ISBN-0-8467-001-8 Hc/1974/USA	$50–65
————	*The Curious Death of Marilyn Monroe* Pinnacle Books $1.95 1 ed. 417 p. ISBN-0-523-00575-3 Pb/1975/USA	$25–35
————	*Enquete sur une mort suspecte: Marilyn Monroe* Julliard 1 ed. 346 p. Sc/1974/FRA	$50–65
————	*Enquete sur une mort suspecte: Marilyn Monroe* Presses pocket 409 p. ISBN-2-266-00021-7 Pb/1976/FRA	$35–45
Robert F. SLATZER	*The Marilyn Files* S.P.I. Books Pb/1992/USA	$10–15
Matteo SOCCIO	*Marilyn in cartellone* Bastogi di Angelo Manuali L7.000 Sc/1983/ITA	$30–40
James SPADA & George ZENO	*Monroe: Her Life in Pictures* Doubleday & Co. $24.95 1 ed. 194 p. ISBN-0-385-17941-3 Hc/1982/USA	$30–50
————	*Monroe: Her Life in Pictures* Doubleday/Dolphin $14.95 1 ed. 194 p. ISBN-0-385-17940-5 Sc/1982/USA	$30–50

Author	Title/Info	Value
________	*Monroe: Her Life in Pictures* Sidgwick & Jackson 8.95 1 ed. 194 p. ISBN-0-283-98871-1 Hc/1982/UK	$30–50
________	*Monroe: Her Life in Pictures* Sidgwick & Jackson 9.95 6 re. 194 p. ISBN-0-283-98998-X Sc/1987/UK	$30–50
________	*Marilyn Monroe: Sa vie en images—Les grands acteurs,3* Jai lu-Cinema 3F 1 ed. 143 p. ISBN-2-277-37003-7 Pb/1988/FRA	$30–50
________	*Marilyn Monroe: Ihr Leben in Bildern* Bussesche 193 p. ISBN-3-87120-813-2 Hc/1983/GER	$35–55
Milo SPERIGLIO	*Marilyn Monroe: Murder Cover-up* Seville $7.95 1 ed. 269 p. ISBN-0-930990-77-3 Sc/1982/USA	$20–40
________	*The Marilyn Conspiracy: by the Private Detective . . .* Pocket Nonfiction $3.50 1 ed. 221 p. ISBN-0-671-62612-4 Pb/1986/ USA	$10–15
________	*The Marilyn Conspiracy—Suicide? Accidental Death? Murder? . . .* Corgi Books 2.50 1 ed. 173 p. ISBN-0-552-13058-3 Pb/1987/UK	$10–15
________	*The Marilyn Conspiracy—Suicide? Accidental Death? Murder? . . .* Corgi Books 2.99 4 re. 173 p. ISBN-0-552-13058-3 Pb/1988/UK	$10–15
________	*A Conspiracao Marilyn* Imago 1 ed. 137 p. Sc/1987/BRA	$20–40
Donald SPOTO	*Marilyn Monroe: The Biography* Harper-Collins $25.00 698 p. ISB--0-06-017987-2 Hc/1993/USA	$25–35
________	*Marilyn Monroe: The Biography* Harper-Collins $6.99 841 p. 1 ed. ISBN-0-06-109166-9 Pb/1994/USA	$8–10
________	*Marilyn La Biografia* Anagrama Pb/1993/ESP	$40–50

Marilyn Monroe—An Uncensored Biography, 1960

Marilyn—An Untold Story, 1973

Author	Title/Info	Value
	Marilyn Finalmente La Verita Sperling & Kupfer Hc/1993/ITA	$40–50
Gloria STEINHEM & George BARRIS	*Marilyn: Norma Jeane* Henry Holt & Co. $24.95 1 ed. 182 p. ISBN-0-8050-0060-7 Hc/ 1986/USA	$30–50

Author	Title/Info	Value
	Marilyn: The Nationwide Bestseller! Plume/N.A.L. $14.95 1 ed. 182 p. ISBN-0-452-2598-7 Sc/1987/USA	$30–50
	Marilyn—Norma Jeane: The Nationwide Bestseller! Signet Book/N.A.L. $4.95 1 ed. 220 p. ISBN-0-451-15596-3 Pb/1988/USA	$10–15
	Marilyn: Norma Jeane Victor Gollancz 12.95 2 re. 182 p. ISBN-0-575-03945-0 Hc/1987/UK	$30–50
	Marilyn Inconnue Sylvie Messinger 195F 1 ed. 182 p. ISBN-2-86583-080-2 Hc/1987/FRA	$30–50
	Marilyn: Un ritrato tenero e realistico Armenia Editore L24.000 1 ed. 268 p. ISBN-88-344-0243-X Hc/1987/ITA	$30–50
	Marilyn: Norma Jeane Informations Forlag 1 ed. 192 p. ISBN-87-7514-0071 Hc/1987/DEN	$30–50
	Marilyn: Norma Jeane Wahlstrom & Widstrand 1 ed. 190 p. ISBN-91-46-15522-8 Hc/1987/SWE	$30–50
Bert STERN	*Marilyn Monroe* (Slipcased/edit. de luxe/limitee a 1,000) #00578 Chene/Hachette 790F. 1 ed. 463 p. ISBN-2-85108-3090 Hc/1982/FRA	$500–1,000
	Marilyn Monroe: The Complete Last Sitting (Slipcased) Schirmer/Mosel 1 ed. 463 p. ISBN-3-88814-103-6 Hc/1982/GER	$500–1,000
Bert STERN & Ann GOTTLIEB	*Marilyn viva* Frassinelli ISBN-88-200-0271-X Hc/1982/ITA	$40–60

Author	Title/Info	Value
Bert STERN	*The Last Sitting* W. Morrow & Co. 1 ed. 188 p. ISBN-0-688-01173-X Hc/1982/USA	$40–60
_____	*The Last Sitting* Black Cat 13.95 1 re. 188p. ISBN-0-7481-0107-1 Hc/1982/UK	$40–60
_____	*Marilyn: Sa Derniere Seance par Bert Stern* Filipacchi 195F 1 re. 188 p. ISBN-2-85018-427-6 Hc/1982/FRA	$40–60
_____	*Marilyn's Last Sitting* Knaur/Biographie DM17.80 242p. ISBN-3-426-02328-8 Pb/1982/GER	$10–15
_____	*Marilyn: haar laatste fotosessie* van holkema en warendorf Sc/1982/HOL	$40–60
Susan STRASBERG	*Marilyn and Me* Warner $21.95 1 ed. 282p. ISBN-0-446-51592-2 Hc/1992/USA	$25–35
_____	*Marilyn and Me* Warner $5.99 1 ed. 254p. ISBN-0-446-36425-8 Pb/1993/USA	$10–15
_____	*Marilyn Et Moi* J'ai lu Pb/1992/FRA	$20–30
Anthony SUMMERS	*Goddess: The Secret Lives of Marilyn Monroe* MacMillan $18.95 1 ed. 415p. ISBN-0-02-615460-9 Hc/1985/USA	$25–45
_____	*Goddess: The Secret Lives of Marilyn Monroe* (Book Club edition) MacMillan/Book Club Ed. 430 p. Hc/1985/USA	$25–45
_____	*Goddess: The Secret Lives of Marilyn Monroe* Onyx Book/N.A.L. $18.95 1 ed. 526p. ISBN-0-451-40014-3 Pb/1986/USA	$10–15
_____	*Goddess: The Secret Lives of Marilyn Monroe* Gollancz 12.95 1 ed. 414p. ISBN-0-575-03641-9 Hc/1985/UK	$25–45

Author	Title/Info	Value
———	*Goddess: The Secret Lives of Marilyn Monroe* Sphere 3.95 1 ed. 619p. ISBN-0-7221-8284-8 Pb/1986/UK	$10–15
———	*Les vies secretes de Marilyn Monroe* Pre. de la renaissance 522p. ISBN-2-35616-370-X Sc/1986/FRA	$25–45
———	*Les vies secretes de Marilyn Monroe* Ed. Club France Loisirs 1 ed. 522p. ISBN-2-277-22282-8 Pb/1987/FRA	$25–45
———	*Les vies secretes de Marilyn Monroe* Jai lu 1 ed. 568p. ISBN-2-277-22282-8 Pb/1987/FRA	$10–15
———	*Las vidas secretas de Marilyn Monroe—Col. Al FILO DEL TIEMPO* Planeta 1400Pt. 1 ed. 349p. ISBN-84-320-4769-4 Sc/1986/ESP	$25–45
———	*Marilyn Monroe: Die Wahrhelt uber ihr Leben und Sterben* Fischer DM16.8 1 ed. 519p. ISBN-3-596-25679-8 Pb/1990/GER	$10–15
———	*Marilyn Monroe: Le vite segrete di una diva* Tascabili sonzogno L8.000 1 ed. 425 p. Sc/1988/ITA	$25–45
———	*De Geheime Levens van Marilyn Monroe* De Bezige Bij 1 ed. 526 p. ISBN-90-234-5297-6 Sc/1986/HOL	$25–45
———	*Gudinnan Marilyn Monroes Hemliga Liv* Forum 1 ed. 516 p. ISBN-91-37-09126-3 Hc/1986/SWE	$25–45
———	*Den nogne gudinde: Sandheden om Marilyn Monroe* Chr. Erichsen 424p. ISBN-87-555-1069-8 Sc/1986/DEN	$25–45
———	*A Deusa as vidas secretas de Marilyn Monroe* Best-Seller 1 ed. 523p. ISBN-85-85091-52-5 Sc/1987/BRA	$25–45
———	*Marilyn* Sonzogno Hc/1992/ITA	$25–40
Roger TAYLOR	*Marilyn Monroe in Her Own Words* Delilah/Putnam 5.95 1 ed. 122p. ISBN-0-399-41014-7 Sc/1983/USA	$40–60

Author	Title/Info	Value
	Marilyn on Marilyn Zachary Kwintner Books 1 ed. 122 p. ISBN-1-872532-01-2 Hc/1983/UK	$40–60
	Marilyn on Marilyn Comet Book 4.95 1 re. 122p. ISBN-0-86379-080-1 Sc/1985/UK	$40–50
	Marilyn in Art Salem House $12.95 1 ed. ISBN-0-88162-169-2 Sc/1984/USA	$40–60
	Marilyn in Art Elm Tree Books 10.00 1 ed. ISBN-0-241-11326-1 Hc/1984/UK	$40–60
William C. TAYLOR	*Marilyn Monroe* Ultramar Hc/1995/ESP	$50–60
Wolfgang TUMLER	*Marilyn Monroe* Dressler/Menschen DM12.80 172p. ISBN-3-7915-5009-8 Sc/1978/GER	$40–60
Michael VENTURA	*Marilyn Monroe: From Beginning to End* Blandford 220p. ISBN-09646873-3-X Hc/1997/UK	$25–40
Orbis VERLAG	*Marilyn Monroe: The Story of Her Life* Colour Library Books, Ltd. 12×14" Hc/1992/GER	$30–50
Ricardo VOLTOLINI	*Marilyn Monroe por ela mesma: Colecao 'O autor por ele mesmo'* Martin Claret 1 ed. 158p. Sc/1991/BRA	$30–50
Edward WAGENKNECHT	*Marilyn Monroe: A Composite View* Chilton Book Co. $5.95 1 ed. 200p. Hc/1969/USA	$70–100
Jane Ellen WAYNE	*Marilyn's Men: The Private Life of Marilyn Monroe* Robson Books 1 ed. 241p. ISBN-0-86051-792-6 Hc/1992/UK	$25–40
	Marilyn's Men St. Martin's $4.50 241p. ISBN-0-312-92943-9 Pb/1993/USA	$5–10

Author	Title/Info	Value
	Marilyn's Men Knauer Pb/1994/GER	$10–15
	Marilyn's Men: The Private Life of Marilyn Monroe Warnerbooks Pb/1993/UK	$10–15
W. J. WEATHERBY	*Conversations with Marilyn* Manson/Charter $7.95 1 ed. 229p. ISBN-0-88405-148-X Hc/1976/USA	$40–70
	Conversations with Marilyn Manson/Charter $7.95 2 re. 229p. ISBN-0-88405-148-X Hc/1976/USA	$40–70
	Conversations with Marilyn Ballantine Nonfiction 1 ed. 178p. ISBN-345-25568-2-175 Pb/1977/USA	$20–35
	Conversations with Marilyn Robson Books 1 ed. 229p. ISBN-0-903895-68-4 Hc/1976/UK	$40–70
	Conversations with Marilyn Sphere Books .95 1 ed. 229p. ISBN-0-7221-8982-6 Pb/1977/UK	$20–35
	Conversations with Marilyn Sphere Books 2.99 1 re. 229p. ISBN-0-7221-8982-6 Pb/1987/UK	$20–30
	Conversaciones con Marilyn: serie conversaciones, n. 7 Gedisa 990Pt. 1 ed. 269p. ISBN-84-7432-051-8 Pb/1978/ESP	$20–30
	Conversations with Marilyn Paragon $12.95 229p. ISBN-1-55778-512-0 Sc/1992/USA	$15–20
Leigh WIERNER	*Marilyn: A Hollywood Farewell* Leigh Wierner 1 ed. 93p. ISBN-0-9619146-3-7 Hc/1990/USA	$70–100

Author	Title/Info	Value
Corrina WINTER	*Marilyn Super-Star Der Funfziger Jahre* Quadro Hc/1992/ITA	$30–45
Maurice ZOLOTOW	*Marilyn Monroe: A Biography* Harcourt Brace $5.75 1 ed. 340 p. Hc/1960/USA	$60–90
	Marilyn Monroe: An Uncensored Biography Bantam Books $0.75 338 p. Pb/1961/USA	$35–45
	Marilyn Monroe—Revised, updated and expanded edition. Perennial Library $9.95 1 ed. 359p. ISBN-0-06-097196-7 Sc/1990/USA	$25–40
	Marilyn Monroe: A Biography W. H. Allen .25 1 ed. 333p. Hc/1961/UK	$60–100
	Marilyn Monroe: An Uncensored Biography Panther Books 1 ed. 287p. Pb/1962/UK	$35–50
	Marilyn Monroe—par Maurice Zolotow—L'air du temps Gallimard 16.50F 1 ed. 416p. Sc/1961/FRA	$60–85
	Marilyn Monroe—Lauro, 99 Plaza & Janes 50Pt. 1 ed. 318 p. Pb/1965/ESP	$35–50
	Marilyn Monroe elama Otava-Kompassikirja 1 ed. 422p. Pb/1964/FIN	$35–50
Several Authors	*Marilyn Sings! The Marilyn Monroe Songbook* Wise Publications 1 ed. 47p. ISBN-0-7119-2712-X Sc/1991/UK	$25–40
	Marilyn Monroe: Cinema d'aujourd'hui-n.1 (nouvelle serie) Film Editions (Pierre Lherminier) 15F 1 ed. 116p. Sc/1975/FRA	$50–70
	Marilyn Monroe: Coleccion Septimo arte, 7 Sedmay Ediciones 250Pt 1 ed. 222p. ISBN-84-7380-122-09 Sc/1976/ESP	$50–70

Author	Title/Info	Value
	Marilyn Monroe: Films/portraits No. 2–Mars/Avril 1978 Editions Cinemania (Solange Devilles) 12F 1 ed. 45p. Sc/1978/FRA	$30–45
	Marilyn Revisitada: Cuadernos Anagrama No. 20 (Serie Cine) Editorial Anagrama (Joaquin Jorda) 1 ed. 95p. Pb/1971/ESP	$35–45
Japanese Books	*Marilyn Monroe # 1–1945–1958* G.I.P. Tokyo 238p. ISBN-4-10-219701-X Pb/1983/JAP	$60–85
	Marilyn Monroe # 1 238p. ISBN-4-8261-0001-9 Sc/1987/JAP	$60–80
	Marilyn Monroe # 3 158p. ISBN-4-8261-0505-3 Sc/1987/JAP	$60–80
	Joe DiMaggio and Marilyn Monroe Kazuo Sayama 261p. ISBN-4-309-010-27-X Hc/1995/JAP	$40–50
	[2] *Flix—Marilyn Monroe: Best Collection 1926–1962* Flix ISBN-89389-042-5 Sc/1991/JAP	$35–45

Books with References to Marilyn
(Many of these feature Marilyn on the front cover)

Author	Title/Info	Value
Patrick AGAN	*The Decline and Fall of the Love Goddesses* Pinnacle Books $20.00 1 ed. 286p. ISBN-0-523-40623-1 Hc/1979/ USA	$20–30
Holmero ALSINA THEVENET	*Cronicas de cine* Ed. de la Flor 1 ed. 330 p. Pb/1973/ARG	$5–10
ANONYMOUS	*The Pocket Playboy* Playboy Press $1.75 1 ed. 224p. Pb/1974/USA	$70–90

The Pocket Playboy, 1974

An assortment of Japanese softcover books entirely on Marilyn

Author

Title/Info

Value

Movie Trivia Quiz Book
Ventura Associates $3.95 Pb/1982/USA — $15–25

500 biografías de personajes célebres
Planeta 1 ed. 249p. ISBN-84-320-6540-4 Pb/1983/ESP — $5–10

Wedding Book
Libro Port 32p. ISBN-8457-0517-6 Pb/1990/JAP — $20–35

Author	Title/Info	Value
Zinn ARTHUR	*Shooting Superstars: Me, My Camera, and the Showbiz Legends* Artique Press $29.95 1 ed. 240p. ISBN-0-9623788-0-1 Hc/1990/USA	$30–40
Carl BAKAL	*How to Shoot for Glamour* Ziff-Davis 2 re. 128p. Hc/1961/USA	$50–75
David BARRACLOUGH	*Hollywood Heaven: The Apple Press* Quintet Publishers $8.95 1 ed. 95p. ISBN-1-85076-298-8 Hc/1991/UK	$10–15
Cecil BEATON	*Cecil Beaton* (Preface de Jean Sagne) Chene/Paris Audiovisuel 185F 1 ed. ISBN-2-264-01372-9 Pb/1989/FRA	$25–35
Robert BLOCH	*Le crepuscule des stars: 10/18 No. 2017, serie 'Nuits Blemes'* Christian Bougois 279p. ISBN-2-264-01372-9 Pb/1989/FRA	$5–10
Claude BONNEFOY	*Le cinema et ses mythes: La nouvell encyclodedie No. 14* Hachette 370F 1 ed. 126p. Pb/1965/FRA	$15–20
Douglas BRODE	*The Films of the Fifties* The Citadel Press 1 ed. 288p. ISBN-0-8065-0510-9 Hc/1976/USA	$20–30
Giovanni CALENDOLI	*Maschere* (Aug. 1962) Ribalta Maschere 300L. 1 ed. 158p. Sc/1962/ITA	$20–30
Jock CARROLL	*Down the Road* Pocket Books Book No. 671-78739-X $1.50 Pb/1974/CAN	$5–10
Colin CLEMENTS	*Bluff your way in Hollywood* Ravette London 1.00 1 ed. 63p. ISBN-0-948456-42-6 Pb/1987/UK	$5–10
Daniel & Susan COHEN	*Screen Goddesses* Hamlyn Bison 1 ed. 128p. ISBN-0-600-34738-9 Hc/1984/UK	$20–30
Gilles COLPART	*Billy Wilder: Filmo 4* Edilig 48F 1 ed. 126p. ISBN-2-85601-040-7 Sc/ /FRA	$15–25

Author	Title/Info	Value
Robin CROSS	*2000 Movies the 1950's* Arlington House 1 ed. 255p. ISBN-0-517-67973-6 Hc/1989/USA	$20–30
Anthony CURTIS	*The Rise and Fall of the Matinee Idol* New English Library 1.95 1 ed. 215p. ISBN-450-02662-0 Sc/1976/UK	$20–30
Lo DUCA	*L'erotisme au cinema* J. Pauvert 1 ed. 218p. Pb/1958/FRA	$30–40
_____	*L'erotisme au cinema: Tome No. 1* J. Paubert 223p. Pb/1962/FRA	$25–35
William A. EWING	*Flora Photographica* Vilo 1 ed. 224p. ISBN-2-7191-0287-3 Hc/1991/FRA	$20–30
Xavier FAUCHE & Christiane NOETZLIN	*Al bacio: Casto, perverso, rubato, mistico . . .* Sugarco Ed. L.22.000 1 ed. 269p. Sc/1987/ITA	$20–30
Joel W. FINLER	*El gran libro del cine* Editorial HMB 1 ed. 171p. ISBN-84-85123-74-3 Hc/1979/ESP	$20–30
Selwyn FORD	*The Casting Couch: Making it in Hollywood* Grafton Books 3.99 1 ed. 229p. ISBN-0-586-20386-9 Pb/1990/UK	$10–15
James GOODE	*The Story of* The Misfits Bobbs-Merrill $5.00 1 ed. 331p. Hc/1963/USA	$45–65
_____	*The Making of* The Misfits Limelight Ed. $9.95 1 ed. 331p. ISBN-0-87910-065-6 Sc/1986/USA	$15–25
Kirk GRIVELLO	*Fallen Angels* Futura 3.99 1 ed. 282p. ISBN-0-7088-4836-2 Pb/1990/UK	$5–10
_____	*Angels caiguts: La vida i la mort tragica de set grans estrelles* Ixia Fahrenheit 451,5 1 ed. 199p. ISBN-84-87530-07-9 Pb/1991/CAT	$5–10

Author	Title/Info	Value
Leslie HALLIWELL	*Halliwell's Film Guide: 7th Edition* Paladin 12.99 7 ed. 1171p. ISBN-0-586-08894-6 Sc/1989/UK	$20–30
Charles HAMBLETT	*Who Killed Marilyn Monroe* Leslie Frewin 1 ed. 175p. Hc/1966/UK	$40–60
————	*Wie Vermoordde Marilyn Monroe?* Flamingo 211p. Sc/1966/HOL	$40–60
————	*The Hollywood Cage* Hart 1 ed. 437p. Hc/1969/USA	$30–40
————	*The Hollywood Cage* Hart 1 ed. 437 p. Sc/1969/USA	$30–40
Joe HEMBUS	*Illustriecte Film: Buhne-50 Hollywood—filme* Monika Nuchtern 1 ed. Sc/1976/GER	$20–30
Danielle HEM-MERT & Alex ROUDENE	*Les Amazones: Hitler et Eva Braun—Marilyn Monroe* rombaldi—lis secrets des amours celebres 1 ed. 292p. Hc/1974/FRA	$20–30
Tom HUTCHINSON	*Deesses de L' Ecran* Edilig 1 ed. 195p. ISBN-2-85601-122-5 Hc/1985/FRA	$20–30
Rodolfo IZAGUIRRE	*Historia sentimental del cine norteamericano* Rodolfo Alonso 1 ed. 119p. Pb/1971/ARG	$5–10
Rene JEANNE & Charles FORD	*Historia ilustrada del cine 3—El libro de bolsillo 512* Alianza 4 re. 436p. ISBN-84-206-1512-9 Pb/1988/ESP	$5–10
Jean-Claude JITROIS	*Parfums de Stars—Edition 01* Filipacchi 230F 1 ed. Hc/1990/FRA	$20–30
John KOBAL	*Film: Star Portraits of The Fifties*—163 glamour photos Dover 1 ed. 163 p. ISBN-0-486-24008-8 Sc/1980/USA	$20–30

Author	Title/Info	Value
John KOBAL	*Hollywood Colour Portraits* (Intro by Carlos Clarens) Aurum 6.95 1 ed. 159p. ISBN-0-906053-83-8 Sc/1985/UK	$20–30
	Hollywood Couleur Henri Veyrier 150F 1 ed. 156p. ISBN-2-85199-295-3 Hc/1983/FRA	$20–30
Madison S. LACY & Don MORGAN	*Hollywood Cheesecake: Sixty Years of America's Favorite Pin-ups* Citadel Press $19.95 1 ed. 286p. ISBN-0-8065-0830-2 Sc/1991/USA	$20–30
Suzanne LLOYD HAYES	*3-D Hollywood Photographs* by Harold Lloyd Simon and Schuster 95p. ISBN-0-671-76948-0 Hc/1992/USA	$35–50
Joshua LOGAN	*Movie Stars, Real People, and Me* Delacorte Press 1 ed. 346p. Hc/1978/USA	$20–30
Elizabeth MACA-VOY & Susan ISRAELSON	*Lovesick: The Marilyn Syndrome* Donald I. Fine $18.95 1 ed. 248p. ISBN-1-55611-220-3 Hc/1991/USA	$20–30
Enrico MAGRELLI	*Hollywood—Party—Quaderni di Filmcritica, 8* Bulzoni 303p. Pb/1979/ITA	$15–20
Daily MAIL	*Films—Two Shillings and Sixpence—Quiz book number 6* Morrison & Gibb 1 ed. 160p. Pb/1957/UK	$20–25
Norman MAILER & Milton H. GREENE	*Of Women and Their Elegance* Simon & Schuster $29.95 1 ed. 288p. ISBN-0-671-24020-X Hc/1980/USA	$30–40
	Of Women and Their Elegance: Photographs by Milton H. Greene Tor $3.50 1 ed. 286p. ISBN-0-523-48015-6 Pb/1981/USA	$10–15
	Of Women and Their Elegance Hodder & Stoughton 1 ed. 288p. ISBN-0-340-23920-4 Hc/1980/UK	$30–40

Author	Title/Info	Value
Tom MALONEY	*U.S. Camera Annual 1964* (Marilyn photos by Bert Stern) U.S. Camera Book-Duell, Sloan & Pearce 1 ed. 231p. Hc/1963/USA	$30–50
Dirk MANTHEY	*Gottinnen des Erotischen Films—Ein Filmbuch von cinema* Redaktion cinema DM24.80 1 ed. 162p. ISBN-3-88724-012-X Sc/1985/GER	$20–30
Doug McCLELLAND	*Star Speak: Hollywood on Everything* Faber & Faber $14.95 1 ed. 337p. ISBN-0-571-12981-1 Sc/1987/USA	$20–30
Terence MOIX	*Hollywood Stories—Lumen/palabra seis No. 8* Lumen 1 ed. 302p. Pb/1971/ESP	$10–15
Edgar MORIN	*The Stars by Edgar Morin: An Account of the Star System* Profile Books/Grove Press $1.35 189p. Pb/1960/USA	$5–10
————	*Les Stars—Le temps qui court* Ed. du Seuil 1 ed. 192p. Pb/1957/FRA	$10–15
————	*Les Stars—Points No.34* Ed. du Seuil 188p. Pb/1972/FRA	$5–10
————	*Las Stars—Servidumbres y mitos: Marilyn, Charlot, James Dean . . .* Dopesa-col. Espectaculo 4/cine 1 ed. 166p. Pb/1972/ESP	$5–10
Michael MUNN	*The Hollywood Murder Casebook* Robson Books 1 ed. 192p. ISBN-0-86051-414-5 Hc/1987/UK	$20–30
————	*The Hollywood Murder Casebook* Headline 3.99 1 ed. 192p. ISBN-0-7472-3112-5 Pb/1989/UK	$5–10
Jean NEGULESCO	*Things I Did . . . and Things I Think I Did . . .* Linden Press/S. & S. $18.95 317p. ISBN-0-671-50734-6 Hc/1984/USA	$20–30

Author	Title/Info	Value
Thomas NOGUCHI	*Les dossiers secrets du medecin legiste de Hollywood Coroner* France Loisirs 211p. ISBN-2-7242-2034-X Hc/1985/FRA	$5–10
——	*Coroner* Pocket Books $3.50 252p. ISBN-0-671-54088-2 Pb/1983/USA	$5–10
Charles NUETZEL	*Whodunit? Hollywood Style* Book Co. of America $0.75 1 ed. 169p. Pb/1965/USA	$10–15
Tilman OSTERWOLD	*Pop Art* Benedikt Taschen 1 ed. 239p. ISBN-3-8228-0667-6 Sc/1992/ESP	$20–30
Toy PICKARD	*Hollywood's Fallen Idols* Batsford Ltd. 1 ed. 192p. ISBN-0-7134-6152-7 Sc/1989/UK	$20–30
R. POMARES & Several Authors	*Churchil/Marilyn Monroe/M. Hernandez: Los revolucionarios siglo* Club Inter. Libro (tomo 11) 319p. ISBN-84-7461-093-1 Hc/1978/ESP	$25–35
Dilys POWELL	*The Golden Screen: Fifty Years of Films* Pavilion 15.95 302p. ISBN-1-85145-342-3 Hc/1989/UK	$20–30
Tom PRIDEAUX	*Life Goes to the Movies* Time-Life Books 304p. ISBN-0-517-62585-7 Hc/1987/USA	$25–35
David ROBINSON	*Panorama du cinema mondial 2—De 1947 anos jours* Denoel/Gonthier 1 ed. 667p. Pb/1980/FRA	$5–10
Eve RUGGIERI	*Raconte . . . quelque femmes remmarquables* Menges (Radio France) 1 ed. 410p. ISBN-2-85620-093 Sc/1980/FRA	$15–25
——	*Raconte . . . quelque femmes remmarquables* France Loisirs 1 ed. 410p. ISBN-2-7242-0797-1 Hc/1980/FRA	$15–25
Enrique SALGADO	*El libro de la vida y la muerte* Nauta 1 ed. 218p. ISBN-84-278-0360-5 Sc/1974/FRA	$20–30
Ken SCHESSLER	*This Is Hollywood: An Unusual Movieland Guide* Ken Schessler $3.95 6 re. 85p. ISBN-0-915633-00-0 Sc/1987/USA	$10–20

Author	Title/Info	Value
Georg SEEBLEN	*Unterhaltung 2—Lexikon zur poplaren kultur—Ro ro ro 6210* Rowohlt 1 ed. 327p. ISBN-3-499-16210-5 Pb/1977/GER	$10–15
Claudius SEIDL	*Billy Wilder: Signo e imagen/cineastas No. 8* Catedra 1 ed. 287p. ISBN-84-376-1023-0 Pb/1991/ESP	$5–10
SESAR	*Hollywood, Hollywood—Glamour Star 3* Glamour International (suplement No. 7) 48p. Sc/1986/ITA	$20–30
Eric SHANES	*Warhol: The Masterworks* Portland House Hc/1991/USA	$20–30
Patricia Fox SHEINWOLD	*Too Young To Die: The Stars the World Tragically Lost* Cathay Books 1 ed. 353p. ISBN-0-86178-051-5 Sc/1979/UK	$20–30
Marianne SINCLAIR	*Those Who Died Young: Cult Heroes of the Twentieth Century* Plexus 8.95 1 ed. 192p. ISBN-0-85965-023-5 Sc/1979/UK	$20–30
Emmeline SNIVELY	*The Models Blue Book* Snively $1.00 128p. Sc/1947-8/USA	$400–600
Penny STALL-INGS & H. MANDELBAUM	*Flesh and Fantasy: The Truth Behind the Fantasy* Perrenial Library $15.95 285p. ISBN-0-06-096343-3 Sc/1989/USA	$20–30
Bert STERN	*Eros: The Last Studio Portraits of Marilyn Monroe* Eros (Ralph Ginzburg) 1 ed. 96p. Hc/1962/USA	$50–80
Ray STUART	*Immortals of the Screen: Over Six Hundred Memorable Photographs* Bonanza Books 1 ed. 224p. Hc/1965/USA	$30–40
Peter UNDERWOOD	*Death In Hollywood* Piatkus 13.95 279p. ISBN-0-7499-1087-9 Hc/1992/UK	$20–25
Edward WAGENKNECHT	*Seven Daughters of the Theater* Da Capo $7.95 1 ed. 234p. ISBN-0-306-80153-1 Sc/1976/USA	$20–25

Author	Title/Info	Value
Alexander WALKER	*Stardom: The Hollywood Phenomenon* Penguin Books .55 385p. ISBN-0-14-003750-0 Pb/1974/UK	$10–15
WEEGEE & Mel HARRIS	*Naked Hollywood* Da Capo Press $6.95 1 ed. ISBN-0-306-80047-0 Sc/1976/UK	$20–30
WEEGEE	*Violenti e violentati* Mazzotta L.18.000 1 ed. Sc/1979/ITA	$20–30
Billy WILDER	*Memories—Et Tout Le Reste Est Folie* Robert L. Sc/1993/FRA	$20–25
Ken WLASCHIN	*Les stars du cinema* Fernand Nathan 1 ed. 232p. ISBN-2-09-293104-0 Hc/1981/FRA	$20–30
Several Authors	*From Broadway to Picadilly: Encore!* (songbook) Wise Pub. 1 ed. 127p. ISBN-0-7119-1425-7 Sc/1988/UK	$20–30
	Memories of Hollywood (songbook) Wise Pub. 1 ed. 64p. ISBN-0-7119-2496-1 Sc/1991/UK	$20–30
	Historia del cine—Biblioteca tematica—tomo 1 Montaner y Simon 1 ed. 190p. ISBN-84-274-0461-1 Hc/1979/ESP	$20–30
	Gran historia ilustrada del cine—Tomo 1 Sarpe 159p. ISBN-84-7291-636-7 Hc/1984/ESP	$20–30

Marilyn Movie-Related Novels:

Author	Title/Info	Value
Matthew ANDREWS	*Let's Make Love*—A2112/2 Bantam Books $0.35 1 ed. 149p. Pb/1960/USA	$25–45
	Let's Make Love—SN914 Corgi Books/Transworld 2.60 188p. Pb/1960/UK	$35–50

Author	Title/Info	Value
George AXELROD	The Seven-Year Itch: A Romantic Comedy—1371/1 Bantam Books $0.25 1 ed. 114p. Pb/1955/USA	$35–50
	The Seven-Year Itch: A Romantic Comedy—1371/1 Bantam Books $0.25 2 re. 114p. Pb/1955/USA	$35–50
W. R. Burnett	La jungla del asfalto—Bibl. Universal Caralt—Serie novela No. 125 Luis de Caralt 450Pt. 2 ed. 242p. ISBN-84-217-4239-6 Pb/1985/ESP	$20–30
	La jungla del asfalto—Bestsellers Serie Negra No. 11 Planeta 1 ed. 201p. ISBN-84-320-8620-7 Pb/1985/ESP	$20–30
	As above, only the Greek version 1 ed. 300p. SC/1987/GRE	$20–30
William INGE	Bus Stop—1518/8 Bantam Books $0.25 1 ed. 113p. Pb/1956/USA	$35–50
	Bus Stop—The story of the 20th Century Fox film starring Marilyn. Charles Buchan's Pub 2.60 1 ed. 96p. Sc/1956/UK	$50–75
Anita LOOS	Les hommes preferent les blondes—Le cinema romanesque—No. 15 Llibrairie Gallimard 3.50F 1 ed. 96p. Sc/1950's/FRA	$50–75
	Les hommes preferent les blondes—No. 54 Llibrairie Gallimard 180p. Pb/1954/FRA	$50–75
	Les hommes preferent les blondes—No. 54 Llibrairie Gallimard 180p. Pb/1956/FRA	$50–75
	Les hommes preferent les blondes—No. 54 Llibrairie Gallimard 180p. Pb/1965/FRA	$50–75
	Les hommes preferent les blondes—Romans—Texte integral N.508 J'ai lu 1 ed. 183p. Pb/1973/FRA	$40–60
	Los caballeros las prefieren rubias—Col. Popular Literaria No. 13 Col Popular Literaria 10Pt. 1 ed. 142p. Sc/1955/ESP	$50–75

Author	Title/Info	Value
	Los caballeros las prefieren rubias—Col. Weekend Noguer 1 ed. 181p. ISBN-84-279-0756-7 Sc/1975/ESP	$30–50
	Los caballeros las prefieren rubias—Cuadernos infimos No. 129 Tusquets 800Pt. 1 ed. 121p. ISBN-84-7223-629-3 Pb/1986/ESP	$20–30
Arthur MILLER	*The Misfits: The New Work by Arthur Miller* The Viking Press 1 ed. 132p. Hc/1961/USA	$50–70
	The Misfits—A Dell Book F115 The Viking Press (book club) 1 ed. 132p. Hc/1961/USA	$50–70
	The Misfits—A Dell Book F115 Dell $0.50 1 ed. 223p. Pb/1961/USA	$30–40
	The Misfits—Penguin Books 1666 Penguin Books $2.60 1 ed. 140p. Pb/1961/UK	$30–40
	De ontvorteiden—Meulenhoff Pockets 86 J. M. Meulenhoff 190p. Pb/1961/HOL	$30–45
Arthur MILLER & other authors	*Film Scripts Three: Charade/The Apartment/The Misfits* Irvingthon $19.95 610p. ISBN-0-8290-2277-5 Sc/1989/USA	$20–30
Terence RATTIGAN	*The Prince and the Showgirl: Marilyn Monroe and Laurence Olivier* Signet Books No. S1409 $0.35 1 ed. 127p. Pb/1957/USA	$30–50
	Plus beau qu'un Reve—Les films pour vous—Hebdomadaire No. 184 Cine-Periodiques (Franco Bozzesi) 0.90F 1 ed. 66p. Magazine/1960/FRA	$30–50
	The Prince and the Showgirl Kenkyusha Pb/ /JAP	$150–200
Billy WILDER	*Some Like It Hot—No. S1656* Signet Book 1 ed. 144p. Pb/1959/USA	$30–50

1960 one-sheet for *Let's Make Love*

Marilyn Bust by Clay Art, 1988

Two cookie jars and "Frame Up" frame

1950s book of paper dolls
by Saalfield

First U.S. book on Marilyn
by Franklin and Palmer, 1953

Censored calendar from the 1950s

1950s–60s head vase by Relpo,
made in Japan

$1,500⁰⁰ — 2000.⁰⁰

Sheet of nine stamps from
Tanzania, 1992

1953 window card for *Niagara*

1956 calendar
(Photo by Laszlo Willinger)

Assorted dolls by Franklin Mint, 1990s

Assorted "world" dolls, 1983

Assorted plates from "The Marilyn Monroe Collection"
by Bradford Exchange, 1990–92

An ad for Lustre-Creme
shampoo, 1953

Porcelain night light
by Vandor, 1984

Porcelain figurines by Royal Orleans, 1982

Plaques by R. J. Ernst, 1992

Earl Moran ink blotter, 1940s

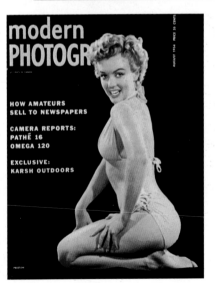

Modern Photography Magazine,
August 1954

Salute Magazine, August 1946

Paris Frou-Frou Magazine, 1950s

Assorted "Marilyn Merlot" wine
from California

Two of three "Lustre-Chrome"
postcards of Marilyn, 1950s

McCormick decanters in large and small, 1984

Two mugs by Clay Art, 1980s

15 - 20.00

An assortment
of movie tie-in
paperbacks,
1955–1961

Novels with References to Marilyn

Author	Title/Info
Jacques ALMIRA	*Le passage du desir—Roman* Gallimard 1 ed. 232p. Sc/1978/FRA

Author	Title/Info	Value
ANONYMOUS	Betty & Gay (contiene los numeros 1 al 7 de esta coleccion) Zinco 325Pt. 1 ed. 34p. Sc/1990/ESP	$20–30
Alvah BESSIE	The Symbol Random House $5.95 1 ed. 305p. Hc/1966/USA	$25–35
——	El simbolo—Edic. de bolsillo Paperback Grijalbo No. 97 Grijalbo 1 ed. 390p. ISBN-84-253-0774-0 Pb/1977/ESP	$20–30
George BERNAU	Candle in the Wind Michael Joseph 8.99 1 ed. 499p. ISBN-0-7181-3543-1 Sc/1991/UK	$20–30
Leonore CANEV-ARI, Jeaneette Van WHYE, Christian & Rachel DIMAS	The Murder of Marilyn Monroe Carrol and Graf 1 ed. Pb/1992/USA	$5–10
James ELLISON	Calendar Girl Pocket Books Pb/1993/USA	$5–10
Jean-Albert FOEX	Satan conduit la belle—Col. Le Mauvais E.D.I.C.A. 1 ed. 159p. Pb/1953/FRA	$30–40
William GOLDMAN	Oropel Plaza & Janes 1 ed. 312p. ISBN-84-01-30320-6 Sc/1981/ESP	$20–30
Ben HECHT	The Sensualists Messner 3 re. 256p. Hc/1959/USA	$20–35
Garson KANIN	Holywood Annees Folles Presses de la Cite 1 ed. 249p. Hc/1975/FRA	$20–30
——	Moviola: Marilyn, Chaplin, Garbo . . . Col. Naranja No. 1501/52 Bruguera 1 ed. 510p. ISBN-84-02-08287-4 Pb/1981/ESP	$10–15

Author	Title/Info	Value
Keith LUGER	*A que hora te mataron Marilyn Monroe?—Servicio Secreto N. 1102* Bruguera 10Pt. 1 ed. 126p. Pb/1971/ESP	$15–20
MARLIT	*La Princesa de los Brezos—Coleccion para mi hija No. 14* Orvy 1 ed. 149p. Pb/ /ESP	$10–20
Arthur MILLER	*After the Fall: A play by Arthur Miller* The Viking Press (limited Edit. 500 Deluxe) 129p. Hc/1964/USA	$20–35
________	*After the Fall: The Most Controversial Play of Our Generation!* Bantam $0.85 1 ed. 164p. Pb/1965/USA	$15–20
________	*Despues de la Caida—Col. Voz Imagen—Serie Teatro No. 8* Ayma 1 ed. 185p. Pb/1965/ESP	$20–30
________	*Despues de la Caida—Teatro en el Teatro* Losada 1 ed. 128p. Pb/1965/ARG	$20–30
________	*Despues de la Caida/Incidente en Vichy—Teatro 2. Gran teatro del . . . Teatro* Losada 144p. Pb/1967/ARG	$20–30
Terenci MOIX	*El dia que va morir Marilyn—El balanci No. 60* Edicions 62 Barcelona 5 re. 336p. ISBN-84-297-0856-1 Pb/1970/CAT	$10–15
________	*El dia que murio Marilyn—Palabra en el tiempo No. 68* Lumen 1 ed. 490p. Pb/1970/ESP	$10–15
________	*El dia que murio Marilyn—Ediciones de bolsillo No. 541* Lumen 490p. ISBN-84-264-4001-0 Pb/1978/ESP	$10–15
________	*El dia en que murio Marilyn—Los JET de Plaza & Janes Vol. 155/2* Plaza & Janes 795Pt. 1 ed. 414p. ISBN-84-01-49502-4 Pb/1990/ESP	$5–10
________	*Le jour ou est morte Marilyn* Le Chemin Vert 127F. 1 ed. 390p. ISBN-2-903-533-26-1 Sc/1987/FRA	$20–30

Author	Title/Info	Value
Neil NORMAN & Son BARRACLOUGH	*Insignificance: The Book* Sidgwick & Jackson 7.95 1 ed. 128p. ISBN-0-283-99218-2 Sc/1985/ UK	$20-30
John RECHY	*Marilyn's Daughter* Carroll & Graf $18.95 1 ed. 531p. ISBN-0-88184-272-9 Hc/1988/ USA	$20-30
Michel SCHETTER	*Le Boulevard de Marilyn—Histoire singuliere No. 4* (comic book) Bedescope 15F. 1 ed. 48p. Hc/1984/BEL	$20-30
Steven SPIRE & Bill O'NEILL	*Marilyn Monroe: Personality Classics No. 2* (comic book) Personality Comics $2.95 1 ed. 24p. Sc/1991/USA	$20-30
Sam STAGGS	*MM II: The Return of Marilyn Monroe* Donal I. Fine $19.95 1 ed. 304p. ISBN-1-55611-179-7 Hc/1991/USA	$20-30
	The Return of Marilyn Monroe S.P.I. $5.50 304p. ISBN-1-56171-181-0 Pb/1992/USA	$10-15
Sam TOPEROFF	*Queen of Desire* Harper-Collins Hc/1992/USA	$10-15
Sergio TOPPI	*Marilyn Monroe—No. 23* (Limited edition comic book) Bedesup 36F. 1 ed. 47p. Sc/1982/BEL	$20-30

Marilyn Postcard Books

Author	Title/Info	Value
American Postcard Co.	*Marilyn Monroe: Nine Detachable Postcards* #11 Printed in Italy	$10-20
Godfrey Cave Associates	*Marilyn Monroe: Twenty Classic Picture Postcards* 1993/USA	$10-20

An assortment
of postcard
books

Author	Title/Info	Value
Magna	*Marilyn Monroe: A Book of Thirty Postcards* ISBN-1-85422-319-4 Sc/1992/UK	$15–25
John MARRIOT	*Marilyn: A Postcard Book* (30) Running Press $7.95 ISBN-0-89471-898-3	$15–20

Author	Title/Info	Value
Pomegranate Artbooks	*Marilyn Monroe: A Book of Postcards* (30 hand colored) 1990/USA	$15–25
Running Press	*Marilyn Monroe: A Postard Book* 30 Cards $6.95 ISBN-0-89471-766-9 1989/USA	$15–25
Running Press	*Warhol*—30 Cards with MM on the cover. 1989/USA	$15–25
Schirmer Art	*Schirmer's Twelve* (No. 2 Film Stills) 1990/ENG	$15–20

The Classic Poster Book, 1990, U.S.

Poster Books

Author	Title/Info	Value
Alice HILLIER	*Marilyn Monroe II: 20 Tear-out Posters* Atlanta Press 1 ed. ISBN-1-870049-20-9 Sc/1989/UK	$25–40
David MALCOLM	*Sex Symbols: Movie Poster Book* Octopus Books 1 ed. 47p. ISBN-0-7064-2371-2 Sc/1985/UK	$25–40
————	*Les Sex Symbols—Un livre a effeuiller* Grum 1 ed. 46p. ISBN-2-7000-6702-9 Sc/1985/FRA	$25–40
Mallard Press	*Marilyn Monroe: The Classic Poster Book* Sc/1990/USA	$20–40
Diego A. MANRIQUE	*Marilyn Monroe Grafic Poster Book* Gaviota/Productions Compac. 1200 Pt. ISBN-84-7693-039-9 Sc/1987/ESP	$25–40
Paul MATHUR	*Marilyn Monroe Poster Book* Alanta Press 1 ed. ISBN-1-8700049-00-4 Sc/1986/UK	$25–40
————	*Marilyn Monroe Poster Book* 20 tear-out posters. Sc/1988/UK	$25–40

MARILYN MONROE
AUTOGRAPH VALUES

Autographs of famous people have been highly collectible for a long time. Certain signed documents can fetch many thousands of dollars. From presidents to dictators to glamorous movie stars and persecuted Native American chiefs, we find a myriad of potentially collectible autographs.

Of all the movie stars that have come and gone since the beginning of motion pictures, Marilyn Monroe commands the highest prices of any in the area of autographs. Marilyn was known to sign many autographs early on in her career. After becoming famous in 1952, due to her "exposure" as a nude model that graced the tops of calendars, Marilyn had less time to sign autographs. The job then fell to her studios' secretaries. However, several photos exist of Marilyn, after her sudden rise to stardom, signing autographs during public appearances. She gave particular attention to young children. During her tour of Korea to entertain the troops, she was known to sign photos, posters, and even casts for the G.I.s.

There are certain things to look for when attempting to authenticate a Monroe autograph. Some tips are listed below to aid you in doing so.

1. Marilyn's signatures have a look of rapidity to them. She always signed with a definite slant to the right and overemphasized the capital letters in her name and those of the inscriptions.

2. "Monroe" is always the more legible half of her name.

3. Marilyn tended to bring the dot in her first name back over the top of the "a."

4. In nearly every example of her signature, her first name is broken into two parts: "Mar" and "ilyn." The "ily" in "ilyn" is written quickly and is not formed well, appearing like a figure eight or a scriptlike "S."

5. The "M-a" in Marilyn and the "M-o" in Monroe are always connected, and there is a sharp angle where "M" meets the following letter.

6. In Marilyn's inscribed signatures (and most of them were), there is a great uniformity in the word "To" in every example.

7. Marilyn nearly always signed her first and last name on the same line.

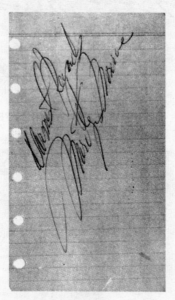

An authentic Monroe autograph on an album page

SECRETARIAL AND FORGERY SIGNATURES

A great many signatures were done by secretaries to appease the droves of Marilyn's fans who wrote to acquire one of her signed photos. These signatures are always slower and more legible than Marilyn's own. The other "footprints" of an authentic Marilyn autograph are always missing, namely the unique formation of the "ily," the lack of a dot over the "a" in "Marilyn," and the more rounded "M's," lacking the sharp lines and definite right slant.

An authentic Monroe autograph

A secretarial signature on an 8 × 10" glossy photo

Authentic Marilyn Autographs

	Value
Marilyn Monroe signed black & white 5 × 7" photo	$1,500–3,000
Marilyn Monroe signed color 5 × 7" photo	$1,500–3,000
Marilyn Monroe signed black & white 8 × 10" photo	$3,000–4,000
Marilyn Monroe signed color 8 × 10" photo	$3,500–4,500
Marilyn Monroe signed black & white 11 × 14" photo	5,000–10,000
Marilyn Monroe signed color 11 × 14" photo	$5,000–10,000
Marilyn Monroe signed and cancelled check	$1,500–2,500
Marilyn Monroe signed studio contract	$4,000–9,000
Marilyn Monroe signed album page (about 4 × 5")	1,500–2,000
Marilyn Monroe signed typed legal document	3,000–4,000
Marilyn Monroe signed typed letter	$2,000–3,000
Marilyn Monroe signed 1940s personal letter	$8,000–12,000
Marilyn Monroe signed record album	$3,000–4,000
Marilyn Monroe signed movie poster	$4,000–5,000

Secretarial Signatures

Marilyn Monroe secretarial signatures are worth one hundred to three hundred dollars per signed photo. The original photos themselves are appealing to collectors because of their sharpness, due to being first-generation prints.

COLLECTIBLE MARILYN MONROE DOLLS

Amazingly, there were only paper dolls produced of Marilyn during her lifetime, and no porcelain or similar dolls such as those made for Shirley Temple, etc. It was not until 1982 that the first dolls were produced of Marilyn Monroe, twenty-one years after her death! A testimony indeed to the eternal love the world has for a fallen angel named Marilyn Monroe.

The first dolls were made by TRISTAR, and it was quite an extensive series, elaborately packaged in cardboard boxes with see-through cellophane. They did not, however, catch a real good likeness of Marilyn, though they did duplicate many of the dresses she wore in her films to some satisfaction. The next series came the following year, 1983, and was done by World Dolls. This series consisted of five dolls, three in porcelain and two in vinyl. They were a vast improvement over the TRISTAR dolls, but still did not capture the greatest likeness of Marilyn. They were infinitely more expensive than the TRISTAR dolls and even included one that was adorned with real fur and jewels! They set the stage for the next series of Marilyn dolls, which was produced by The Franklin Mint, beginning in 1990 and continuing still today. This series is by far the most exquisite of all, capturing an extremely good likeness of Marilyn and adorning her with replicas of elaborate gowns actually worn in her various movies, with the exception of one doll called *Sweater Girl*. For the first time, these dolls were offered in "posed" positions instead of the traditional "stiff" dolls. They are generally priced in the two hundred dollar range, but one five hundred dollar doll was produced in 1997 and featured leather shoes and a sequined gown from *There's No Business Like Show Business*. It is twice the size of the rest in the series. In 1997 a set of three *Barbie* Marilyns were produced by Mattel that were fitted in costumes from Marilyn's films and were very well done, though a bit out of the ordinary.

The only dolls that were produced during Marilyn's lifetime were the four different paper doll books done by Saalfield, beginning in 1952. These four books were in full color and basically replicated each other, just changing color arrangements and composition of the dolls on the front cover. These are now highly prized by Marilyn collectors, with the uncut and intact books being preferred.

Porcelain and Vinyl Doll Values

	Value
1982-TRISTAR/20th Century Fox Film Corp.-*There's No Business Like Show Business*; 16" tall; vinyl; dressed in a gold lamé gown. First series	$125–160
1982-TRISTAR/20th Century Fox Film Corp.-*How to Marry a Millionaire*; 16" tall; vinyl; dressed in a red gown. First series	$125–160
1982-TRISTAR/20th Century Fox Film Corp.-*The Seven-Year Itch*; 16" tall; vinyl; dressed in the famous blowing white dress. First series	$125–160
1982-TRISTAR/20th Century Fox Film Corp.-*Gentlemen Prefer Blondes*; 16" tall; vinyl; dressed in a pink gown from the movie. First series	$125–160

The four 16" Tri-Star Dolls, 1982

An assortment of 11½" Tri-Star Dolls, 1982–83

Value

1982-TRISTAR/20th Century Fox Film Corp.-*How to Marry a Millionaire*; 11½" tall; vinyl; dressed in a red gown. First series — $50–100

-TRISTAR/20th Century Fox Film Corp.-*There's No Business Like Show Business*; 11½" tall; vinyl; dressed in gold gown that was actually designed for *Gentlemen Prefer Blondes*. First series — $50–100

1982-TRISTAR/20th Century Fox Film Corp.-*The Seven-Year Itch*; 11½" tall; vinyl; dressed in the famous white blowing dress from the movie. First series — $75–100

1982-TRISTAR/20th Century Fox Film Corp.-*Gentlemen Prefer Blondes*; 11½" tall; vinyl; dressed in a pink gown from the movie. First series — $75–100

1983–TRISTAR/20th Century Fox Film Corp.-*River of No Return*; 11½" tall; vinyl; dressed in a red and blue gown and holding a guitar. This dress not worn in the movie. Second series — $75–100

1983-TRISTAR/20th Century Fox Film Corp.-*Let's Make It Legal*; 11½" tall; vinyl; dressed in a green gown not actually worn in the movie. Second series — $75–100

Value

1983-TRISTAR/20th Century Fox Film Corp.-*Niagara;*
11½" tall; vinyl; dressed in a red gown with a pink
shawl and carrying a record. Second series $75–100

1983-TRISTAR/20th Century Fox Film Corp.-*Gentlemen Prefer Blondes;* 11½" tall; vinyl; dressed in a
beige and black bodysuit with black stockings and
wearing a black top hat. Second series $75–100

1983-WORLD DOLL-An original portrait doll; one-
year edition only; 18½" tall; vinyl; dressed in the
famous blowing white dress from *The Seven-Year
Itch;* came with a Certificate of Authenticity. Part
of the World Doll Celebrity Series. Original price
was $150.00 $250–400

1983-WORLD DOLL-An original portrait doll; one-
year edition only; 18½" tall; vinyl; dressed in a red
formal gown with a white feather boa; came with a
Certificate of Authenticity; part of the World Doll
Celebrity Series. Original price was $75.00 $125–200

1983-WORLD DOLL-An original portrait doll; one-
year edition only; 16½" tall; porcelain; dressed in
a white-sequined gown; came with a Certificate of

An assortment of 1983 World Dolls

Value

Authenticity; part of the World Doll Celebrity Series. Original price was $300.00 — $300–400

1983-WORLD DOLL-An original portrait doll; one-year edition only; 16½" tall; porcelain; dressed in a black-sequined gown; came with a Certificate of Authenticity; part of the World Doll Celebrity Series. Original price was $400.00 — $300–500

1983-WORLD DOLL-An original portrait doll; porcelain; limited and numbered edition; dressed in a gold metallic mesh gown and wearing a real white mink fur; fitted with glass eyes and one-fourth karat diamond earrings; part of the World Doll Celebrity Series; came with a Certificate of Authenticity. Original price was a whopping $3,000.00! — $1,200–1,800

1990-FRANKLIN MINT-*Gentlemen Prefer Blondes;* 19"; porcelain; dressed in a pink gown; came with a Certificate of Authenticity. Original price was $200.00 — $200–225

1991-FRANKLIN MINT-*The Seven-Year Itch;* porcelain; 19"; dressed in the famous blowing white dress; came with a Certificate of Authenticity. Original price was $200.00 — $200–225

1992-FRANKLIN MINT-*Gentlemen Prefer Blondes;* 19"; porcelain; dressed in a red-sequined gown;

An assortment of 1990s Franklin Mint Dolls

	Value
came with a Certificate of Authenticity. Original price was $200.00	$200–225

1993-FRANKLIN MINT-*Sweater Girl;* porcelain; 19"; dressed in a gray skirt and a pink sweater; came with a Certificate of Authenticity. Original price was $200.00 $200–225

1994-FRANKLIN MINT-*Golden Marilyn;* porcelain; 19"; dressed in a gold lamé gown; came with a Certificate of Authenticity. Original price was $200.00 $200–225

1996-FRANKLIN MINT-*Some Like It Hot;* porcelain; 19"; dressed in a black dress; came with a Certificate of Authenticity. Original price was $200.00 $200–225

1996-FRANKLIN MINT-*River of No Return;* porcelain; 19"; dressed in a red and gold gown; came with a Certificate of Authenticity. Original price was $200.00 $200–225

1996-FRANKLIN MINT-*The Ultimate Marilyn;* 24"; porcelain; dressed in a beige bejeweled gown from Marilyn's role as Vicky in *There's No Business Like Show Business;* came with a Certificate of Authenticity; limited edition of 9,500. Original price was $500.00 $500–525

1997-FRANKLIN MINT-*All About Eve;* 19½"; porcelain; dressed in a white gown with a fur coat from Marilyn's 1950 movie; came with a Certificate of Authenticity. Original price was $200.00 $200–225

1997-FRANKLIN MINT-*There's No Business Like Show Business;* 19"; porcelain; dressed in a blue gown from the movie; came with a Certificate of Authenticity. Original price was $200.00 $200–225

1998-FRANKLIN MINT-*Vinyl Portrait Dress-Up Doll;* 15⅛"; dressed in the pink dress from *Gentlemen Prefer Blondes;* wardrobe trunk and additional outfits were available. Original price was $110.00 $110–120

1993-DSI-*Fur Fantasy Marilyn;* 11½" tall; vinyl; dressed in a gold gown with a black fur; individually numbered; limited edition with a Certificate of Authenticity; 50,000 made. Original price was $34.99 $50–65

1993-DSI-*Silver Sizzle Marilyn;* 11½" tall; vinyl; dressed in a silver gown; individually numbered;

The Ultimate Marilyn. The Franklin Mint Doll, 1996

	Value
limited edition with a Certificate of Authenticity; 50,000 made. Original price was $34.99	$50–65
1993-DSI-*Sparkle Superstar Marilyn;* 11½" tall; vinyl; dressed in a red and black gown; individually numbered; limited edition with a Certificate of Authenticity; 50,000 made. Original price was $34.99	$50–65
1993-DSI-*Emerald Evening Marilyn;* 11½" tall; vinyl; dressed in a green gown; individually numbered; limited edition with a Certificate of Authenticity; 50,000 made. Original price was $34.99	$50–65
1993-DSI-*Spectacular Marilyn;* 11½" tall; vinyl; dressed in a blue gown with a blue boa; individually numbered; limited edition with a Certificate of Authenticity; 50,000 made. Original price was $34.99	$50–65
1993-DSI-*Spotlight Splendor Marilyn;* 11½" tall; vinyl; dressed in a black gown with a white fur; individually numbered; limited edition with Certificate of Authenticity; 50,000 made. Original price was $34.99	$50–65
1993-DSI-*Silver Dazzle Marilyn;* 11½" tall; vinyl; dressed in a silver gown; individually numbered; limited edition with a Certificate of Authenticity;	

An assortment of DSI Dolls, 1993

	Value
limited to an edition of only 15,000 and available at such places as QVC	$80–100
1997-MATTEL-*The Seven-Year Itch;* 11½"; vinyl; Barbie as Marilyn in the famous white blowing dress from the movie; Hollywood Legends Collection	$50–70
1997-MATTEL-*Gentlemen Prefer Blondes;* 11½"; vinyl; Barbie as Marilyn in a red-sequined gown from the movie; Hollywood Legends Collection	$50–70
1997-MATTEL-*Gentlemen Prefer Blondes;* 11½"; vinyl; Barbie as Marilyn in a pink gown from the movie; Hollywood Legends Collection	$50–70
1982-CMSR IMPORTS-Marilyn Monroe Musical Doll; 8" tall; porcelain from the waist up; costumed in the famous white blowing dress from *The Seven-Year-Itch;* has a diamond ring on the right hand and rotates on a plastic base; plays "Diamonds Are a Girl's Best Friend"	$85–95

Paper Doll Values

	Value

American Beauties-(Saalfield #1338)-Stiff cover with two Marilyn dolls on the front and a punch-out dressing table on the back. This set was issued

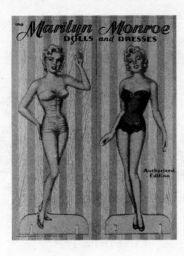

**No. 4308 book
of paper dolls by
Saalfield, 1953**

<u>Value</u>

after the company's contract was up and they were
unable to use Marilyn's name on them, though
they are identical to the identified Marilyn paper
doll books that follow. This set was most likely is-
sued in the late 1950s. $150–200

Marilyn Monroe Paper Dolls-(Saalfield #4323-1954)-
This book features two standing Marilyn dolls made
of heavy cardboard on the cover, which has a blue-
and-white-striped background. A complete wardrobe
is inside. These dolls are known as "statuette" dolls
and are scarce because there were few made. $300–400

Marilyn Monroe Paper Dolls-(Saalfield #4308–25;
1953)-An original edition of MM paper dolls. Features two hard cardboard "statuette" dolls affixed
to the front cover. The book jacket doors swing
open to reveal the pages of clothes inside. A dress-
ing table is featured on the back cover. $300–400

Marilyn Monroe Paper Dolls-(Saalfield #158610; 1953)-
This book features two dolls on the front cover.
"Authorized Edition" is printed in the lower right
corner of the cover. $300–400

Marilyn Monroe Paper Dolls by Tom Tierney-
(1979)-All-color book includes cut-out doll and
thirty-two costumes from twenty-four of Marilyn's
films. By Dover Publications. $20–25

**Paper dolls by
Tierney, 1979**

Value

Talking paper doll of Marilyn by Adult Toys-(circa
1970's)-Shows Marilyn in the famous white blowing dress from *The Seven-Year Itch* and says, "I
Love You"; image is in b/w. $15–25

MARILYN FIGURAL COLLECTIBLES

	Value
Marilyn Monroe Bear by Enesco; 1990; ceramic; part of the "Lucy & Me" collection by Lucy Rigg. Made in Sri Lanka. The bear is wearing the famous white blowing dress from *The Seven-Year Itch*.	$15–20
Marilyn Monroe Bisque Porcelain Night Light by Vandor; 1984; 9" tall; featuring Marilyn in the famous blowing white dress from *The Seven-Year Itch*. Made in Japan and unauthorized.	$125–175
Marilyn Monroe Bobbing Head Doll; 1996; 9" tall; porcelain; limited edition of 5,000; came with a Certificate of Authenticity and was individually numbered; packed in a generic box; shows MM in the gold lamé dress.	$45–55
Marilyn Monroe Bust; year and maker unknown; approximately 20" tall, made of paper mache or similar "mannequin" material; hollow on inside; used in stores to display jewelry and scarfs, etc.	$100–200
Marilyn Caricature Statue by Continental Studios of Burbank, CA; 1970s; plaster; features Marilyn in the famous white blowing dress; has a bumble bee stamped in the bottom of the statue.	$100–150
Marilyn Monroe Caricature Statue by Enesco; 1980s–90s; 16½" tall, plaster; features Marilyn in a black gown; distributed by Tobacco Stores; shows Marilyn's head to be much bigger in proportion to her body as is typical with the caricature statues.	$50–70

**Caricature
statue by Enesco**

Value

Marilyn Monroe Coin Operated Bank; circa 1982;
12" tall; featuring a vinyl Marilyn doll on top of a
plastic base in the famous blowing white dress
pose from *The Seven-Year Itch*. Simply insert a
coin into the slot and a small fan blows Marilyn's
dress up; came in white dress with black base or
red dress with white base. Made by Funtime Sav-
ings of China. $40–80

Marilyn Monroe Cookie Jar by Enesco; 1997; ceramic; features a bust of Marilyn in a halter dress;
available in pink, white, or teal; Limited Edition.
Very nicely done. Original price was $300.00. $300–320

**Funtime Savings
Bank, 1982**

Value

Marilyn Monroe Glass Dome Music Box; 1995; The
Franklin Mint; 5½" tall; plays "Diamonds Are a
Girl's Best Friend"; Limited Edition. $60–80

Marilyn Monroe Glass Dome Music Box; 1998; The
Franklin Mint; 5½" tall; plays "Two Girls From
Little Rock"; Limited Edition; shows Marilyn in a
red sequined dress. $60–70

Marilyn Monroe Head Vase by Relpo; 1950s–early
1960s; 6¾" tall; ceramic; featuring Marilyn in a
black halter dress with large pearl earrings and a silver bow in the back left bottom corner of her hair,
barely visible from the front. Distributed in floral
shops with flower bouquets in them. Very scarce. $1,500–2,000

Marilyn Monroe Head Vase by Malena; 1988; 8½"; plas-
ter; not a good likeness of Marilyn; done in pastel hues. $30–40

Marilyn Monroe Head Vase; 1980s; 4" tall; ceramic;
maker unknown; featuring Marilyn holding a micro-
phone and wearing a white dress. Not a great likeness. $40–60

Marilyn Monroe McCormick Decanter by the
McCormick Distilling Co.; 1983; 15" tall; featuring Marilyn in the famous blowing white dress

Value

from *The Seven-Year Itch*; Copyright 20th Century
Fox Film Corp.; packed in a decorative box. $250–400

Marilyn Monroe McCormick Decanter by the
McCormick Distilling Co.; 1983; 7"; featuring Mar-
ilyn in the famous blowing white dress from *The
Seven-Year Itch*, as above; Copyright 20th Century
Fox Film Corp.; packed in a decorative box. $100–200

Marilyn Monroe Metal Figurine; 1979; 2¼" tall; featuring Marilyn in the famous blowing white dress from
The Seven-Year Itch; sculpted in the old toy soldier
style; made in England; limited to an edition of 200
and made special for Gerry Alingh in Iowa. $40–60

Marilyn Monroe Plastic Figure; 1991; 3½" tall; made
in China; features Marilyn in a gold lamé gown
with her hands resting at her sides. $10–15

Marilyn Monroe Porcelain Sculpture by The Franklin
Mint; 1997; 10" tall; featuring Marilyn in the famous
blowing white dress from *The Seven-Year Itch*; limited

Decanters in two sizes by McCormick, 1983

Value

to forty-five firing days and accented with twenty-four-karat gold and platinum. Original price was $200.00. $200–210

Marilyn Monroe Street Light Lamp from the Crosa Collection; 1996; porcelain; about 28" tall; showing Marilyn standing by a street light in the famous blowing dress. $75–120

Marilyn Monroe Clay Figure sitting on a piano; early 1980s; 7½" tall. $80–95

Royal Orleans Items

Value

Marilyn Monroe Figurine by Royal Orleans; 1982; 9"; featuring Marilyn in the famous white blowing dress from *The Seven-Year Itch;* Limited and Numbered Edition of 20,000; produced with a matching plate. $250–350

Marilyn Monroe Figurine by Royal Orleans; 1982; 9"; featuring Marilyn in a pink dress from *Gentlemen Prefer Blondes;* Limited Numbered Edition of 20,000; produced with a matching plate. $250–350

Marilyn Monroe Figurine by Royal Orleans; 1982; 9"; featuring Marilyn in a red dress from *Niagara;*

Set of Royal Orleans Figurines, 1982

	Value
Limited Numbered Edition of 20,000; produced with a matching plate.	$250–350

Marilyn Monroe Figurine by Royal Orleans; 1982; 9"; featuring Marilyn in a red one-piece bathing suit from *How to Marry a Millionaire*; Limited numbered edition of 20,000; produced with a matching plate. $250–350

Marilyn Monroe Figurine by Royal Orleans; 1982; 4" tall; featuring Marilyn in a pink dress from *Gentlemen Prefer Blondes*; Limited Edition; matches its counterpart in the above set. $50–75

Marilyn Monroe Figurine by Royal Orleans; 1982; 4" tall; featuring Marilyn in the famous white blowing dress from *The Seven-Year Itch*; Limited Edition; matches its counterpart in the above set. $50–75

Note: The two 4" figurines immediately above also came with a small eyelet affixed to the top of Marilyn's head so that they could be used as ornaments. These are valued the same.

Clay Art Items

	Value
Marilyn Monroe Ceramic Mask by Clay Art; 1988	$40–60
Marilyn Monroe Ceramic Mask by Clay Art with a star-shaped background; 1988	$50–70

Clay Art powder dish, 1988

Value

Marilyn Monroe Ceramic Bust by Clay Art; 1988; featuring Marilyn in a white halter dress; done in pastel hues and glazed; came in a decorative box. $50–70

Marilyn Monroe Ceramic Circular Powderbox; 1988; done in black and white with a color Marilyn on the handle; came in a decorative box. $25–35

Marilyn Monroe Ceramic Cookie Jar by Clay Art; 1997; original price of $45.00. $45–50

Marilyn Monroe Ceramic 3-D Pin by Clay Art; 1988; came with rhinestones affixed to it and was mounted on a piece of cardboard. $8–12

Marilyn Monroe Covered Heart Box by Clay Art; 1988; featuring Marilyn's face on top; came in decorative packaging. $25–35

Marilyn Monroe Figural Picture Frame by Clay Art; 1988; featuring Marilyn's picture in the frame; came with a decorative box. $25–35

Marilyn Monroe Head Mug in 3-D by Clay Art; 1988; came in a decorative box. $15–20

Marilyn Monroe Heart Shaped Dish by Clay Art; 1988; featuring Marilyn's reclining figure on top and came in a decorative box. $25–35

Marilyn Monroe Light Switch Plate by Clay Art $15–20

Marilyn Monroe Salt and Pepper Shakers by Clay Art; 1988; 3½" tall; featuring Marilyn in a white and a black dress. $16–20

Marilyn Monroe Welcome Plaque by Clay Art featuring a heart shape with "Welcome" on it, affixed to a Marilyn bust. $25–40

Clay Art dish, 1988

MOVIE-RELATED COLLECTIBLES

From the art departments of the major Hollywood studios came a myriad of beautiful advertising posters, lobby cards, pressbooks, publicity stills, and other materials. Today, these items are exceedingly collectible. Some posters featuring big-name stars and movies are bringing tens of thousands of dollars. Marilyn posters and related items are fortunately (for the collector) bringing much less. America has had a long-standing fascination for the movies, and the collectibles listed below appeal not only to Monroe collectors, but to collectors of Hollywood memorabilia as well.

Pressbooks (Campaign Books)

Nearly every movie has had a pressbook produced for publicity purposes. There is no set size, but they generally are 14 x 18". They consist of a variety of ads, articles, and photos that may be clipped and run in local newspapers by the theater owners. Of great help to the Marilyn collector is the fact that they show each of the various movie posters, lobby cards (in many cases), banners, slides, and publicity stills produced for the movie. Pressbooks are usually valued at 5 to 20 percent of the price of a one-sheet movie poster for the film involved. Pressbooks vary slightly in size and content from one film to another. In some cases supplements were produced in addition to the main pressbook; note that these must not be mistaken for the original release—these will almost always be identified as supplements on their front covers.

Film Title	Year	Studio	Value
A Ticket to Tomahawk	1950	Fox	$40–80
All About Eve	1950	Fox	$75–125

Pressbook, *The Seven-Year Itch*, 1955

Film Title	Year	Studio	Value
As Young As You Feel	1951	Fox	$40–80
Bus Stop	1956	Fox	$100–275
Clash by Night	1952	RKO	$40–80
Dangerous Years	1947	Fox	$50–100
Don't Bother to Knock	1952	Fox	$50–100
Gentlemen Prefer Blondes	1953	Fox	$100–200
Home Town Story	1951	MGM	$40–80
How to Marry a Millionaire	1954	Fox	$75–125
Ladies of the Chorus	1948	Columbia	$75–125
Let's Make Love	1960	Fox	$40–80
Love Happy	1950	United Artists	$50–100
Love Nest	1951	Fox	$40–80
Monkey Business	1952	Fox	$40–80
Niagara	1953	Fox	$100–200
O. Henry's Full House	1952	Fox	$40–80
Right Cross	1950	MGM	$30–60
River of No Return	1954	Fox	$50–100
Scudda Hoo! Scudda Hay!	1948	Fox	$30–50
Some Like It Hot	1959	United Artists	$100–200

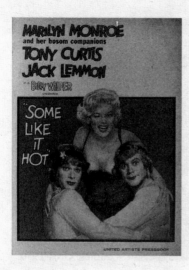

Pressbook, *Some Like It Hot*, 1959

Film Title	Year	Studio	Value
The Asphalt Jungle	1950	MGM	$100–175
The Fireball	1950	Fox	$40–80
The Misfits	1961	United Artists	$40–70
The Prince and the Showgirl	1957	Warner Bros.	$100–200
The Seven-Year Itch	1955	Fox	$100–300
There's No Business Like Show Business	1954	Fox	$100–200
We're Not Married	1952	Fox	$40–80

Note: Marilyn was to appear in the 1962 film *Something's Got to Give* but she died before filming was completed. It is possible that there are a few posters, pressbooks, and other materials that were produced for this film, but I have never seen any.

Publicity Stills

These photos were usually taken by a studio photographer and measure 8 x 10" or 11 x 14". These were produced in both glossy and matte form and came in color and in black and white. Other sizes that were produced are generally smaller than those listed above. Most were made in conjunction with Marilyn's current film and included the photographer's name, studio name, and information on the film itself, and were numbered either on the front or the back. Quite often this information was typed on a sheet of paper and affixed

**Publicity still sold
with picture
frames, circa 1950**

to the bottom border or the back of the photo. All of these photos
are very sought after by Marilyn collectors, as they are first generation
and of high quality/sharpness.

Values

5 x 7"	$20–40
8 x 10"	$60–100
11 x 14"	$200–400

Film Stills

For each of the films produced by the studios, a series of between
eight and twelve 8 x 10" stills were produced to be displayed in
theater lobbies. These featured scenes from the films and were done
in black and white, in color, or in both. They were produced on
glossy stock paper and featured an information strip along the bottom
half inch or so of the photo. This information strip included a listing
of the actors/actresses, producer, director, studio, copyright date, title
of the movie, and other information. They also featured a number,
usually in the bottom right corner, and are especially known for their
sharpness. The earlier color versions were simply hand tinted, and in
the late 1950s they became more like color photographs as we know
them today.

Values

8 x 10" (black & white)	$25–45
8 x 10" (color)	$45–65

Note: The prices for the stills listed above are pretty general and would pertain to all of those produced during Marilyn's lifetime.

Miscellaneous Movie-Related Collectibles

Heralds

These promotional "mini newspapers" consisted of four pages printed on newsprint paper and opened to reveal a centerfold featuring artwork similar to the film's poster. More information and graphics were printed on the front and back. They were made in various sizes over the years and ranged from 10½ to 17" wide and 15 to 22 ½" long when folded.

VALUES

For films where MM has top billing	$50–100
For early MM films (with MM appearing in graphics)	$40–80
For MM films with no graphics featuring her	$20–40

Door Panel Posters

Produced for selected films, these featured similar graphics to the film's posters. Many were done in a three-color process and measured 20 x 60". The few that have survived are extremely collectible.

VALUE

For films where MM has top billing	$300–500
For films with MM in bit parts with small pic of Marilyn	$100–200
For MM films with no graphic of MM	$50–100

Cardboard Promo Posters

Several promo posters were done to advertise products or books tied in with Marilyn's various movies. These were generally done on hard cardboard and in at least three colors. All are quite scarce.

1956 Promo Poster for the movie tie-in book *Bus Stop*; 11 x 14"; featuring a large Duo-tone picture of Marilyn and stating "Read the Book! See the Movie!" $100–150

Program, *How to Marry a Million-aire,* **1954**

Souvenir Programs

These were handed out at select theaters to moviegoers and consisted of several pages of black and white and color photos of the stars and/or scenes from the film. They are very attractive and very collectible. Those that feature color throughout are the most valuable, but all are highly prized.

VALUE

For films where MM has top billing $80–125
For films with MM in bit parts with small pics of
   Marilyn $40–80
For MM films with no graphic of Marilyn $20–40

Note: Foreign programs for Marilyn's films tend to be much less elaborate and consist of either black-and-white graphics, or Duo-tone or tinted graphics. They are done on much lighter-weight paper and are valued at one quarter the value of those prices listed above.

TV Tel-ops/Slides

These were distributed by the studios through their promotional pressbooks and are extremely rare. They were generally done in sets of three or four and would show scenes from the film. A script would accompany them to be read by the TV announcer as each particular slide appeared on the screen. These were available on cardboard or in glass slide form. These are so scarce that it is difficult to affix a value.

VALUE

For those showing MM (per set)	$100–200
For those not showing MM (per set)	$40–80

Playbills/Handbills

These were single-page handouts that would reproduce a film's poster, or similar artwork to that of the poster, on their fronts. They also stated (usually at the top) when a movie was to be shown at a particular theater. They were printed on various shades of paper.

VALUE

For films where MM has top billing	$25–50
For those not featuring an image of MM	$10–20

Standees

These were produced for most films and may feature a small image of Marilyn in those films in which she did not have top billing. Some of these cardboard standees reproduced the film's poster, but the ones that featured a large blowup of Marilyn are the most valuable and highly prized by Monroe collectors. For some of Marilyn's bigger films, two or three different standees were often made that featured her prominently. They were generally about five feet tall and could be ordered with or without an easel. They were printed in at least three colors and cost between twelve and fifteen dollars to the theater owners. Few examples remain.

VALUES

For those featuring only Marilyn	$800–1,500
For those with a small image of Marilyn	$300–700
For those with no image, but from an MM film	$100–200

Miscellaneous Movie Posters and Lobby Cards

- Three Sheet—These came in two sections generally and are three times the size of a one-sheet movie poster. As well, they are valued at approximately three times the value of a one sheet.
- Six Sheet (81 x 81")—These came in three or four sections and are very scarce. They are valued at six times the value of a one sheet for any particular film.
- Twenty-four sheet (billboard size)—Done on light stock paper and almost nonexistent.
- 40 x 60"—These posters were done on a heavy stock paper using a rare silk-screening process. They were meant to hang

outside at bus stops, etc., and therefore most were destroyed
by the weather. They are highly sought after and are valued at
one and a half to two times the value of a one sheet for the
particular film.

• Banners—These were done on light stock and are very rare.

Note: Foreign posters are valued at much lower prices than U.S.
posters and were issued in different sizes than the U.S. posters. Buyers
beware. Usually along the bottom right- or left-hand corner of all
posters is a copyright statement that will give a name of the studio
and the year of release, along with a number, such as 32–41. If the
number is preceded by an R, such as R32-14, it signifies that the
poster was a reissue at a later date, sometimes many years later. A
reissue is in essence a reproduction and does not have the value of
the original release. However, some of the reissues are now quite old
themselves and are bringing decent prices. Beginning in the 1960s
and continuing through the present, there were many reproductions
made of Marilyn's classic films by such companies as Portal Publications. Many are dated and identified as such, but if they're not, look
for an address that includes a zip code along the bottom edge of the
poster, as there were no zip codes in use during Marilyn's day.

The following descriptions will be followed by a film-by-film listing of their values for the corresponding Marilyn Monroe films.

One Sheet (27 × 41")

These were the posters most often seen by the public, which still
holds true today. They are the most sought after size of poster. Because these posters were printed on a lighter-stock paper, many collectors choose to have them backed with linen or paper to help
stabilize them. They appeal to collectors because they are of a size
easy to display, and most of our movie poster memories are associated
with the standard one sheet that hung either in or out of the theater's lobby.

Half Sheet (22 × 28")

These were done on a heavier-stock paper than the one sheets.
In general, they sell for about 30 to 35 percent of the value of a one
sheet and can feature graphics equal to or at times better than the
one sheets. In these instances the value increases considerably.

Window Card (14 × 17–22")

Printed on very heavy-stock paper, these posters were made for
window displays, as their name implies. They came with a blank area

on their tops, where the local theaters could print show dates and times. This information was sometimes just handwritten and in other instances is printed professionally. Often the border that displayed this information has been trimmed away, which reduces the value of the card.

Inserts (14 × 36")

These are tall, narow posters usually printed on heavy stock. They sometimes feature more attractive graphics than the one sheets. In these cases, they are worth more. Inserts are valued at about the same price as the half sheets, or about 30 to 35 percent of the one-sheet value.

Lobby Cards (11 × 14")

These generally feature scenes from the film and can be quite colorful. They are printed on heavy stock paper and come in sets of eight as a rule, but sets of ten were also created. Those that feature Marilyn are of course worth more than those that do not. For some of Marilyn's earlier movies, she may only be featured in one or two. The cards are all numbered along the bottom margin and include the studio's name and year of release. Card number one is always called the "Title Card" and is different from the rest in that it features pics of the star players and bold letters featuring the film's title. As a rule, these are valued at higher levels than the remainder of the cards.

The theaters were required to return all posters and lobby cards to the studios. Fortunately, not all theaters complied, and many examples of these wonderful items exist today.

Selected Poster, Lobby Card, and Related Values

Note: Prices below pertain only to those items that feature Marilyn Monroe. Information is given in alphabetical order of films in which Marilyn appeared.

	Value
ALL ABOUT EVE—1950—FOX STUDIOS	
One Sheet	$300–500
Lobby Title Card	$400–600
Lobby Card (MM only on card #3)	$300–500
Insert	$250–400
THE ASPHALT JUNGLE—1950—MGM STUDIOS	
Lobby Title Card	$250–500
Lobby Card (MM on card #8 only)	$200–400

	Value
AS YOUNG AS YOU FEEL—1951—FOX STUDIOS	
One Sheet	$100–200
Half Sheet	$50–100
Window Card	$50–100
Lobby Title Card	$75–125
Lobby Card	$50–75
Insert	$100–200
BUS STOP—1956—FOX STUDIOS	
One Sheet	$300–500
Half Sheet	$200–375
Three Sheet	$1,200–1,500
Window Card	$200–300
Lobby Title Card	$200–300
Lobby Card (MM on seven of the eight)	$75–125
Insert	$200–375
CLASH BY NIGHT—1952—RKO STUDIOS	
One Sheet	$150–250
Half Sheet	$200–375

1956 lobby card, *Bus Stop*

	Value
Window Card	$100–200
Lobby Title Card	$100–175
Lobby Card (MM only on card #3)	$100–200
Insert	$150–275

DANGEROUS YEARS—1947—FOX STUDIOS

Lobby Title Card	$300–500
Lobby Card (MM only on card #8)	$300–475

DON'T BOTHER TO KNOCK—1952—FOX STUDIOS

One Sheet	$475–750
Half Sheet	$175–375
Three Sheet	$2,000–2,500
Window Card	$125–250
Lobby Title Card	$100–175
Lobby Card (Marilyn on all)	$75–125
Insert	$375–750

THE FIREBALL—1950—FOX STUDIOS

Lobby Card (MM on card #5 only)	$175–225

GENTLEMEN PREFER BLONDES—1953—FOX STUDIOS

One Sheet	$450–800
Half Sheet	$200–400
Three Sheet	$1,500–1,800
Window Card	$150–250
Lobby Title Card	$100–175
Lobby Card (MM on seven of eight)	$75–100
Insert	$125–200

HOME TOWN STORY—1951—MGM STUDIOS

One Sheet	$125–225
Half Sheet	$75–125
Window Card	$50–100
Lobby Title Card	$65–125
Lobby Card (MM on card #2)	$125–175
Insert	$50–100

HOW TO MARRY A MILLIONAIRE—1954—FOX STUDIOS

One Sheet	$400–800
Half Sheet	$175–375

	Value
Three Sheet	$1,100–1,300
Window Card	$150–225
Lobby Title Card	$60–125
Lobby Card (MM on all)	$50–100
Insert	$175–375

Ladies of the Chorus—1948—Columbia Studios

Lobby Title Card	$300–500
Lobby Card (Marilyn on cards #4, 7, and 8)	$200–400

Let's Make It Legal—1951—Fox Studios

One Sheet	$175–300
Half Sheet	$100–200
Window Card	$75–125
Lobby Title Card	$100–150
Lobby Card	$50–100
Insert	$200–300

Let's Make Love—1960—Fox Studios

One Sheet	$150–275
Half Sheet	$75–150

Window card,
How to Marry a
Millionaire, 1954

	Value
Window Card	$70–125
Lobby Title Card	$60–100
Lobby Card (MM on cards #2, 3, 4, 5, 7, 8)	$40–75
Insert	$70–125

LOVE HAPPY—1950—UNITED ARTISTS

Lobby Card (MM on card #8 only)	$500–900

Note: Certain posters and lobby cards for this film were rereleased in 1953 with larger MM graphics. These are valued at less than the originals, of course, so look for the capital "R" before the year printed on the items.

LOVE NEST—1951—FOX STUDIOS

One Sheet	$150–275
Half Sheet	$75–125
Window Card	$75–125
Lobby Title Card	$200–250
Lobby Card	$100–150
Insert	$175–225

THE MISFITS—1961—UNITED ARTISTS STUDIOS

One Sheet	$150–300
Half Sheet	$70–125
Window Card	$70–125
Lobby Title Card	$60–100
Lobby Card (MM on cards, #2, 3, 4, 5, 6, and 7)	$50–70
Insert	$100–200

MONKEY BUSINESS—1952—FOX STUDIOS

One Sheet	$175–375
Half Sheet	$100–200
Window Card	$100–200
Lobby Title Card	$75–125
Lobby Card (MM on cards, #2, 5, and 8)	$50–100
Insert	$100–200

NIAGARA—1953—FOX STUDIOS

One Sheet	$500–700
Half Sheet	$200–350
Window Card	$175–300
Lobby Title Card	$100–150

Window card,
Niagara, **1953**

	Value
Lobby Card (MM on six of eight)	$60–125
Insert	$250–400

O. HENRY'S FULL HOUSE—1952—FOX STUDIOS

One Sheet	$150–250
Half Sheet	$60–125
Window Card	$50–100
Lobby Title Card	$100–200
Lobby Card (MM on card #4)	$50–100
Insert	$60–100

THE PRINCE AND THE SHOWGIRL—1957—FOX STUDIOS

One Sheet	$500–1,000
Half Sheet	$250–450
Three Sheet	$1,500–1,700
Window Card	$200–400
Lobby Title Card	$125–175
Lobby Card (MM on all)	$75–125
Insert	$200–400

RIVER OF NO RETURN—1954—FOX STUDIOS

One Sheet	$400–800
Half Sheet	$200–350

Lobby card no. 2, *The Prince and the Showgirl*, 1957

	Value
Window Card	$150–250
Lobby Title Card	$75–125
Lobby Card (MM on all)	$60–100
Insert	$125–200

THE SEVEN-YEAR ITCH—1955—FOX STUDIOS

One Sheet	$800–1,400
Half Sheet	$500–1,000
Three Sheet	$2,000–2,500
Window Card	$200–500
Lobby Title Card	$200–400
Lobby Card (Marilyn on all)	$75–150
Insert	$200–400

SOME LIKE IT HOT—1959—UNITED ARTISTS STUDIOS

One Sheet	$400–800
Half Sheet	$200–400
Three Sheet	$1,500–2,000
Window Card	$200–400

Lobby card no. 7, *The Seven-Year Itch*, 1955

	Value
Lobby Title Card	$100–200
Lobby Card (MM on cards #5, 6, 7, and 8)	$75–125
Insert	$250–450

THERE'S NO BUSINESS LIKE SHOW BUSINESS—
1954—FOX STUDIOS

One Sheet	$100–225
Half Sheet	$60–100
Window Card	$60–100
Lobby Title Card	$50–80
Lobby Card (MM on cards, #3, 4, 5, 6, and 8)	$60–100
Insert	$100–200

A TICKET TO TOMAHAWK—1950—FOX STUDIOS

Lobby Title Card	$125–175
Lobby Card (MM only on card #4)	$200–250

WE'RE NOT MARRIED—1952—FOX STUDIOS

One Sheet	$100–225
Half Sheet	$60–100

1954 lobby card, *There's No Business Like Show Business*

	Value
Window Card	$60–100
Lobby Title Card	$50–80
Lobby Card (MM on cards #4 and 6)	$75–125
Insert	$60–100

MARILYN—1963—FOX STUDIOS—NARRATED BY
ROCK HUDSON

One Sheet	$100–200
Half Sheet	$75–150
Three Sheet	$200–300
Window Card	$60–125
Lobby Title Card	$40–80
Lobby Card (MM on all)	$40–65
Insert	$50–90

VINTAGE MARILYN PERSONALITY POSTER

1954—It is widely believed that only one poster featuring Marilyn was made available to the general public during her lifetime. This poster measures 21½ x 62" and is in color, showing a photo of Marilyn in a two-piece red-and-white-striped bikini against a white background. Marilyn's hands are drawn to her left side, as if she's tucking in some fabric; her legs are spread apart, and she's wearing an ankle bracelet and a pair of pumps. Most of these are printed very clearly, but some are not. The original issue price was $2.00; the photo is done in Kodachrome, and the posters were made by a Boston company. An ad featuring this poster for sale can be found in the January 1954 issue of *Ebony* magazine, and a photo of Marilyn exists signing one of the posters for a GI during her trip to Korea in 1954 to entertain the troops. Valued at $300–400.

Contemporary Marilyn Posters

A great many posters of Marilyn were printed after her death in 1962, the bulk of which were done in the 1980s and 90s. The list is endless, but a good cross section of the more valuable editions are listed below. Any poster created after 1975 and not in a limited edition is generally worth ten to twenty dollars.

	Value
1967—Poster of Marilyn measuring 30 x 42" and in black and white; features a photo of Marilyn as Roslyn from *The Misfits*; produced by Famous Faces.	$50–75
1979—Poster entitled *Marilyn 62—Bert Stern Photographs*; 23 ½ x 30"; by Boris Gallery of Photography—Boston; shows a nude Marilyn holding a see-through scarf over her body.	$75–100
1980s—Poster of Marilyn measuring 23 x 27" and entitled *The Last Sitting*; promotional poster for Bert Stern's book of the same title; shows ten different images of Marilyn.	$50–75
1980s—As above, only showing Marilyn nude holding a see-through scarf in front of her; color photo.	$50–75
1980s—As above, only showing Marilyn on her stomach in a black-and-white photo.	$50–75
1980—As above, only from Germany and showing Marilyn lying nude on her side; measures 23 x 31"	$75–125
1989—Phil Stern photo of Marilyn in black and white and measuring 18 x 24"; printed on heavy paper.	$100–200
Date Unknown—*Art America Proudly Presents Two Legends* by Earl MacPherson; featuring John Wayne on one side, and Marilyn on the other—with four lovely drawings by MacPherson.	$100–150

NEWSPAPERS

Newspapers have been instrumental in recording everyday and historical events. Papers headlining Abraham Lincoln's assassination, the sinking of the *Titanic*, or the death of a famous person are all highly collectible in today's market.

Since newspapers were printed on such thin and perishable paper, few have held up against the test of time. Furthermore, most were thrown out shortly after they were read. A few people had the foresight to save what they deemed important issues, and safely stashed them away to be enjoyed by future generations.

Marilyn Monroe made the papers often, beginning very early on in her career. Most of the earliest references and photos appeared in the Hollywood-related papers and those in the immediate area of Hollywood, chronicling Marilyn's various roles and/or promotional campaigns for the studios. The earliest that I have been able to buy is a Chicago paper featuring a prominent photo of Marilyn on its front cover. Marilyn is holding on to several baseball bats and was part of a Hollywood baseball team on a promotional tour to promote her film *Love Happy*. Whenever Marilyn is featured on the paper's front-page headlines, the value is increased considerably. The most collectible of these are the issues that carried a full report of Marilyn's death in August 1962. The following is a selection of collectible Marilyn newspapers from across the country. They are listed by title, date, description, and value.

	Value
Chicago Herald American—July 9, 1949. "Today! Film Stars 'World Series' "; "Film Stars Stage World Series Here"; "It'll Be a Lovely Game With Marilyn Monroe As Bat Girl." A large pic of Marilyn holding six baseball bats is shown along with the above headlines.	$100–300

July 9, 1949, issue of *Chicago Herald American*

	Value
Chicago Sun-Times—Aug. 6, 1962. Headline reads, "Marilyn Monroe Dies of Drug Overdose."	$80–120
Evening Sentinel (Keene, NH)—Aug. 6–9, 1962. Four consecutive days of the paper, with articles throughout. (set of four)	$60–70
The Honolulu Advertiser—Aug. 6, 1962. Headline reads: "Movie Star Marilyn Monroe Dies from Overdose of Pills." Articles inside include, "Studios Halt Stars' Rule"; "Movie Colony's Reaction: 'Can't Believe She's Dead' "; "Highlights of a Career That Ended in Tragedy."	$150–175
Los Angeles Times—Aug. 6, 1962—Monday Preview Extra. Headlines include, "Marilyn Monroe Dies—Blame Pills"; "First Details of Actress' Death in Brentwood"; "Nude Body Found in Bed, Empty Capsule Bottle at Her Side"; "Help She Sought Eluded Marilyn." Large pic of MM on the front cover, with articles and pics inside.	$150–200

EXTRA
Los Angeles Times PREVIEW

MARILYN MONROE DIES: BLAME PILLS

First Details of Actress' Death in Brentwood

Help She Sought Eluded Marilyn

Nude Body Found in Bed, Empty Capsule Bottle at Her Side

Aug. 6, 1962, issue of *Los Angeles Times*

	Value
New York Journal American—Oct. 6, 1954. Front-page report: "Louella O. Parsons Reveals: Joe Fanned on Jealousy." Pics of Marilyn and drama coach on cover. Articles inside on filed divorce papers.	$60–80
New York Journal American—Oct. 12, 1956. Headlines include, "Bombshell in London—Tightly Clad Marilyn Steals London Show." Pics of MM and Arthur Miller.	$60–80
New York Journal American—June 23, 1959. Headlines include, "Marilyn Under Knife"; "Doctor Calls Condition Excellent." Pictures of Marilyn on cover.	$60–80
New York Journal American—Nov. 13, 1960. Headlines include, "Dorothy Kilgallen Exclusive: Inside Story of the Marilyn-Yves Romance"; "MM: Secrets of Her Life by Zolotow (Part One)"; "Marilyn Won't Talk About Divorce." All are lengthy articles.	$40–60
New York Journal American—Mar. 29, 1961. Headlines include, "Don't Grab Joe." Pictures of Marilyn and Joe DiMaggio on the cover and one more inside.	$20–40

New York Journal American—Aug. 6, 1962. Headlines include, "Why did Marilyn End Life?" One large pic is

Value

featured on the cover, as well as six small ones. Inside articles include, "Star's Last Hours Being Checked"; "A Girl Who Found Stardom, But Not Happiness"; "Star's Death Stunning Blow to Film World"; "Three Ex-husbands React—As MM Foretold"; "MM Was Many Things to Many People"; "A Stairway to Stardom—Bit By Bit—A Star Is Born—and Glows—and Dies." $150–200

New York Mirror—Oct. 5, 1954. Headline reads, "Dimag's Split!"; "Boredom, Sexy Photos Split Dimag's"; "Some of the Reasons Why." Features large pics of Marilyn on the cover. $60–80

New York Mirror—Oct. 6, 1954. Headline reads, "Marilyn Sobs, Joe Gets Walking Papers." Inside articles include: "Nights Were Dull at Joe and Marilyn's"; "Marilyn Starts Suit, Wept All Night Over It." Pics of MM on cover. $60–80

New York Mirror—Oct. 7, 1954. Headlines read: "Joe Goes: 'I'll Never Be Back' Any Other Man? Marilyn Weeps." Big pic of Marilyn and Joe on the cover. $70–90

New York Mirror—Nov. 12, 1960. Headlines read: "Marilyn Miller All Washed Up." Pics of MM and Arthur Miller and Yves Montand on cover. Articles inside include: "MM Admits It's Over"; "See No Break-Up for Montands." $50–75

New York Mirror—Aug. 6, 1962. Headlines read, "Marilyn Monroe Kills Self. Found Nude in Bed . . . Hand on Phone . . . Took 40 Pills." No pics on cover. Inside articles include, "Marilyn's Tragic Life: World's Golden Girl"; "MM Witty Philosopher"; "Friends Here and Abroad Stunned by News"; "MM's Toughest Role—Life." This issue includes a centerfold of photos. $100–130

New York Mirror—Aug. 6, 1962. Same issue as above, only MM is featured on the cover. $200–250

New York Mirror—Aug. 7, 1962. Headlines include, "Marilyn's Last Day of Life." Two pics of MM on the cover. Inside articles include, "Story of MM's Last Days"; "Marilyn's Tragic Life . . . Her World of Pretending"; "Pill Victim's Pattern: Nearly All Want Back." $100–140

Value

New York Mirror—Aug. 9, 1962. Headline reads, "Joe's Goodbye: A Kiss, a Tear." Several inside articles and a two-page centerfold of photos. $100–140

New York Mirror—Aug. 15, 1962. Headline reads, "Marilyn's Last Happy Day." Large MM pics on cover. Inside article reads, "Gaiety That Death Stilled." Photos of Marilyn at her thirty-sixth birthday party. A centerfold of pics is also featured. $100–140

New York Mirror—Aug. 18, 1962. Headlines include, "Find Marilyn 'Wanted to Die' "; "Left Over 500G." Articles inside include, "MM Often Wished to Die . . . She Left 500G, 142G To Coach." $30–40

New York News—Jan. 15, 1952. Headlines include, "Dimaggio and Marilyn Wed." More on page 3 inside. $50–90

New York News—May 31, 1956. Headline reads, "Marilyn's Next Near Divorce." No pics of MM on cover. Article inside reads, "Marilyn And Miller Tune Wedding Bells." $30–40

New York News—Nov. 12, 1960. Headline reads, "Miller Walks Out on MM." Pics of MM on cover. Inside article reads, "Arthur Packs His Pulitzer Prize, Walks Out on MM." More photos featured inside. $40–60

New York News—Aug. 6, 1962. Headline reads, "Did He Make a Mystery Call?" Inside article reads, "Seek Mexican in MM's Mystery Call." More articles inside. $50–70

New York News—Aug. 9, 1962. Headline reads, "Joe Whispers 'I Love You.' " Pics of DiMaggio and son on cover. Articles inside include, "Joe to Marilyn At Rites: 'I Love You' " and Lawford: "I Phoned MM on Death Night." $75–100

New York News—Aug. 9, 1962. As above, only a different edition. Headline reads, "Last Goodbye." Joe DiMaggio photo on cover. Articles inside include, "Joe to Marilyn At Rites"; "MM's Mexican Pal Is in Beverly Hills"; "Stars Barred at Rites—Lawford's 'shocked.' " Features a two-page centerfold of pics. $80–100

New York News—Aug. 14, 1962. Headlines read, "Marilyn Speaks . . . Star's Own Words to Biographer

Value

in Last Weeks Before Death . . . MM's Last Picture." Has a large pic of MM on the cover. Inside article reads, "Twilight of a Star: Here's MM, Barefoot and Bubbly." Lots of pictures and includes a centerfold of photos. $100–140

New York News—Aug. 15, 1962. Headline reads, "MM Relives Tragic Childhood." Large pic of MM on cover. Inside article reads, "The Tragic Childhood Days." More pics featured inside. $80–100

New York News—Aug. 18, 1962. Headlines read, "MM's Estate May Hit Million. Death Held 'Probable Suicide.'" Pics of Jose Bolanos at crypt and beneficiary of will. Articles inside read, "Marilyn Returns the Fire in Last Tiff With Gossips"; "MM Left the Million $ She Looked Like"; "Final Verdict on Finale: Probable Suicide"; "Bolanos Says Last Good-bye with Flowers." Many photos inside. $60–80

New York Post—Aug. 6, 1962. Headline reads, "Marilyn's Last Days." $100–150

New York Post—Aug. 10, 1962. Headline reads, "Marilyn—Tragedy's Child." $80–100

New York Post—June 21, 1965. Headline reads, "Taxes Take Marilyn's Millions"; more inside. $40–60

Philadelphia Bulletin—Aug. 6, 1962. "Marilyn Monroe's Death Starts Hunt for Motive"; "Officials Wonder If She Intended to Kill Herself!" Pics of MM, DiMaggio, Arthur Miller, and Yves Montand. $150–200

Philadelphia Daily News—Feb. 2, 1952. "No diva, film lassie Marilyn Monroe attains glamor in other lines. Like them?" Features a large photo of Marilyn on the cover sitting on a diving board with more information on the inside pages. $60–80

Philadelphia Evening Bulletin—Aug. 8, 1962. Headline reads, "MM Found It Impossible to Live Up to Her Screen Reputation." $20–30

PLATES AND PLAQUES

Marilyn Plates

Bradford Series One

	Value
Bradford Exchange—*The Seven-Year Itch*; 1990; 8½"; plate one in the Marilyn Monroe Collection; Limited Numbered Edition; limited to 150 firing days; a Delphi plate painted by Chris Notorile. Original price was $27.94. Bradex No. 84-D19-5.1	$40–60
Bradford Exchange—*Gentlemen Prefer Blondes*; 1990; 8½"; plate two in the Marilyn Monroe Collection; Limited Numbered Edition; limited to 150 firing days; a Delphi plate painted by Chris Notorile. Original price was $27.94. Bradex No. 84-D19-5.2	$40–60
Bradford Exchange—*How to Marry a Millionaire*; 1991; 8½"; plate three in the Marilyn Monroe Collection; Limited Numbered Edition; limited to 150 firing days; a Delphi plate painted by Chris Notorile. Original price was $27.94. Bradex No. 84-D19-5.3	$40–60
Bradford Exchange—*Niagara*; 1992; 8½"; plate four in the Marilyn Monroe Collection; Limited Numbered Edition; limited to 150 firing days; a Delphi plate painted by Chris Notorile. Original price was $27.94. Bradex No. 84-D19-5.4	$35–55
Bradford Exchange—*There's No Business Like Show Business*; 1992; 8½"; plate five in the Marilyn Monroe Collection; Limited Numbered Edition; limited to 150 firing days; a Delphi plate painted by Chris Notorile. Bradex No. 84-D19-5.5	$35–55

Value

Bradford Exchange—*How to Marry a Millionaire*; 1992; 8½"; plate six in the Marilyn Monroe Collection; Limited Numbered Edition; limited to 150 firing days; a Delphi plate painted by Chris Notorile. Bradex No. 84-D19-5.6 $35–55

Bradford Exchange—*My Heart Belongs to Daddy*; 1992; 8½"; plate seven in the Marilyn Monroe Collection; Limited Numbered Edition; limited to 150 firing days; a Delphi plate painted by Chris Notorile. Bradex No. 84-D19-5.7 $35–55

Bradford Exchange—*Bus Stop*; 1992; 8½"; plate eight in the Marilyn Monroe Collection; Limited Numbered Edition; limited to 150 firing days; a Delphi plate painted by Chris Notorile. Bradex No. 84-D19-5.8 $35–55

Bradford Exchange—*All About Eve*; 1992; 8½"; plate nine in the Marilyn Monroe Collection; Limited Numbered Edition; limited to 150 firing days; a Delphi plate painted by Chris Notorile. Bradex No. 84-D19-5.9 $35–55

Six of the *Marilyn Monroe Collection* of plates by
The Bradford Exchange, 1990–92

Value

Bradford Exchange—*Monkey Business;* 1992; 8½"; plate ten in the Marilyn Monroe Collection; Limited Numbered Edition; limited to 150 firing days; a Delphi plate painted by Chris Notorile. Bradex No. 84-D19-5.10 $35–55

Bradford Exchange—*Don't Bother to Knock;* 1992; 8½"; plate eleven in the Marilyn Monroe Collection; Limited Numbered Edition; limited to 150 firing days; a Delphi plate painted by Chris Notorile. Bradex No. 84-D19-5.11 $35–55

Bradford Exchange—*We're Not Married;* 1992; 8½"; plate twelve and the final plate in the Marilyn Monroe Collection; Limited Numbered Edition; limited to 150 firing days; a Delphi plate painted by Chris Notorile. Bradex No. 84-D19-5.12 $35–55

Bradford Series Two

Value

Bradford Exchange—*For Our Boys in Korea—1954;* 1992; 8¼"; plate one in the *Magic of Marilyn* Collection; Limited Numbered Edition; limited to 95 firing days; a Delphi plate painted by Chris Notorile. Bradex No. 84-D19-12.1 $35–55

Bradford Exchange—*Opening Night;* 1992; 8¼"; plate two in the *Magic of Marilyn* Collection; Limited Numbered Edition; limited to 95 firing days; a Delphi plate by Chris Notorile. Bradex No. 84-D19-12.2 $35–55

Bradford Exchange—*Rising Star;* 1993; 8¼"; Plate three in the *Magic of Marilyn* Collection; Limited Numbered Edition; limited to 95 firing days; a Delphi plate painted by Chris Notorile. Bradex No. 84-D19-12.3 $35–55

Bradford Exchange—*Stopping Traffic;* 1993; 8¼"; plate four in the *Magic of Marilyn* Collection; Limited Numbered Edition; Limited to 95 firing days; a Delphi plate painted by Chris Notorile. Bradex No. 84-D19-12.4 $35–55

Bradford Exchange—*Strassburg's Student;* 1993; 8¼"; plate five in the *Magic of Marilyn* Collection; Limited Numbered Edition; limited to 95 firing days; a

Two plates in the *Magic of Marilyn* series by The Bradford Exchange, 1992–93

	Value
Delphi plate painted by Chris Notorile. Bradex No. 84-D19-12.5	$35–55
Bradford Exchange—*Photo Opportunity*; 1993; 8¼"; plate six in the *Magic of Marilyn* Collection; Limited Numbered Edition; limited to 95 firing days; a Delphi plate painted by Chris Notorile. Bradex No. 84-D19-12.6	$35–55
Bradford Exchange—*Shining Star*; 1993; 8¼"; plate seven in the *Magic of Marilyn* Collection; Limited Numbered Edition; limited to 95 firing days; a Delphi plate painted by Chris Notorile. Bradex No. 84-D19-12.7	$35–55
Bradford Exchange—*Curtain Call*; 1994; 8¼"; plate eight and final plate in the *Magic of Marilyn* Collection; Limited Numbered Edition; limited to 95 firing days; a Delphi plate painted by Chris Notorile. Bradex No. 84-D19-12.8	$35–55

Bradford Series Three

	Value
Bradford Exchange—*All That Glitters*; 1994; 8⅛"; plate one in the *Reflections of Marilyn* Collection; Limited Numbered Edition; limited to 95 firing days; artwork by Chris Notorile. Original price was $29.90; Bradex No. 84-B10-169.1	$35–50

Value

Bradford Exchange—*Shimmering Heat;* 1994; 8⅛";
plate two in the *Reflections of Marilyn* Collection;
Limited Numbered Edition; limited to 95 firing
days; artwork by Chris Notorile. Bradex No. 84-
B10-169.2 $35–50

Bradford Exchange—*Million Dollar Star;* 1994; 8⅛";
plate three in the *Reflections of Marilyn Collection;*
Limited Numbered Edition; limited to 95 firing
days; artwork by Chris Notorile. Bradex No. 84-
B10-169.3 $35–50

Bradford Exchange—*A Twinkle in Her Eye;* 1995; 8⅛";
plate four in the *Reflections of Marilyn* Collection; Limited Numbered Edition; limited to 95 firing days; artwork by Chris Notorile. Bradex No. 84-B10-169.4 $30–40

Bradford Exchange—*A Glimmering Dream;* 1995; 8⅛";
plate five in the *Reflections of Marilyn* Collection;
Limited Numbered Edition; limited to 95 firing
days; artwork by Chris Notorile. Bradex No. 84-
B10-169.5 $30–40

Bradford Exchange—*Sparkling Cherie;* 1995; 8⅛";
plate six in the *Reflections of Marilyn* Collection;
Limited Numbered Edition; limited to 95 firing
days; artwork by Chris Notorile. Bradex No. 84-
B10-169.6 $30–40

Postage stamp
plate by The
Bradford Ex-
change, 1995

Value

Bradford Exchange—*Luminous Lorelei;* 1995; 8⅛"; plate
seven in the *Reflections of Marilyn* Collection; Limited
Numbered Edition; limited to 95 firing days; artwork
by Chris Notorile. Bradex No. 84-B10-169.7 $30–40

Bradford Exchange—*Dazzling Dreamgirl;* 1995; 8⅛";
plate eight and final plate in the *Reflections of Marilyn* Collection; Limited Numbered Edition; limited
to 95 firing days; artwork by Chris Notorile. Bradex No. 84-B10-169.8 $30–40

Bradford Series Four

Value

Bradford Exchange—*Sultry Yet Regal;* 1995; 8½"; *Marilyn—The Gold Collection;* Limited Numbered Edition;
limited to 95 firing days; reproduces the U.S. Postage
Stamp of Marilyn. Bradex No. 84-B10-339.1 $35–45

Bradford Series Five

Value

Bradford Exchange—*Isn't It Delicious;* 1997; 8⅛"; plate
one in the *Silver Screen Marilyn* Collection; Limited
Numbered Edition; artwork by Gadino; banded in
platinum; Bradex No. 84-B10-550.1 $30–40

Bradford Exchange—*I Don't Mean Rhinestones;* 1997;
8⅛"; plate two in the *Silver Screen Marilyn* Collection; Limited Numbered Edition; artwork by Gadino; Bradex No. 84-B10-550.2 $30–40

Bradford Series Six

Value

Bradford Exchange—*Forever Marilyn;* 1997; 8⅛"; plate
one in the *Marilyn By Milton H. Greene: Up Close
and Personal* Collection; Limited Numbered Edition; limited to 95 firing days; featuring an actual
photo by Milton Greene. Bradex No. 84-B10-
809.1. Original price was $34.95. $30–40

Bradford Exchange—*Body and Soul;* 1997; 8⅛"; plate
two in the *Marilyn By Milton H. Greene: Up Close
and Personal* Collection; Limited Numbered Edition; limited to 95 firing days; featuring an actual
photo by Milton Greene. Bradex No. 84-B10-809.2 $30–40

Value

Bradford Exchange—*Blonde Passion;* 1997; 8⅛"; 22-
karat gold rim; shows Marilyn putting on Chanel
No. 5 perfume. Original price was $29.95. $30–35

Bradford Sculptural Plate

Value

Bradford Exchange—*Satin Sensation;* 1996; 7.5" high ×
5.5" wide; plate one in the *Showstoppers: The Glamour of Marilyn Monroe* Collection; Limited Edition
of 9,000; numbered; shows MM in the pink gown
from *Gentlemen Prefer Blondes,* standing with her
hands above her head parting curtains onstage; Bradex No. 84-B10-266.1; designed by Chris Notorile;
original price was $64.84. $65–75

Hamilton Plates

Value

The Hamilton Collection—*Free Spirit;* 1995; 8¼";
23K gold border; limited to 28 firing days; featuring artwork by Franco based on photos by André
de Dienes; Certificate of Authenticity. $30–40
The Hamilton Collection—*A Star Is Born;* 1995; 8¼";
23K gold border; limited to 28 firing days; featuring artwork by FRANCO based on photos by
André de Dienes; Certificate of Authenticity. $30–40
The Hamilton Collection—*Remembering Norma Jean;*
1995; 23K gold border; limited to 28 firing days;
featuring artwork by FRANCO based on photos by
André de Dienes; Certificate of Authenticity. $30–40
The Hamilton Collection—*A Country Girl at Heart;*
1995; 23K gold border; limited to 28 firing days;
featuring artwork by FRANCO based on photos by
André de Dienes; Certificate of Authenticity. $30–40
The Hamilton Collection—*Girl Next Door;* 1995;
8¼"; 23K gold border; limited to 28 firing days;
featuring artwork by FRANCO based on photos by
André de Dienes; Certificate of Authenticity. $30–40
The Hamilton Collection—*A Day in the Sun;* 1995;
8¼"; 23K gold border; limited to 28 firing days;
featuring artwork by FRANCO based on photos by
André de Dienes; Certificate of Authenticity. $30–40

Value

The Hamilton Collection—*In The Spotlight;* 1995;
8¼"; 23K gold border; limited to 28 firing days;
featuring artwork by FRANCO based on photos by
André de Dienes; Certificate of Authenticity. $30–40

The Hamilton Collection—*Young and Carefree;* 1995;
23K gold border; limited to 28 firing days; featuring artwork by FRANCO based on photos by
André de Dienes; Certificate of Authenticity. $30–40

The Hamilton Collection—*Beauty Secrets;* 1995; 23K
gold border; limited to 28 firing days; featuring artwork by FRANCO based on photos by André de
Dienes; Certificate of Authenticity. $30–40

The Hamilton Collection—*Home Town Girl;* 1995;
23K gold border; limited to 28 firing days; featuring artwork by FRANCO based on photos by
André de Dienes; Certificate of Authenticity. $30–40

Please Note: There were two or three more plates done in the above series that I have not been able to get information on. Furthermore, several plates in the series are already unavailable from the company, which suggests that this series will hold its value well.

R. J. Ernst Plates

Value

R. J. Ernst—Marilyn Monroe plate with two images
of Marilyn painted by Susie Morton; 10"; painted
in blue, pink, and purple hues. $100–175

R. J. Ernst—Marilyn Monroe plate painted by Susie
Morton; 8½"; featuring Marilyn in a black dress. $65–95

Royal Orleans Plates

Value

Royal Orleans/20th Century Fox—*The Seven Year Itch;*
1982; *Marilyn—An American Classic* Series; Limited
Numbered Edition of 20,000; with a Certificate of
Authenticity; first plate in series. Original price was
$25.00. $80–100

Royal Orleans/20th Century Fox—*Gentlemen Prefer
Blondes;* 1982; *Marilyn—An American Classic* Series;
Limited Numbered Edition of 20,000; with a Cer-
tificate of Authenticity. Second plate in the series. $60–80

Two of the *Royal Orleans* series of plates, 1982

	Value
Royal Orleans/20th Century Fox—*Niagara;* 1982; *Marilyn—An American Classic* Series; Limited Numbered Edition of 20,000; with a Certificate of Authenticity. Third plate in the series.	$60–80
Royal Orleans/20th Century Fox—*How to Marry a Millionaire;* 1982; *Marilyn—An American Classic* Series; Limited Numbered Edition of 20,000; with a Certificate of Authenticity. Fourth (final) plate in the series.	$60–80

Miscellaneous Plates

	Value
Unidentified 10" hard plastic plate featuring Marilyn in the famous white skirt scene from *The Seven-Year Itch;* unauthorized by her estate; another variation or two known to exist; value each	$10–20

MARILYN PLAQUES

	Value
Ernst, Inc.—*Marilyn;* 1991; 7 × 9" (including whitewashed hardwood frame); Limited Numbered Edition with a Certificate of Authenticity; 1st in the set featuring Marilyn in a glamorous bust pose by artist Susie Morton; limited to 30 firing days.	$40–50

Value

Ernst, Inc.—*New York, New York;* 1991; 7 × 9" (including frame); Limited Numbered Edition with a Certificate of Authenticity; 2nd in the set featuring Marilyn standing near a car by artist Susie Morton; Limited to 30 firing days. $40–50

Ernst, Inc.—*Lights, Camera, Action!;* 1991; 7 × 9" (including frame); Limited Numbered Edition with a Certificate of Authenticity; 3rd in the set featuring Marilyn in three different bust poses by artist Susie Morton; limited to 30 firing days. $40–50

Ernst, Inc.—*Manhattan Heat;* 1992; 7 × 9" (including frame); Limited Numbered Edition with a Certificate of Authenticity; 4th and last in the set featuring Marilyn in the famous blowing white dress from *The Seven-Year Itch* by artist Susie Morton; limited to 30 firing days. $40–50

POSTCARDS AND RELATED COLLECTIBLES

Postcards

Black and White

	Value
Bromofoto—#1196—Italian—larger 4 × 6" card of Marilyn lying in the grass in a tight sweater and blowing on a dandelion with one hand behind her head.	$35–45
Celebrity Autograph Series—British—#100—early 1950s vintage. Shows Marilyn with her hand to her chin and with a big smile. Published by L. D. Ltd.	$20–25
Celebrity Publishers—#84—British card showing Marilyn and her facsimile autograph.	$25–35
Celuloide Stars—Spain—Shows Marilyn in a candid-type pose from *Some Like It Hot*.	$25–35
Celuloide Stars—#423—Spain—Shows a publicity photo of Marilyn and Richard Widmark from *Don't Bother to Knock*; edges of card are serrated.	$25–35
Celuloide Stars—#48—Spain—Shows Marilyn in a costume-check pose from *Gentlemen Prefer Blondes*; card has serrated edges.	$25–35
Cliche International—#529—French—mid-1950s vintage full-length pose of Marilyn in a one-piece bathing suit with arms outstretched above her head.	$20–30
Editions P. I.—#674—French—early 50s vintage bust portrait of MM in sleeveless sweater.	$20–30
Editions P. I.—No number—French—Candid mid-50s shoulder shot of Marilyn in a cotton shirt with collar up.	$20–35

Value

Film Star Autograph Portrait Series—British—#98—early 50s portrait of Marilyn in a gold lamé strap dress, with a facsimile autograph at bottom of postcard. Published by L. D., Ltd. $20–30

Geburtstag—#54—Dutch-mid 50s bust portrait of Marilyn in gold lamé halter gown with mink wrap on one shoulder and a facsimile autograph in the corner that reads, "Best Always, Marilyn Monore." $20–30

Greetings—British—Featuring Marilyn in a low-cut gown with a pearl-beaded halter and pearl-drop earrings. $30–40

Mexican—No number—early 50s bust portrait of Marilyn with her hand to her chin and a big smile. $20–30

Mexican—#58—early 50s bust portrait of Marilyn, bare shouldered, with long black gloves and a rhinestone bracelet. $20–30

Mexican—#68—early 50s waist shot of Marilyn in a gold lamé gown with "Marilyn" printed on the front. $20–30

Niagara Promo Postcard—Possibly British—Shows Marilyn in front of Niagara Falls and has her facsimile autograph. The card reads, "Greetings From Niagara, Love Marilyn Monroe." $25–35

Personality Posters—#25—01—U.S.—5 × 8"—1960s or early 70s vintage. Large heavy cardboard postcard of Marilyn wearing a white blouse and standing in a doorway. $20–30

Picturegoer Series—British—#D—154—Shows Marilyn in a circa 1950 bust portrait holding roses. $20–30

Picturegoer Series—British—#D333—early 50s bust portrait in a gold lamé dress. $20–30

Rotalfoto—#662—Shows Marilyn seated in a black thin-strap gown. $30–35

Souvenir Postcard of the National Postmasters Convention held Oct. 12–16, 1947 at Los Angeles, California. Marilyn is one of four people on the card. Exceedingly rare. $100–200

Soveranas—#344—Spain—Shows Marilyn in a publicity photo for *The Seven-Year Itch*. $25–35

Soveranas—#321—Spain—Shows Marilyn in an early 1950s publicity pose. $25–35

Soveranas —#440—Spain—Shows Marilyn in a publicity pose for *Niagara*. $25–35

Picture postcards
for promotion of
Some Like It Hot,
1959

	Value
Turismofoto—#40—Italy—A close-up pic of Marilyn with her chin resting on her hand; a slightly larger 4 × 6" card.	$35–45
United Artists—1959—Set of twelve 3½ × 5" postcards in an envelope released for publicity purposes to promote *Some Like It Hot;* envelope reads, "Hot! Twelve beautiful picture postcards." Colors on envelope are in black, white, and red.	$100–200

Color

	Value
Andy Warhol—circa 1980s–90's—Set of eight cards reproducing different Warhol silkscreened versions of the familiar head shot from *Niagara*. Five cards with single images in vivid pop-art colors, and three cards featuring two and four reverse images. Published by Nouvelle Images	$6–8
Archivo Bermejo—Spain—#8—shows Marilyn in a publicity pose for *The Seven-Year Itch*.	$25–35
Archivo Bermejo—Spain—Shows Marilyn in a publicity pose for *River of No Return*.	$25–35

Value

CK-10—Germany—Shows a bust shot of Marilyn in a green blouse underneath a tree looking up at the sky. $25–35

CK-73—British—A waist shot of Marilyn in a gold lamé dress with her hands behind her. Published by D. Constance Ltd. $40–50

Classico—1980s–90s—Set of five color postcards featuring French posters for *The Seven-Year Itch*, *Niagara*, *Gentlemen Prefer Blondes*, and *Bus Stop*, plus the American poster for *The Seven-Year Itch*. $5–8

Editions P. I.—France—Shoulder shot of Marilyn in a black halter gown with a white collar and a red background. $30–35

ISV-A89—Germany—Features a color bust shot of Marilyn in a gold lamé gown. $35–45

ISV-IV/6—Germany—Full-length shot of Marilyn in a yellow one-piece bathing suit, leaning on an up-turned iron table, with one hand behind her head. $20–30

ISV-IV/6—Germany—As above, only MM is standing, and the background is blue. Marilyn has one hand on her hip and the other behind her head. $20–30

ISV-A10—Germany—Shows a waist shot of Marilyn in a gold lamé gown viewed from the side. The back of the card advertises "How to Marry a Millionaire." $25–35

Lusterchrome—U.S.A.—L.38—Shows Marilyn in a blue-and-white-striped bikini kneeling down with her hands on her knees; background of the card is red, and the photo is captioned "Beautiful Eyeful." $20–30

Lusterchrome—U.S.A.—L.39—Shows Marilyn lying down on her side in a two-piece yellow bikini with white tie strings; background of the card is red, and the photo is captioned "Thinking of You." $20–30

Lusterchrome—U.S.A.—L.40—Shows Marilyn in a blue-and-white-striped bikini sitting on the beach in a pair of wedge shoes. $20–30

Lusterchrome—U.S.A.—JL.13—Jumbo 6 × 9" card of Marilyn with the same pose as card L-38, above entitled "A Beautiful Eyeful." $25–35

Lusterchrome—U.S.A.—JL.14—Jumbo 6 ×9" card of Marilyn with the same pose as card L-39, above entitled "Thinking Of You." $25–35

Value

Lusterchrome—U.S.A.—JL.15—Jumbo 6 × 9" card of
Marilyn entitled "The Charmer," with the same
outfit as the one Marilyn is wearing on card L-38
above, only Marilyn is sitting on the beach and
wearing wedge shoes. $25–35

Lusterchrome—U.S.A.—L.38—REPRO of the above
card on Marilyn (L-38). $5–10

Lusterchrome—U.S.A.—L.40—REPRO of the above
card on Marilyn (L-40). $5–10

Mexico—#23—Shows a full-length shot of Marilyn in
a potato sack dress and Lucite pumps leaning on a
white pillar. $35–45

Quality Postcards of San Francisco—circa 1980s–90s-
Six different color cards, numbered #360, #365,
#367, #374, #953, and #954, showing Marilyn in a va-
riety of poses (the set). $6–8

Rotolfoto #36—Italy—Beautiful bust shot of Marilyn
in a pink dress, gold ring earrings, looking down
with her hand up to her head. A publicity pose for
Niagara. $25–35

Rotolfoto #109—Italy—Shows Marilyn in a publicity
photo for *How to Marry a Millionaire*. $25–35

Sam Shaw—Circa 1993; Uncut sheet of Marilyn postcards measuring 27 × 41". $80–100

20th Century Fox—U.S.—Beautiful shot of Marilyn
standing in white shorts next to a railing with a facsimile autograph on the front. This card was sent
to fans who had written in to request Marilyn's autograph, with a list of charges for an additional
photo given on the back. $35–45

#67—Unknown country—Possibly Holland or En-
gland—Nice color shoulder pose of Marilyn in a
white fur wrap. $25–35

MUTOSCOPE (ARCADE) CARDS

Value

Marilyn Mustoscope Card—3¼ × 5¼" with a black-
and-white image of Marilyn in a one-piece bathing
suit with a large polka-dot scarf blowing in the
wind. $25–35

**Mutoscope card
of an early Mari-
lyn, late 1940s**

	Value
Marilyn Mutoscope Card—3¼ × 5¼" with a black-and-white image of Marilyn in a one-piece bathing suit and wearing fur mittens, hands on her hips, and Eskimo-type fur boots on. Card is tinted purple.	$25–35
Marilyn Mutoscope Card—3¼ × 5¼" with a color-tinted image of Marilyn in a red showgirl outfit (circa 1954) and sitting on the edge of a table.	$25–35
Marilyn Mutoscope Card by artist Earl Moran—Late 1940s artwork of Marilyn seated on an ottoman with a caption that reads, "Now, this is just between you and me." Card is in color.	$35–45
Marilyn Mutoscope Card by artist Earl Moran—Late 1940s artwork of Marilyn seated and hand raised in a toast with a wineglass with a caption that reads, "The doctor said I needed glasses." Card is in color.	$35–45

Greeting Cards

	Value
Marilyn Greeting Card—5 × 7¼"—U.S.—Shows Marilyn in a full-length pose wearing a negligee with a caption that reads, "Marilyn Monroe, Star of 20th Century Fox Productions."	$25–35
Marilyn Greeting Card—6 × 8¼"—U.S.—Shows Marilyn in a waist shot and wearing a black strapless gown, long black gloves, and with her hand up to her cheek. Caption at bottom reads, "Marilyn Monroe—20th Century Fox."	$25–35
Marilyn Greeting Card—7 × 9¼"—U.S.-Shows Marilyn in a full-length pose, seated, wearing a negligee, with one hand on her thigh and the other on her midrif. Similar caption at bottom to those just above.	$25–35
Ambassador Greeting Cards of Marilyn; circa 1995; set of five; four in color and one in black and white; 5 × 7"; labeled for the occasion of "Birthday," "Love," "Goodbye," "Inspirational," and blank (for a personalized note); the set	$10–12

Cigarette, Gum, and Assorted Cards

	Value
Italian Cigarette Card—#95—1½ × 2"—Shows a color image of Marilyn from *How to Marry a Millionaire* in a single-strap dress. Printed on the back is "Marylin Monroe."	$35–45
British Cigarette Card—Cinema & Television Stars #24—Barbers Teas (1953)—1¼ × 2¾"—Has a color pic of Marilyn on it.	$20–30
Marilyn Gum Card—British—2½ × 4"—Has color artwork of Marilyn and is number 15 in a series. Has her name at the bottom of the card and mentions *The Seven-Year Itch*.	$35–45
Australian Licorice Card—Film Stars #23—1½ × 2½"—Circa 1957 with a color pic of Marilyn.	$35–45
Australian Weeties Vita—Brits Crispies Card—Popular Film Stars #11—2¼ × 3¼"—Circa 1955 with a color pic of Marilyn.	$35–45

Value

Chocolate Card—Holland—Geburtstag 1. Juni—2¼ ×
3¾"—Heavy stock card. Has a color pic of Marilyn
from *Some Like It Hot* and is numbered 30. $35–45

Topps Flip Book Card—1950 Card # 2 out of a set;
shows MM and Groucho Marx in a scene that was
meant for the 1949 film *Love Happy* but was never
used in the film. MM is in a one-piece bathing
suit. Card measures 1¼ × 2" and has indents on
each side of one end where a rubber band could be
wrapped around after the entire set was completed
and the cards could then be flipped with your fin-
gers. Set is listed in guides as R-710-2. $50–100

RECORDS AND RELATED COLLECTIBLES

LP and EP Records

	Value

Con Plumas Marilyn Monroe
  Date: 1982
  Label: Liberty $40–60

Fabulous Marilyn/Reissue of *Deux Jolies Blondes*
  Date: Not available.
  Label: Classic Original Productions, Marquis Disque
  (LP)—1450–50103
  Personal appearances never before on LP $25–35

Gentlemen Prefer Blondes/Los Caballeros Las Prefieren Rubias
  Date: 1982
  Label: Belter serie La Musica en el Cine 2–90.014
  (Spain) $30–50

Gentlemen Prefer Blondes (Original Soundtrack—10")
  Date: 1953—Reissued in 1957
  Label: MGM Records—E208 (33 RPM)
  Songs: "Bye Bye Baby"; "A Little Girl from Little
  Rock"; "Diamonds Are a Girl's Best Friend";
  "When Love Goes Wrong," plus other musical selec-
  tions from the movie $60–75

Gentlemen Prefer Blondes/Til The Clouds Roll By—Compi-
  lation Album
  Date: 1957, Reissued in 1972
  Label: MGM 2353067
  Songs: "Bye Bye Baby"; "A Little Girl from Little
  Rock"; "Diamonds Are a Girl's Best Friend";
  "When Love Goes Wrong" $30–50

233

*Gentlemen Prefer
Blondes,* **EP,**
1953

Value

Goodbye, Primadonna
Date: 1982
Label: German Import, Ultra Phone, LC-0001
Includes a poster calendar $20–30
Goodbye, Primadonna
Date: 1980
Label: Ariston AR/LP 12382 (Italy)
Songs: Ten $25–35
Goodbye Yellow Brick Road
Date: 1973
The song "Candle in the Wind" is on this album. $20–30
Hear Them Again (Compilation Album)
Date: 1968
Label: Reader's Digest (RCA—A 10–Album
Collection)
Song: "You'd Be Surprised" $20–30
Hi-Fi Story #2 LP
Date: 1980s
Compilation featuring Johnny Guitar with color
cover of MM and a fold-out jacket with more pics $20–40
Hi-Fi Story #17 LP
Date: 1980s
Compilation not featuring MM songs, but MM is on
the cover in color pic and there's a fold-out jacket
with pics $20–40

Hi-Fi Story No.
2, Italian LP.
1980s

Value

Hollywood On the Air Presents: The Feminine Touch (Compilation Album)
Date: Not available.
Label: Star-Tone Records
Comedy skit featuring Marilyn, Edgar Bergen and
Charlie McCarthy $20–40
Hurray for Hollywood (Compilation Album)
Date: 1972
Label: RCA Victor LSA 3085—produced by Don
Schlitter
Vintage re-issue of original from 1930–1957; fifteen
other stars singing on album.
Song: "I'm Going to File My Claim" $20–40
Joe Droukes Shadowboxing
Date: 1984
Label: Southwind Productions by Buddah Records Inc. $20–40
La Fantastica (E Indimenticabile) Marilyn
Date: 1980
Label: Ri-Fi serie Penny Oro RPO/ST 72017 (Italy)
Songs: Nine $30–40
La Voce, Le Musiche Ei Films—Marilyn Monroe
Date: 1973
Label: Italian—TPL 1 7025—RCA Victor
Songs: "You'd Be Surprised"; "My Heart Belongs to
Daddy"; "Kiss"; "A Fine Romance"; "Heat Wave";
"After You Get What You Want You Don't Want It";
"Bye Bye Baby"; "River of No Return"; "Diamonds
Are a Girl's Best Friend"; "I'm Going to File My
Claim"; "She Acts Like a Woman Should"; "Lazy" $50–60

Let's Make Love,
**LP No. ACS
8327**

Value

Le Milliardaire
   Date: 1960
   Label: French Import, Phillips 6325–150 $40–50
Let's Make Love (Original Sound track)
   Date: 1960
   Label: Columbia-CL1527
   Songs: "My Heart Belongs to Daddy"; "Incurably
   Romantic"; "Let's Make Love"; "Specialization,"
   plus other musical numbers from the show $40–50
Let's Make Love (Original Sound track Collector Series)
   Date: 1973
   Label: ACS8327—Columbia (Also available on
   cassette)
   Songs: As above $25–35
L' Indimenticabile Marilyn Monroe
   Date: 1970
   Label: Movietone Records MTL 2603 (Italy)
   Songs: Nine $40–60
L' Intramontabile Mito Di Marilyn LP
   Date: 1983
   Label: RCA CL89167 Italy
   Songs: MM sings eleven from her sound tracks
   (Color cover of MM) $35–45
Marilyn
   Date: 1963
   Label: 20th Century Fox Records FXG 5000 GEMS
   Came with black-and-white ready-to-frame photo of
   MM. This album was released in conjunction with
   the film *Marilyn*, narrated by Rock Hudson and re-
   leased in 1963.

Marilyn by 20th Century Fox, LP No. FXG 5000

	Value
Songs: "Heat Wave"; "A Little Girl from Little Rock"; "One Silver Dollar"; "Diamonds Are a Girl's Best Friend"; "Lazy"; "When Love Goes Wrong"; "Bye Bye Baby"; "I'm Going to File My Claim"; "After You Get What You Want You Don't Want It"; "River of No Return"	$60–75

Marilyn Monroe
Date: 1973
Label: Japanese Import RA5640
Includes ten pages of photos and a double-page layout $40–60

Marilyn
Date: 1978
Label: German Import UAS 295601 $40–60

Marilyn Monroe
Date: 1962
Label: Ascot, United Artists ALS 16008
Songs: "I Wanna Be Loved by You"; "River of No Return"; "I'm Through with Love"; "Running Wild," plus other selections from Marilyn's movies $80–90

Marilyn Monroe
Date: 1988
Label: Ricordi serie Orizzonte ORL 8781 (Italy)
Songs: Seventeen $30–40

Marilyn Monroe Bravo
Date: 1973
Label: Made in Germany. 6370–201 $30–50

Marilyn Monroe Chante EP
Date: 1960 (France)

Value

Label: Philips Medium 432.812 be
  Songs: "My Heart Belongs to Daddy"; "Specializa-
  tion"; "Let's Make Love" $50–70
Marilyn Monroe—Diamonds Are a Girl's Best Friend
  Date: 1985
  Label: NCB Records (Denmark)
  Songs: "Heat Wave"; "Lazy"; "After You Get What
  You Want You Don't Want It"; "You'd Be Sur-
  prised"; "A Fine Romance"; "One Silver Dollar";
  "River of No Return"; "I'm Going to File My
  Claim"; "A Little Girl from Little Rock"; "When
  Love Goes Wrong"; "Diamonds Are a Girl's Best
  Friend"; "Bye Bye Baby" $30–50
Marilyn Monroe (From the original soundtrack of *Mari-
  lyn* the movie)
  Date: 1963
  Label: Great Britain Import, Pleasure MFP mono
  1176
  Five pics of MM on cover $80–95
Marilyn Monroe—Goodbye Primdonns
  Date: 1981
  Label: Ariston AR/LP/12382—Italy
  Contains poster calendar of MM $45–60
Marilyn Monroe—Goodbye Primadonna
  Date: Early 1980s
  Label: Telefunken 10174—Made in Mexico
  Songs: Titles all listed in Spanish $30–50
Marilyn Monroe: Greatest Hits
  Date: 1986
  Label: Neon Records (Belgium)
  Songs: "My Heart Belongs to Daddy"; "After You
  Get What You Want You Don't Want It"; "Dia-
  monds Are a Girl's Best Friend"; "One Silver Dol-
  lar"; "River of No Return"; "Heat Wave"; "I'm
  Going to File My Claim"; "When I Fall in Love";
  "Bye Bye Baby"; "Specialization" $35–50
Marilyn Monroe: Legends (For The First Time)
  Date: 1974
  Label: Legends 1000/1
  Includes numerous songs, film scenes, and appear-
  ances—twenty-three total; has color MM cover and
  a fold-out jacket $30–40

Value

Marilyn Monroe: Musica Per I Tuoi Sogni
   Date: 1982
   Label: Dischi Ricordi SRIC 1005—Ariston (Italian
   Import) Includes a sixteen-page booklet with a gate-
   fold sleeve $35–45
Marilyn Monroe—Never Before and Never Again
   Date: 1978
   Label: Stet Records DSI5005
   Songs: "Do It Again"; "Diamonds Are a Girl's Best
   Friend"; "Kiss"; "A Little Girl From Little Rock";
   "This Is a Fine Romance"; "Bye Bye Baby"; "You'd
   Be Surprised"; "A Little Girl from Little Rock-Re-
   prise"; "She Acts Like a Woman Should"; "When
   Love Goes Wrong"; "Heat Wave"; "Happy Birth-
   day, Mr. President" $35–45
Marilyn Monroe—Rare Recordings 1948–1962
   Date: 1979
   Label: Sandy Hook SH2013
   Includes numerous songs, film scenes, interviews,
   commercials, etc. $35–45
Marilyn Monroe
   Date: Not available

*Marilyn Monroe—
Never Before and
Never Again, LP,
1978*

MM—*Rare Recordings* by Sandy Hook, LP No. 2013, 1979

	Value
Recorded directly from *Gentlemen Prefer Blondes* Label: Italian Import	$30–45

Marilyn Monroe Sings Her Movie Hits
    Date: 1988
    Label: The Entertainers ENT LP 13052 (Italy)
    Songs: Sixteen
	$30–40

Marilyn Monroe Special (World Star Collection)
    Date: Not available.
    This is a double album with two full-page black-and-white photos inside.
	$30–45

Marilyn Monroe—The Best from Her Movies
    Date: 1986
    Label: Lotus Records of Italy
    Songs: "Bye Bye Baby"; "Diamonds Are a Girl's Best Friend"; "When Love Goes Wrong"; "A Fine Romance"; "She Acts Like a Woman Should"; "Specialization"; "When I Fall In Love"; "Heat Wave"; "River of No Return"; "Lazy"; "After You Get What You Want You Don't Want It"; "I'm Going To File My Claim"; "You'd Be Surprised"; "My Heart Belongs to Daddy"; "A Little Girl from Little Rock"; "Kiss"
	$35–45

Marilyn, Poo Poo Pa Doop
    Date: 1978
    Label: United Artists-EP
    Songs: "I Wanna Be Loved By You"; "Running Wild"; "I'm Through With Love"
	$30–40

More Original Soundtracks and Hit Music from Great Motion Picture Themes (Compilation Album)	

	Value

Date: 1961
Label: United Artists
Songs: "I Wanna Be Loved by You" $20–30
No Hay Edad Para El Recuerdo
Date: 1976
Label: RCA Victor AVS 4376 (Argentina)
Song: "I'm Gonna File My Claim" $25–35
Norma Jean
Date: 1979
Label: RCA
Includes a song sung by Sammi Smith, with nine
other songs included on the album $20–30
Portrait of Marilyn Monroe
Date: 1973
Label: Jamaican Import, United Artists FML-3
Songs: "I Wanna Be Loved by You"; "Runnin
Wild"; "I'm Through with Love" $30–50
RCA Promo Disc
Date: 1954
Label: RCA M-146-2 (78 RPM)
This was released for DJ use only and not sold to
the public.
Labels include pics of MM.
Songs: "I'm Gonna File My Claim"; "River of No Return" $100–175
RCA Promo Disc, as above
Date: 1954
Label: RCA (Swedish cut)
Has different pics on the label than the above $100–175
Recordando A Marilyn Monroe
Date: Not available.
Label: Diana LPD 201
Songs: All spelled in Spanish $20–40
Remember Marilyn
Date: 1972
Label: 20th Century Fox—T901 (Re-release of the
1963 album *Marilyn*)
Contains a 12-page photo book on Marilyn from the
Legend and the Truth photo exhibition; color cover
and foldout jacket $30–40
Remember Marilyn
Date: 1974
Label: Fontana 9286865 (Italy) $40–60

                                                              Value

Remember Marilyn
    Date: 1970s
    Label: Philips 637021 (Germany)
    Has color pic of MM on cover and came with a
    twelve-page booklet $40–60
Remember Marilyn Monroe
    Date: 1974
    Label: Japanese Import V2005
    Album opens to a full cover of Marilyn $50–70
Remember Marilyn
    Date: 1980
    Label: Made in Jamaica. RPL-6002
    Songs: Ten $50–70
Remember Marilyn (in a plastic cannister)
    Date: 1989
    Label: TVP Records 1022 SLX 02261 (Italy)
    Comes with album, button, T-shirt, ten photos (8 x
    10"), 3D photo, and twenty postcards $30–40
Some Like It Hot
    Date: 1978
    Label: Import from England. UAC 5097 $30–40
Some Like It Hot Cha Cha Cha
    Date: 1959
    Label: United Artists UA3029 (Yellow Background) $70–90

*Some Like It
Hot—Cha Cha
Cha* **LP, 1959**

Value

Some Like It Hot (Original Sound track)
  Date: 1959—Reissue, 1964
  Label: UA 4030 (Ascot)
  Songs: "Running Wild"; "Some Like It Hot";
  "I'm Through with Love"; "I Wanna Be Loved
  by You," plus other musical selections from the
  movie $40–80
Some Like It Hot
  Date: 1960
  Label: Philips P 08436 L (Italy)
  Songs: "Runnin Wild"; "I Wanna Be Loved By
  You"; "I'm Through with Love" $60–80
Some Like It Hot
  Date: 1975
  Label: UA-LA 272-G
  Songs: "Runnin Wild"; "I Wanna Be Loved By
  You"; "I'm Through with Love" $25–35
Star Fur Millionen
  Date: 1973
  Label: 20th Century Fox Phonogram 6370 201
  (Germany)
  Songs: Nine $60–80
Super Album: Selections from Original Soundtracks and
  Scores (Compilation Album)
  Date: 1963
  Label: ASCOT—United Artists
  Songs: "I Wanna Be Loved by You"; "I'm Through
  with Love"; "Running Wild" $20–30
The Edgar Bergen Show with Charlie McCarthy: With Spe-
  cial Guest Marilyn Monroe (Comedy Series #13)
  Date: 1974
  Label: Radiola MR 1034 (CBS Radio Broadcast) $25–35
The Marilyn Monroe Collection (20 Golden Greats)
  Date: 1984
  Label: Dejavu—DVLP 2001 Italian Import $30–40
The Marilyn Monroe Story
  Date: 1988
  Label: Five FM 14203 (Italy)
  Songs: Twenty-nine songs! $35–45
The Misfits (Limited Edition Collector's Series)
  Date: 1961
  Label: UAL A273-G $40–60

The Misfits
sound track, No.
UAS 5087, 1961

	Value
The Misfits (Original Sound track)	
Date: 1961	
Label: UAL 4087	$40–60
The Story of Marilyn Monroe	
Date: 1976	
Label: Ariston Oxford OX 3039 (Italy)	
Has color pic of MM on cover	$50–70
The Unforgettable Marilyn Monroe	
Date: 1967	
Label: Movietone Records (a division of 20th Century Fox Records)—S72016	
Marilyn sings songs from her sound tracks.	$50–70
The Very Best of Marilyn Monroe	
Date: Not available	
Label: Artisian Import FUN 9001	
Was also available on cassette	$30–50
The Voice, Songs and Films of Marilyn Monroe	
Date: 1976	
Label: RCA	
Contains a selection of songs from Marilyn's movies	$30–45

45 RPM Records

	Value
Elvis and Marilyn	
Date: 1978	
Label: PDS 8667	
Sung by Leon Russell	$10–15

Value

Goodbye Yellow Brick Road
   Date: 1973
   Song: "Candle in the Wind" by Elton John $10–15
Marilyn Monroe Sings
   Date: 1963
   Label: 20th Century Fox (Promotional for the film
   Marilyn)—Narrated by Rock Hudson—#311
   Songs: "One Silver Dollar"; "River of No Return" $40–50
Marilyn Monroe Sings
   Date: 1978
   Label: United Artists 36484 (England)
   Has fold-out picture sleeve.
   Songs: "I Wanna Be Loved by You"; "Running
   Wild"; "I'm Through With Love" $20–25
Marilyn Monroe Sings
   Date: 1982
   Label: Planeta P-181 (Spain)
   Has color picture sleeve.
   Songs: "I'm Gonna File My Claim"; "After You Get
   What You Want You Don't Want It" $20–25
Marilyn Monroe Sings—Some Like It Hot
   Date: 1959

**45 RPM record
from Spain by
Planeta**

Value

Label: UA 1005
Came in hardcover box with photo jacket
Songs: "Some Like It Hot"; "Running Wild"; "I'm
Through with Love"; "I Wanna Be Loved by You" $80–90
Marilyn Monroe Sings—Some Like It Hot (as above)
Date: 1959
Label: UA RE-T-1231 (England)
Has different cover from the U.S. edition $80–95
*Recorded from the Soundtrack of "Gentlemen Prefer
Blondes"*
Date: 1953
Label: MGM Records—X208 EP
Two-record set
Songs: "Bye Bye Baby" by Marilyn and "Bye Bye
Baby" by Jane Russell $60–80
Recorded from the Soundtrack of "River of No
Return"
Date: 1954
Label: RCA
Sold 75,000 copies in the first three weeks of
release.
Songs: "I'm Going to File My Claim"; "River of
No Return" $60–80
*The River of No Return (il fiume senza ritorno)/I'm Gonna
File My Claim (L'uomo che voglio)*
Date: 1954
Label: RCA 45N 0120 (Italy) $60–80
*Recorded Songs from "There's No Business Like Show
Business"*
Date: 1954
Label: RCA Records EP-EPA 593
Songs: "You'd Be Surprised"; "Heat Wave"; "Lazy";
"After You Get What You Want You Don't Want
It" $60–80
There's No Business Like Show Business (Follie Dell'Anno)
Date: 1954
Label: RCA A72V 0004 (Italy) $60–80
There's No Business Like Show Business (Follie Dell'Anno)
Date: 1954
Label: RCA EPA 593 (Italy) $60–80
Some Like It Hot
Date: 1983

	Value
Label: UA-Liberty serie Dance for ever n.26 2C 008-83377 (France)	$20–30
Some Like It Hot Chante	
Date: 1983	
French made	$15–20
Some Like It Hot—"I wanna be loved by you/I'm through with love"	
Date: 1959	
Label: London 45 HL 8862 (Italy)	$60–80
Sidney Skolsky Interviews Marilyn Monroe and Marilyn Sings	
Date: June 1954	
Label: Dell Publishing Company, Inc. MM-SS-1	
Songs: "I'm Gonna File My Claim" and "Diamonds Are a Girl's Best Friend"	$150–200

Picture Discs

	Value
Hurray for Hollywood	
Date: 1984	
Label: Astan PD 20106 (Germany)	
Marilyn sings one song.	$40–50
Marilyn Monroe—The Latest Blonde (Let's Make Love Soundtrack)	$40–50
Marilyn Monroe	
Date: Circa 1986	
Label: (stemra-PD 83003)—Made in Denmark.	
Features MM in a black-and-white nude pose on one side and a black-and-white pose from *Bus Stop* on the other side	$40–50
Marilyn Monroe	
Date: Circa 1980s	
Label: PD 83006	
Features MM in the nude pose and the fishnet stocking pose	$40–50
Marilyn Monroe	
Date: 1984	
Label: AR 30031	
Features MM in the nude pose and standing with an umbrella; features twelve songs	$40–50

Value

Marilyn Monroe—Rare Recordings
   Date: 1979
   Label: Sandy Hook—Limited Edition of 25,000
   MM featured in the nude pose $40–50

Marilyn Monroe/Runnin' Wild
   Date: 1985
   Label: AR 30038 (Denmark)
   Features MM in a black negligee and in nude pose; in-
   cludes an everlasting calendar; features ten songs $40–50

Some Like It Hot
   Date: 1979
   Label: UASP 30226A
   Features six small head shots of MM $35–45

The Legend Lives On
   Date: 1986
   Label: Sandy Hook Limited Edition—(83003-stemra-PD)
   Features MM in the gold lamé pose and white fur
   pose; made in Denmark; features ten songs $40–55

The Legend Lives On **picture disc by Sandy Hook, 1986**

Value

The Ten
  Date: Circa 1980s
  Label: PD50–005
  Features MM in an uncommon nude pose $35–45

Cassettes

Value

Ladies of Burlesque
  Date: 1979
  Label: Sandy Hook
  MM sings from *Ladies of the Chorus* $10–15
Let's Make Love (Original Sound track Collector's
  Series)
  Date: 1973
  Label: Columbia $15–20
Marilyn Monroe—Rare Recordings
  Date: 1979
  Label: Sandy Hook $10–15
1953—Do You Remember?
  Date: 1985
  Label: The Great American Gift Co., Inc., New Ro-
  chelle, N.Y.
  Features news of 1953 and says, "Startling new maga-
  zine begins publication featuring nude calendar
  photo of MM." $10–15
The Very Best of Marilyn Monroe
  Label: FUN 9001 Artisian Import $10–15

CDs

Value

Ladies of Burlesque
  Date: 1979
  Label: Sandy Hook—#19
  Songs from *Ladies of the Chorus* $15–30
Las Canciones Favoritas de Marilyn Monroe
  Date: Not available.
  Label: EMI 2187996782—made in Mexico $20–40

Value

Legends—Marilyn Monroe
   Date: 1994
   Label: Wise Pack LECD 067—made in England $15–20
Legends—Marilyn Monroe
   Date: 1995
   Label: Wise Pack—Vol. 2 LECD 130—made in
   England $15–20
Marilyn Monroe
   Date: Not available.
   Label: MEC 949029 arc records—made in Holland $15–20
Marilyn Monroe—Great American Legends Series
   Date: 1992
   Label: Delta Music, Inc. $15–20
Marilyn Monroe—16 Greatest Songs
   Date: 1990
   Label: 12012 $20–30
Marilyn Monroe—24 Great Songs
   Date: 1995
   Label: BXCL 284—made in Holland $20–40
Marilyn Monroe—Gold
   Date: 1993
   Label: Gold 034—made in Holland $15–20
Marilyn Monroe—Goodbye Primadonna
   Date: 1984
   Label: AZ 339372 $20–30
Marilyn Monroe—I Wanna Be Loved by You
   Date: 1986
   Label: Solid Gold CD SG 8602 $20–30
Marilyn Monroe—Never Before and Never Again
   Date: Not available
   Label: DRG CDXP 15005—made in Japan $25–35
Marilyn Monroe—The Complete Recordings
   Date: 1988
   Label: RARECD 06/07—made in Switzerland $20–30
Marilyn Monroe—The Legend Lives On
   Date: 1986
   Label: DARTS CD 180003 $20–30
Marilyn Monroe—Some Like It Hot
   Date: 1989
   Label: CDMX 101 DRG $20–30
Presenting Marilyn Monroe—The Essential Collection
   Date: Not available

	Value
Label: Wisepack lec dd 621—made in England.	
Two pack	$20–40
Showgirls—Yesterday Gold	
Date: 1989	
Label: YDG 2513—made in Belgium.	
Set of five CDs, one of which is MM; features	
twenty-one songs	$30–40
Super Stars—Marilyn Monroe	
Date: 1994	
Label: Super 027—made in Holland	$15–25
The Marilyn Monroe Collection	
Date: 1987	
Label: DVCD 2001-Dejavu—made in Switzerland	$20–30
The World of Marilyn Monroe—Heatwave	
Date: Not available	
Label: Trace 0401092	
Features ten songs	$10–20

CD-ROMs

	Value
Marilyn and André	
Date: 1995	
Publisher: Gazelle Technologies, Inc.	
Available for MAC or MPC; an interactive biography; contains 250 black-and-white and color photos, various film clips and narration.	
Original Price: $54.95	$55–60

8-Track Tapes

	Value
Remember Marilyn	
Date: 1972	
Label: TVP Records—8T-TVP-1022. By 20th Century Fox Records.	
Features ten songs	$20–30

8-track tape by Fox, 1972

FILMS ON LASER DISC

Value

All About Eve
  Date: 1987
  Label: Fox-1076-80
  138 min.—b/w $20–30
The Asphalt Jungle
  Date: 1987
  Label: Voyager CC1126L
  112 min.—b/w $20–30
Bus Stop
  Date: 1985
  Label: Fox 1031-80
  94 min.—color $20–30
Clash By Night
  Date: 1991
  Label: Image 8299TU
  105 min.—b/w $20–30
Gentlemen Prefer Blondes
  Date: 1988
  Label: Fox 1019-80
  92 min.—color $20–30
How to Marry a Millionaire
  Date: 1988
  Label: Fox 1023-80
  96 Min.—color $20–30

Value

How to Marry a Millionaire
Date: 1992
Label: Fox-1023-85
96 min.—color $20–30

Love Happy
Date: 1988
Label: Image 6234RE
85 min.—b/w $20–30

The Misfits
Date: 1988
Label: Fox
124 min.—b/w $20–30

The Misfits
Date: 1990
Label: MGM/UA ML101650
124 min.—b/w $20–30

Monkey Business
Date: 1988
Label: Fox 5140–80
97 min.—b/w $20–30

Niagara
Date: 1987
Label: Fox 5138-80
89 min.—color $20–30

Remembering Marilyn
Date: 1989
Label: Image 6526VE-Documentary
60 min.—color $20–30

River of No Return
Date: 1988
Label: Fox 5139-80
91 min.—color $20–30

Some Like It Hot
Date: 1988
Label: Fox 4577-80
121 min.—b/w $20–30

Some Like It Hot
Date: 1989
Label: MGM/UA 103848
121 min.—b/w $20–30

Some Like It Hot
Date: 1989

Value

Label: Voyager CC1180L
121 min.—b/w $20–30
Some Like It Hot
Date: 1992
Label: MGM—UA 102699
121 min.—b/w $20–30
Some Like It Hot
Date: 1992
Label: Voyager CC1180L
121 min.—b/w $20–30
There's No Business Like Show Business
Date: 1987
Label: Fox 1086-80
117 min.—color $20–30
The Prince and the Showgirl
Date: 1992
Label: Warner WB11154
117 min.—color $20–30
The Seven-Year Itch
Date: 1987
Label: Fox 1043-80
105 min.—color $20–30

Films on Videocassette

Value

Ladies of the Chorus
Date: 1992
Label: No. 51013—Columbia Tristar Home Video—
ISBN-0-8001-1278-4
61 min.—b/w $20–30
Love Happy
Date: 1988
Label: No. 2467—Republic Pictures Home Video—
ISBN-1-55526-025-X
85 min.—b/w $15–25
Marilyn and the Kennedys (Say Goodbye to the President)
Date: 1988
Label: American Video—No. 947—Nominated for a
British Academy Award
71 min.—color $15–25

	Value
Marilyn and the Kennedys (A 30 Year Cover-up unveiled at last!) Date: 1992 Label: Goodtimes Video—No. 7055 72 min.—color	$15–25
The Legend of Marilyn Monroe (Narrated by John Huston) Date: 1987 Label: Goodtimes Home Video Corp.—No. 5164-ISBN-1-55510–065–1 34 min.—b/w	$15–25
The Legend of Marilyn Monroe (Narrated by John Huston) Date: 1986 Label: Goodtimes Home Video Corp.—No. VGT 5164—MM in white fur shot on cover 34 min.—b/w	$15–25
The Marilyn Files (Based on Robert Slatzer's book) Date: 1991 Label: entertainment KVC—No. 11168—ISBN-0-8043-1168-4 55 min.—color	$15–25
The Prince and the Showgirl Date: 1987 Label: Warner Home Video, Inc.—No. 11154 117 min.—color	$15–25
There's No Business Like Show Business Date: 1991 Label: Fox Video, Inc.—No. 1086 117 min.—color	$15–25

CBS Fox Video Series:

	Value
Bus Stop Date: 1987 Label: 20th Century Fox—No. 1031 Please note that this particular movie was not licensed for release in the 1992 series of Fox MM movies, because of copyright problems with the writer's family, thus making this a very desirable item at present. This may change if the movie is rereleased. 94 min.—color	$75–125

1987 series of films on video by Fox

	Value
Gentlemen Prefer Blondes Date: 1987 Label: 20th Century Fox—No. 1019 92 min.—color	$25–35
How to Marry a Millionaire Date: 1987 Label: 20th Century Fox—No. 1023 96 min.—color	$25–35
Let's Make Love Date: 1987 Label: 20th Century Fox—No. 1141 118 min.—color	$25–35
Monkey Business Date: 1987 Label: 20th Century Fox—No. 5140 97 min.—b/w	$25–35
Niagara Date: 1987 Label: 20th Century Fox—No. 5138 89 min.—color	$25–35
River of No Return Date: 1987 Label: 20th Century Fox—No. 5139 91 min.—color	$25–35
Some Like It Hot Date: 1987 Label: 20th Century Fox—No. 4577 122 min.—b/w	$25–35

	Value
The Misfits Date: 1987 Label: 20th Century Fox—No. 4584 125 min.—b/w	$25–35
The Seven-Year Itch Date: 1987 Label: 20th Century Fox—No. 1043 105 min.—color	$25–35

Fox Video Series—1992:

	Value
As Young As You Feel Date: 1992 Label: 20th Century Fox—No. 1951—ISBN-0-7939-1951-7	$20–30
Don't Bother to Knock Date: 1992 Label: 20th Century Fox—No. 1231—ISBN-0-7939-1231-8 76 min.—b/w	$20–30
Gentlemen Prefer Blondes Date: 1992 Label: 20th Century Fox—No. 1019—ISBN-0-7939-1019-6 92 min.—color	$20–30
How to Marry a Millionaire Date: 1992	

1992 series of films on video by Fox

Value

Label: 20th Century Fox—No. 1023—ISBN-0-7939-
1023-4
96 min.—color $20–30
Let's Make It Legal
Date: 1992
Label: 20th Century Fox—No. 1950–ISBN-0-7939-
1950–9
79 min.—b/w $20–30
Let's Make Love
Date: 1992
Label: 20th Century Fox—No. 1141—ISBN-0-7939-
1141-9
118 min.—color $20–30
Love Nest
Date: 1992
Label: 20th Century Fox—No. 1957—ISBN-0-7939-
1957-6
84 min.—b/w $20–30
Monkey Business
Date: 1992
Label: 20th Century Fox—No. 5140–ISBN-0-7939-
5140–2
97 min.—b/w $20–30
Niagara
Date: 1992
Label: 20th Century Fox—No. 5138—ISBN-0-7939-
5138-0 $20–30
River of No Return
Date: 1992
Label: 20th Century Fox—No. 5139—ISBN-0-7939-
5139-9
91 min.—color $20–30
Something's Got to Give
Date: 1992
Label: 20th Century Fox—No. 1955
46 min.—color $20–30

Sound Cards

(All 33 rpm measuring about 5½" x 7½"):

	Value
"After You Get What You Want"—Featuring a photo from *Somethings Got to Give*; made in Denmark	$25–35
"Anyone Can See I Love You"—Heart-shaped with Marilyn's image on it; made in Denmark	$25–35
"Bye Bye Baby"—Photo of Marilyn by Milton Greene on card; made in Denmark	$25–35
"Diamonds Are a Girl's Best Friend"—Richard Avedon photo of Marilyn on card; made in Denmark	$25–35
"My Heart Belongs to Daddy"—Marilyn wearing a gold lamé dress on the card; made in Denmark	$25–35
"When I Fall in Love"—Milton Greene photo on the card; made in Denmark	$25–35

Super-8 Film Reels

	Value
Gentlemen Prefer Blondes—Boxed; shows selected scenes from the movie in color and with sound	$100–150
There's No Business Like Show Business; boxed	$100–150
The Seven-Year Itch; boxed	$100–150

My Heart Belongs to Daddy sound card, 1980s

8mm Black and White Movie

Value

The Story of Marilyn Monroe by Official Films; No. A-
  101; released shortly after Marilyn's death in 1962 $80–120

The Story of Mar-
ilyn Monroe, Of-
ficial Films,
8mm film, 1960s

SHEET MUSIC

While Marilyn Monroe was no Whitney Houston, she was by no means a bad singer. She had received training early on from a half dozen vocal coaches, most of whom were provided by the studios, and she performed at least one song in ten of the twenty-nine films she made from 1948–1961.

After her 1953 movie, *Gentlemen Prefer Blondes*, some skeptics doubted that it was indeed Marilyn who performed the songs in the film. Fox studio boss Darryl Zanuck promptly offered ten thousand dollars to the first person who could prove that Marilyn did not sing in her own voice in the film. Not a soul ever collected!

Marilyn had a rather soft and sensual singing voice, which matched her soft and sensual persona! In 1954, while on her honeymoon in Asia with second husband Joe DiMaggio, Marilyn sang to thousands of U.S. troops in Korea. During one of the shows, Marilyn forgot the words to a song. One of the GIs yelled out, "Don't sing and don't talk, just walk!" The crowd roared. Asked later how she held up in the freezing cold of Korea, she replied, "It was the highlight of my life. I swear I didn't feel a thing but good."

Other nonmovie-related Marilyn sheet music has been produced over the years and is very much sought after by collectors. The earliest of these pieces is the song "Marilyn," performed by Ray Anthony and Orchestra for Marilyn at a party thrown in her honor by Mr. Anthony at his poolside in Brentwood. Mickey Rooney played the drums, and even "Lassie" attended the party!

Many foreign countries produced sheet music simultaneous to, or within a year or two after, the U.S. releases of her movies. Quite often the foreign covers used entirely different images of Marilyn. These are equally as sought after by collectors.

As always, condition is a factor in determining the value of sheet music. The most common problems are the occasional pen or pencil signature on the cover by a previous owner. Another common occurrence is a rubber stamp stating the store's name and a selling price. Neither of these take a great deal away from the value, unless they are placed on Marilyn's image. More serious defects are punched holes near the spine from having been bound, significant tears, stains, and badly split or detached spines. These problems have a more drastic impact on the value of the sheet music.

Marilyn performed her very last songs on the evening of May 19, 1962 at Madison Square Garden. The occasion was a birthday party for President John F. Kennedy. The songs were "Happy Birthday" and "Thanks for the Memories."

Sheet Music Values
(Arranged in order of Movie Title/Year/Song/Value)

	Value
LADIES OF THE CHORUS (1948)	
"Anyone Can See I Love You"	$100–200
"Every Baby Needs a Da Da Daddy"	$100–200
A TICKET TO TOMAHAWK (1950)	
"Oh, What a Forward Young Man You Are"	$100–200
NIAGARA (1953)	
"Kiss"	$35–55

"Kiss," 1953
Australian sheet
music

Value

GENTLEMEN PREFER BLONDES (1953)

"We're Just Two Little Girls from Little Rock"	$35–55
"Bye Bye Baby"	$35–55
"Diamonds Are a Girl's Best Friend"	$35–55
"When Love Goes Wrong"	$35–55
"Ain't There Anyone Here for Love"	$35–55

Note: The last two have different cover graphics from the rest of the score.

RIVER OF NO RETURN (1954)

"River of No Return"	$35–55
"I'm Going to File My Claim"	$35–55
"One Silver Dollar"	$35–55
"Down in the Meadow"	$35–55

THERE'S NO BUSINESS LIKE SHOW BUSINESS (1954)

"If You Believe"	$35–45
"Let's Have Another Cup of Coffee"	$35–45
"After You Get What You Want You Don't Want It"	$35–45
"Heat Wave"	$35–45
"Lazy"	$35–45
"There's No Business Like Show Business"	$35–45
"A Man Chases a Girl"	$35–45

"The River of No Return," 1954 U.S. sheet music

	Value
"A Sailor's Not a Sailor"	$35–45
"When the Midnight Choo-Choo Leaves"	$35–45

Note: The above sheet music features a very small rendition of Marilyn on the cover and is generally worth less to collectors because of this.

THE SEVEN-YEAR ITCH (1955)
"The Girl Upstairs" $35–55

BUS STOP (1956)
"That Old Black Magic" $35–55
"The Bus Stop Song" $35–55

THE PRINCE AND THE SHOWGIRL (1957)
"I Found a Dream" $75–125

SOME LIKE IT HOT (1959)
"I'm Through with Love" $50–100
"I Wanna Be Loved by You" $50–100
"Runnin' Wild" $50–100

LET'S MAKE LOVE (1960)
"Let's Make Love" $35–45
"Incurably Romantic" $35–45
"Specialization" $35–45

"The Bus Stop Song," 1950s Australian sheet music

"I'm Thru' with
Love," 1959
British sheet
music

	Value
"Hey You with the Crazy Eyes"	$35–45
"My Heart Belongs to Daddy"	$40–50

Note: The last song has a different cover from the rest, thus the
higher price.

MISFITS (1961)

Theme Song	$25–35

Miscellaneous Marilyn Sheet Music

	Value
• "Goodbye Norma Jean" from the movie *Norma Jean Wants to Be a Movie Star*, starring Misty Rowe (1976)	$8-15
• "Mamba a La Marilyn Monroe" by Perez Prado (1954)	$25–45
• "Marilyn" by Ervin Drake and Jim Shirl (1952)	$75–125
• "Oh Baby Mine I Get So Lonely"—Sung by Bing Crosby and The Four Nights, this is the New Zealand release and has MM pictured prominently on the front of the score. (1954)	$60–80
• "Old Forgotten Lane"—Dedicated to Marilyn Monroe. Words by Mary Hale Woolsey. Music	

"Oh Baby Mine
I Get So
Lonely," 1954
sheet music
from New
Zealand

Value

by Neil Moret and George Date. MM's photo
on front. circa 1950 $75–125
• "The Rock and Roll Waltz" (1955)—British
  sheet music for a song Kay Starr sang with a
  photo cover of various performers, including
  MM, dancing onstage. $60–80
• "Sentimental Rhapsody"—From MM's film,
  How To Marry A Millionaire, featuring MM,
  Betty Grable, and Lauren Bacall on the cover—
  Italian (1950s) $80–100

Note: More modern pieces are generally worth five to ten dollars. The foreign releases are generally worth one-fourth more than
the U.S. releases.

STAMPS AND RELATED COLLECTIBLES

(Arranged Alphabetically by Country)

Value

Country: Antigua and Barbuda
  Date: May 11, 1987
  Description: Single stamp and the fourth stamp
  ever issued featuring Marilyn.
  Original Face Value: $9.00 $10–12

Country: Antigua and Barbuda
  Date: 1990
  Description: A single stamp that reads, "Marilyn
  Monroe 1926–1962."
  Original Face Value: $0.30 $8–10

Country: Burkina Faso (Africa)
  Date: 1994
  Description: Three single-stamp sheetlets featuring
  Marilyn on the insert and other stars on the sheet
  and an additional stamp/sheetlet all on Marilyn.
  Came as a set. $60–80

Country: Burkina Faso (Africa)
  Date: 1995
  Face Value: 3000F
  Description: Set of two silver and 23K gold foil
  stamps inserted into two sheets; one shows Dean
  Martin and space ships and the other shows Frank
  Sinatra, a rocket, three images of MM, and one of
  John F. Kennedy; each $15–20

Country: Burkina Faso (Africa)
  Date: September 1995
  Description: Shows MM leaning on an auto on the
  sheetlet and is titled, "Entertainment Series." $30–40

Value

Country: Burkina Faso (Africa)
  Date: 1995
  Face Value: 1500F
  Description: A single stamp inserted on a sheetlet
  featuring two images of MM and one of a train on
  the sheetlet and two images of Marilyn on the
  stamp; measures 4 7/8 × 3 3/4" $8–12
Country: Burkina Faso (Africa)
  Date: 1995
  Face Value: 750F
  Description: Set of two sheetlets featuring numer-
  ous stars with a single stamp insert featuring two
  artists' renditions of Marilyn; each measures 5 5/16
  × 3 11/16": each $8–12
Country: Batum
  Date: 1995
  Description: A sheetlet consisting of two stamps,
  one of Elvis and one of Marilyn, and another sheet-
  let featuring an additional two stamps of other stars.
  Value (two-stamp sheetlet) $8–10
  Value (four-stamp sheetlet) $10–15
Country: Congo Republic
  Date: 1971
  Description: Single stamp and the second ever is-
  sued on MM $40–50
Country: Dominica
  Date: December 1994
  Face Value: $0.90 (single) and $6.00 (sheet)
  Description: Nine-stamp sheetlet and two single-
  stamp sheetlets with the stamps inserted.
  Value (singles) $7–9
  Value (sheets) $12–15
Country: Fujeira
  Description: Sheet of twenty movie star postage
  stamps, each with color art of a star and a black-
  and-white scene from one of their films. Stars in-
  cluded are Marilyn Monroe, Jean Harlow, Jayne
  Mansfield, James Dean, Sharon Tate, Vivien Leigh,
  Clark Gable, Martine Carol (Lola Montes), Ru-
  dolph Valentino, etc. $20–30
Country: Fujaira
  Date: 1972

Value

Face Value: Range from 5–100 DM for each
stamp.
Description: Twenty-stamp sheet picturing different
movie stars, one of which is Marilyn. $15–20
Country: Gambia
  Date: 1992
  Face Value: D3
  Description: Nine-stamp sheetlet entitled "Famous
  Entertainers." Stamps read, "Marilyn Monroe"
  1926–1962 and measure 4 7/16 × 6 1/4" $9–12
Country: Gambia
  Date: 1995
  Face Value: D4 (single stamp within sheet) and
  D25 (each single-stamp sheetlet)
  Description: One nine-stamp sheetlet and two sin-
  gle stamps inserted on each of two different
  sheetlets.
  Value: (sheet of nine) $20–30
  Value: (each of two single sheets) $5–8
Country: Grenada
  Date: 1995
  Face Value: $0.75 each
  Description: Sheet of sixteen stamps with one large
  image of MM on the right side of the sheet, styled
  after the U.S. sheet of Marilyn stamps. Titled "Hol-
  lywood Legends." An edition of 50,000 Limited
  and Numbered $15–20
Country: Grenada
  Date: September 1995
  Face Value: $1.00 each
  Description: Marilyn is one of the stamps; also fea-
  tured are Tom Cruise, Charlie Chaplin, Shirley
  Temple, Spencer Tracy, Katharine Hepburn, John
  Wayne, and Marlon Brando; celebrates the 100th
  birthday of cinema $15–20
Country: Guyana
  Date: 1995
  Description: Nine-stamp sheet with a genuine sil-
  ver-foil-insert stamp of Elvis; sheet also pictures
  John Wayne, Marilyn Monroe, Ava Gardner, Hum-
  phrey Bogart, James Dean, Errol Flynn, and Rita
  Hayworth $16–20

Value

Country: Hungary
Date: 1994
Face Value: 19Ft
Description: Marilyn's image is featured among that
of two soccer players; Hungary salutes the U.S. $5–8

Country: Madagascar
Date: 1994
Face Value: 140 Fmg
Description: Sheet of six stamps, two of which are
Marilyn and entitled "Show Must Go On" $10–15

Country: Madagascar
Date: 1995
Face Value: 100,550,5000 Fmg (respectively)
Description: Set of three stamps celebrating the
69th anniversary of Madagascar; represents three of
Marilyn's films, *Niagara, Some Like It Hot,* and *Gen-
tlemen Prefer Blondes;* measures 5 7/8 wide × 3 1/4"
high; each $10–12

Country: Madagascar
Date: 1995
Face Value: 10000 Fmg
Description: Sheetlet with a single-stamp insert fea-
turing several artists' renditions of Marilyn; well
done; measures 3 × 4" $8–12

Country: Mali
Date: July 27, 1970
Description: First stamp of Marilyn ever to be issued! Celebrates the discovery of the motion picture machine by the Lamere Brothers; features
Marilyn, Jean Harlow, and the brothers on the
stamp $45–55

Country: Mali
Date: 1994
Face Value: 225F
Description: Single stamp inserted on a sheet; came
perforated or unperforated $15–20

Country: Mongolia
Date: 1995
Face Value: Graduate from 60 to 350 in Mongo-
lian currency on nine stamps.
Description: Sheet of nine color stamps entitled
Marilyn "Cinema"; great artwork and colors $15–20

Country: Mongolia
    Date: 1995
    Face Value: 300
    Description: A sheetlet with a single-stamp insert
    featuring artists' rendition of Marilyn on stamp
    from her film *Niagara* and Marilyn's nude image
    on the sheetlet with flames and Niagara Falls; mea-
    sures 5 11/16 × 4 1/2"; entitled "Marilyn Monroe
    dans 'Niagara' " $8–12
Country: Mongolia
    Date: 1995
    Face Value: 300
    Description: Sheetlet with a single-stamp insert fea-
    turing three artists' renditions of Marilyn and of a
    cruise ship; measures 5 5/16 × 3 1/2" $8–12
Country: Mongolia
    Date: 1995
    Face Value: 300
    Description: Sheetlet with a single-stamp insert;

Sheetlet with inset of Mongolian Marilyn stamps, 1995

Value

entitled "Marilyn Monroe 'Lifetime' "; features
three artists' renditions of Marilyn on the sheetlet
and one on the stamp; shows MM as a baby on the
sheetlet; measures 5 1/4 × 4 2/16" $8–12
Country: Marshall Islands
    Date: 1995
    Description: Sheet of twelve stamps $12–15
Country: Montserrat
    Date: 1995
    Face Value: $1.15
    Description: Sheet of nine stamps featuring various
    artists' renditions of Marilyn; each stamp says "100
    Years of Movies" and "Marilyn Monroe
    1926–1962"; measures 5 wide × 6 1/2" long $15–20
Country: Montserrat
    Date: 1995
    Face Value: $6
    Description: Sheet featuring an artist's rendition of
    MM and Elvis in embrace; entitled "100 Years of
    Movies" and gives birth and death dates for both
    of them; measures 4" wide × 5 3/16" high $15–20
Country: République Centrafricaine
    Date: 1995
    Face Value: 2000F
    Description: One stamp inserted on a sheet that fea-
    tures three images of Marilyn, one of John Ken-
    nedy and several space vehicles. $16–20
Country: République Centrafricaine
    Date: 1995
    Description: Single-stamp sheetlet featuring MM
    with the new Gyron car; measures 3 × 4" $6–10
Country: République Centrafricaine
    Date: 1997
    Description: Sheet of nine MM stamps, all
    different. $10–20
Country: São Tomé e Principe
    Date: January 12, 1994
    Face Value: Db10
    Description: Sheet of eight stamps featuring Elvis,
    Marilyn, Bette Davis, Humphrey Bogart, James
    Dean, John Lennon, and Audrey Hepburn. Titled
    "Happy Birthday Elvis." $16–20

Value

Country: São Tomé e Principe
  Date: January 12, 1994
  Description: Single stamp of MM inserted onto a
  sheetlet. $5–9
Country: São Tomé e Principe
  Date: January 12, 1994
  Face Value: Db 10
  Description: Sheet of nine stamps , all of MM with
  just so-so artistry; measures 4 15/16 × 7 5/16" $10–20
Country: St. Vincent
  Date: 1994
  Face Value: $1.00
  Description: Sheet of nine Marilyn stamps $10–15
Country: Tanzania
  Date: 1991
  Face Value: 500/-
  Description: Single stamp inserted on sheetlet mea-
  suring 3 × 4 1/4." $10–15
Country: Tanzania
  Date: 1992
  Face Value: 75/-
  Description: Nine stamp sheet measuring
  5 1/2 × 7" $8–12

Sheet of nine *St.*
Vincent **stamps,**
1994

	Value
Country: Touva	
Face Value: Many different.	
Description: One sheet of ten stamps with Marilyn's image occupying one and one half	$10–20
Country: Touva	
Date: 1995	
Face Value: 1800	
Description: Two different two-stamp sheetlets, each featuring one stamp of MM and one of other stars; Titled, "Hollywood Stars."	
Value (each sheetlet)	$5–10
Country: Touva	
Date: May 1996	
Description: Sheet of six MM stamps, plus one single stamp of MM	
Value (sheet)	$10–15
Value (single)	$5–7
Country: United States	
Date: June 1, 1995	
Face Value: $0.32	
Description: Single or sheet of twenty MM stamps	
Value (single)	32 cents
Value (sheet)	$7–9

Items Related to the U.S. Postage Stamp (1995 Releases)

	Value
Marilyn Stamp Program	$10–15
Marilyn Commemorative Panel with four stamps	$8–10
Marilyn Stamp Folio	$5–10
22nd Postal Guide with MM on the cover (paperback)	$12–15
Marilyn Stamp Pin with gold metal edging	$5–8
Marilyn Stamp Magnet	$5–8
Marilyn Stamp Key Chain	$5–8
Marilyn Stamp Money Clip	$9–12
Marilyn Stamp Paper Weight (on a marble base)	$12–15
Marilyn Stamp T-Shirt	$20–30
Marilyn Stamp Beach Towel	$20–30
Marilyn Stamp First Day Cover—Universal City Postmark	$2–5
Marilyn Stamp Poster—two styles	$50–90

	Value
Marilyn Stamp Placemat—MM stamp was one of several shown—displayed on counter at post office.	$25–40
Marilyn Stamp First Day of Issue Cancellation Cachet. Set of five standard-sized-envelopes with special artwork in color on silk. Produced by Colorano Co.	$25–35
Marilyn Stamp First Day of Issue Cancellation Cachet. Single standard envelope with special artwork in color on silk. Produced by Colorano Co.	$6–8
Marilyn Stamp First Day of Issue Cancellation Cachet. Single standard envelope with special artwork printed in sepia-tone by Washington Press.	$6–8

CALENDARS
AND ADVERTISING
COLLECTIBLES

Marilyn was destined to be a calendar girl. One of her very first modeling assignments was for pinup artist Earl Moran. Moran's work was very well known and was widely distributed in the 1940s and 50s. It was in 1947 that a young Marilyn posed for Moran in various stages of undress. Moran's renditions of Marilyn were featured not only on calendar tops but on other items such as advertising blotters, matchbook covers, and notepads. Moran's series of paintings entitled "Maid In Baltimore" command the highest prices. These feature Marilyn in a two-piece yellow bikini, in different poses. They were also done in a much larger format than the rest of the Moran calendars and were sold between 1947 and 1950. A selection of the original photos Moran took of Marilyn recently appeared in an article *Playboy* did on MM.

Another photographer by the name of Laszlo Willinger took many early modeling photos of Marilyn in the late 1940s that were later resurrected after Marilyn achieved superstar status in the 1950s. These became the tops for calendars primarily, and are printed in beautiful, clear color. All are of the cheesecake variety and were available on different-sized calendars. The photos were taken both in the studio and out on a sunny California beach. In some cases props were used, such as a giant Mexican sombrero, which Marilyn holds over her nude body.

The most famous of all the Marilyn calendars is, of course, the nude pose on red velvet, taken by photographer Tom Kelley in 1949. Kelley had offered Marilyn a "lift" a few years earlier after he discovered her next to her disabled car on a California street. He presented his business card to her at the time and said that he'd enjoy photographing her sometime. The year 1949 was not a lucrative one for Marilyn. Out of work and hungry, she needed the fifty dollars Kelley would pay her for posing nude. Marilyn did insist that Kelley's wife

276

be present for the session. A series of shots were taken against a red velvet backdrop, but only two ever have appeared on calendar tops. The most common of these is entitled *Golden Dreams* and the less common is entitled *A New Wrinkle*. Each pose is slightly different, but the *New Wrinkle* pose is the rarer of the two, and calendars that feature it are worth double those with *Golden Dreams* poses.

Mr. John Baumgarth of Chicago, Illinois, purchased the *Golden Dreams* pose for a mere five hundred dollars, and his calendar company went on to gross more than $1 million in sales with it. Remember, Marilyn was paid just fifty dollars! These calendars were both released in 1952, coinciding with Marilyn's rapid rise to stardom. When asked what she had on during the photo session, Marilyn coyly replied, "the radio." The *Golden Dreams* pose was later chosen as *Playboy*'s very first centerfold in their premiere issue of December 1953. The *Golden Dreams* pose continued to grace calendar tops through the 1950s, but dropped off dramatically thereafter, with a few reproductions made in the late sixties and early seventies. These reproductions were usually printed on a light cardboard, whereas the originals were printed on a heavy-stock paper but were still very pliable. Telltale signs that a calendar is old include rusty staples where the calendar pad is affixed, yellowed paper on the front and back of the calendar, and the name of the calendar company and the phrase "Litho—Made in U.S.A." In addition, the originals nearly always featured metal strips along the top and bottom borders of the calendar, with a loop built into the middle of the top metal strip for hanging purposes. The reproductions show the red velvet background as an orange-red versus the crimson-red found on authentic calendars.

Collectors generally favor calendars with the pad intact, beginning with January, and an advertisement for a store, gas station, etc., on its front somewhere. The old addresses and phone numbers used in these ads are also telltale signs of the age of the calendar. The last of the beautiful Marilyn advertising calendars were printed around 1960 and, with the exception of a few reproductions of the nude pose years later, have been replaced with our modern twelve-month calendars.

U.S. Calendars

Note: These are in order by year (oldest to newest).

Vintage Calendars

Value

1947–1949. Earl Moran did at least two different
   paintings of Marilyn in a two-piece yellow bathing

H. E. AYLSWORTH
818 Main Street - WARREN, RHODE ISLAND   Phone 6254
Replacement Parts — Accessories — Tires
American Hammered Piston Rings
KOPPERS COMPANY, INC.

KOPPERS

1949 Earl Moran's *Maid in Baltimore* calendar

Value

suit entitled *Maid In Baltimore*. There is some
question as to whether the '49 calendar is indeed
MM. These calendars advertise American Hammered Piston Rings. Values for each are the same.
Please note that Earl Moran did about a dozen
paintings entitled "Maid in Baltimore," but only
the '47 and '48 are MM. Dimensions are approximately 16 x 34".

$300–600

Late 1940s–Early 1950s. Earl Moran Handout Calendars. These small calendars feature various artists'
renditions of Marilyn that can be bent back to pro-
duce a 3D effect. These are printed on a heavy
cardboard and feature the calendar and advertisement on the bottom. A number of titles for the
paintings include *Little Miss Muffet, What Little
Girls Are Made Of, Don't Hope for the Best, Hop For*

Calendar from 1953, *A New Wrinkle*

	Value
It, Peter, Peter Pumpkin Eater, Rosie's Are Red . . . , etc. These generally measure 5 x 10".	$40–80
1952. A calendar entitled *Dame and Dane*, which features a young Norma Jean seated next to a Great Dane. Done in both a vertical and a horizontal cut, with the vertical showing more of Marilyn and the dog. Both valued the same. These generally measure 8 x 10" and 8 x 11" respectively.	$100–300

1952. Famous nude calendar of Marilyn entitled *Golden Dreams*. Features Marilyn lying on red velvet in a 1949 photo by Tom Kelley. A more scarce version with an alternate photo was also done and is entitled *A New Wrinkle*. Available in at least four different sizes between 1952 and 1959. Those not featuring Marilyn's name, but just the titles above, are worth about one-third more than those that feature her name. Those that feature the rarer *New Wrinkle* pose are worth double those featuring the *Golden Dreams* pose. Some of the calendars featuring the *Golden Dreams* pose featured a sheet of acetate with a lace nightie printed on it that could be lifted up to reveal Marilyn in her birthday suit below. These are basically worth the same price as the standard *Golden Dreams* and carry such a title as *Lure of Lace*. A number of the calendars simply came with the lace nightie printed right on the calendar itself. A few of the calendars came with an informational sheet bound in by the metal strip that ran along the top of the calendar. This informational sheet included a brief biographical sketch on Marilyn. Beware of reproductions.

Values (approximate sizes):

9 x 14"	$60–125
11 x 22 ½"	$100–200
16 x 34"	$200–300
Larger Sizes	$250–400

1952. RKO Studio handout calendar of Marilyn. Features Marilyn in a one-piece bathing suit to promote her new film *Clash By Night*. Duotone in color. Measures about 4 x 8". $50–100

1953-1956. Laszlo Willinger photographed Marilyn in the mid-1940s, and these photos were later resurrected after Marilyn's sudden rise to fame and were used as calendar tops beginning in 1953. All are of the cheesecake variety and are very colorful and clearly printed. All are very scarce. They usually feature a brief bio on Marilyn under the calendar pad (you must lift the pad up), and she is usually identified on the front of the calendar, just below her image. A few of the titles used were *Vivacious Marilyn* (which featured her in a two-piece yellow bathing suit) and *Friendly Smile* (which featured her in a striped two-piece bathing suit). There are also at least two different calendars featuring MM on the beach with windswept hair and wearing a two-piece striped bathing suit. Yet another features Marilyn holding a huge Mexican sombrero over her nude body, and another features MM seated in a Hawaiian grass skirt outfit.

Value (approximate sizes):

9 x 14"	$75–125
11 x 22 ½"	$150–250

Salesmen's sample calendar, *Vivacious Marilyn*, 1950s

	Value
16 x 34"	$300–500
Larger Sizes	$400–600

1952–1956? Marilyn is said to have appeared in a Pabst Blue Ribbon calendar in the early to mid-1950s. The photo was taken by Tom Kelley, the same man who photographed her in the nude. It is in full color, and it shows Marilyn holding a large beach ball above her head. It is believed that she is featured on one of the summer months of the calendar. $200–300

1954. *Studio Sketches* Pin-up Calendar by T. N. Thompson. Features Marilyn on the first two months.The first page is a painting of Marilyn by Thompson that features Marilyn in the *Golden Dreams* pose, but with a black negligee painted over strategic places. The second page features a painting of a young Marilyn in a white "cowgirl" outfit. The image was also featured on the envelope the calendar came in. She is dressed in a white cowboy hat, shorts, and boots and is topless. The calendar is spiral bound and measures about 8 x 10". $100–200

1955. A calendar that came in an envelope that featured a cutout circle that showed Marilyn's upper torso from the first page of the inside calendar.

Value

Featured four-page calendar with three months on
each page. The first page shows Marilyn in the famous *Golden Dreams* pose, but with a black negligee painted over strategic places. The next three
pages feature a young Marilyn in various "cowgirl"
poses entitled *Coming Out On Top, Caught Short*,
and *Southern Exposure*. Marilyn is topless in all of
them and has on white cowboy boots, white shorts,
and a white cowboy hat. It measures about 8 x 11". $100–200

1956. A calendar featuring the artwork of Ben Hur
Baz and showing Marilyn kneeling in a two-piece
bathing suit. A very nice rendition of Marilyn. Approximately 16 x 34". $150–200

1959. A calendar, consisting of seven pages, released
as a promotional item for Marilyn's 1959 film *Some
Like It Hot*. The calendar features several images of
Marilyn in black and white. The outside of
the calendar reads, "The New Marilyn Monroe Calendar—Very Hot For March!" It is colored in
black, red, and white. Approximatley 8 ½ x 11". $125–200

**1956 Salesmen's
sample calendar**

Value

1960. Pocket calendar made in Italy. Features Marilyn in full color on the front and was sold in a glassine envelope. Other stars are featured throughout. Measures about 2 x 3". $35–60

1961. A calendar featuring the artwork of Ben Hur Baz and showing Marilyn in an oversized yellow shirt, which is quite revealing. Approximately 16 x 34". $100–200

1974. Marilyn calendar produced in conjunction with Norman Mailer's biography on Marilyn. It is spiral bound and features eight color and four black and white portraits of the star. Was sold in a colorful envelope featuring a large Bert Stern photo of Marilyn's face. Measures about 8 ½ x 13". $25–40

1975. Poster-Calendar of Marilyn in black and gray tones with red lips. Released in conjunction with the movie *Goodbye Norma Jean,* starring Misty Rowe as Marilyn. Measures about 21 x 35". $25–35

Note: Quite a few vintage salesmen's sample calendars are on the market that feature the images described above. These date generally from 1952–1960. They are often blank on the top, bottom, or midsection where the advertisements would later go, and are either void of

1974 calendar by Norman Mailer

a calendar pad or have simply the month of January glued on as a single sheet. They are worth up to one quarter less than the price of the full calendars unless they are one of the scarcer releases.

Marilyn Monroe Calendars (1980–1998)

Beginning around 1983, many calendars have been printed on Marilyn in the modern square format and measuring about 12 x 12". Most are twelve-month calendars. These have been produced by such companies as Pomegranate, Portal, Landmark, and Hallmark. They feature a wide assortment of Marilyn portraits on each calendar. Some came spiral bound, and most were shrink-wrapped. An extensive listing of most of them follows.

Note: Calendars from 1980 through 1990 are worth twenty to thirty dollars each, and those from 1991 through 1998 are worth fifteen to twenty dollars each.

1980. Marilyn Monroe Calendar with fold-out double exposure and scenes from MM's movie *The Misfits*.

1981. Unfolds to 22 x 32"; has double-exposure nude on one side and the complete story of the making of *The Misfits* on the other side; with color pics.

1983. Marilyn Monroe Calendar with photography by Milton Greene. Beautiful b/w photos of MM.

1984. Marilyn Monroe Calendar—12 x 14" with photos by Milton H. Greene. Pomegranate.

1984. Marilyn Monroe Pin-up Calendar—Compiled by James Spada with color and b/w photos. Harmony Books.

1986. Marilyn Monroe Calendar. By Landmark.

1987. Marilyn 25th Anniversary Calendar. Commemorative edition by Landmark. Ken Galente Collection.

1988. Marilyn Monroe Calendar by Portal. No. 895.

1988. Marilyn Monroe Twentieth Century Fox Calendar by Design Look, Inc. Has fold-out poster, organizer, and planner.

1988. Marilyn Monroe Calendar by Landmark.

1989. Marilyn Monroe Calendar by Landmark.

1989. Marilyn Monroe Calendar by Portal.

1989. Marilyn Monroe Calendar by Portal with same cover as the 1989 Landmark calendar.

1989. Marilyn Monroe Calendar by Joseph Jasgur. Design Look, Inc. Early pics of Norma Jean; 16-month calendar.

1990. Marilyn Monroe Calendar by Landmark.

1990. Marilyn Monroe Calendar by Portal.

**1993 12-month
Hallmark
calendar**

1990. Marilyn Monroe Calendar by Joseph Jasgur. Design Look, Inc. Has early Norma Jean pics.

1990. Marilyn Monroe Calendar by Pomegranate with b/w pics.

1990. Marilyn Monroe Engagement Calendar by Landmark; 52-week spiral bound. Each week has new b/w portrait. 7 x 9".

1990. Andy Warhol Engagement Calendar with painting of Marilyn on the cover.

1991. Marilyn Monroe Calendar by Portal.

1991. Marilyn Monroe Calendar by New Seasons Publishing.

1991. Marilyn Monroe Calendar by Greystone.

1991. Marilyn Monroe Calendar by Landmark General.

1992. Marilyn Monroe Calendar by Portal.

1992. Marilyn Monroe Calendar by New Seasons Publishing.

1992. Marilyn Monroe Calendar by Bernard of Hollywood. Landmark.

1992. Marilyn Monroe Calendar by Pomegranate.

1992. Marilyn Monroe Calendar—*Playboy*'s Marilyn; 16-month calendar by Day Dream Calendars, Inc.

1993. Marilyn Monroe *Bernard of Hollywood* Calendar by Landmark.

1993. Marilyn Monroe Calendar by Portal; 16-month calendar.

1993. Marilyn Monroe Calendar by Hallmark. Different cover than the one below.

1993. Marilyn Monroe Calendar by Hallmark. Spiral bound.

1993. Marilyn Monroe Calendar by Neues Publishing.

1994. Marilyn Monroe Calendar by Portal; 16-month calendar.

1994. Marilyn Monroe Calendar by Hallmark.

1994. Marilyn Monroe Calendar by Bernard of Hollywood.

1994. Marilyn Monroe Calendar by Landmark General Corp.

1994. Marilyn Monroe Quote-A-Day Calendar.

1994. Marilyn Monroe's Collector's Edition Calendar. Measures 15 x 15". By Avalanche Publications.

1995. Marilyn Monroe Calendar by Landmark.

1995. Marilyn Monroe Calendar by Avalanche. Has 12 b/w pics of Marilyn by André de Dienes. 12 x 12".

1996. Marilyn Monroe Pocket Calendar by Pomegranate. Photos by Sam Shaw.

Foreign Calendars (1983-1996)

	Value
1983—Marilyn Monroe Pocket Calendar with color gatefold. Italy.	$30–45
1980s—Marilyn Monroe Calendar—Il Mito—Italian two-year calendar.	$30–40
1987—Marilyn Monroe Calendar by Acorn of London, England.	$25–35
1987—Marilyn Monroe Calendar by Culture Shock of England.	$20–30
1987—Marilyn Monroe Calendar by Danilo of England.	$20–30
1988—Marilyn Monroe Calendar by Danilo Promotions of England. 12 x 16½". Color and b/w pics; spiral bound with laminated pages.	$30–40
1988. Marilyn Monroe Calendar by Atlanta Press of England.	$20–30
1989. Marilyn Monroe Calendar by Danilo of England.	$20–30
1989. Marilyn Monroe Calendar by Culture Shock of England.	$30–40
1989. Marilyn Monroe Big Big Poster Calendar by Culture Shock of England.	$30–40
1990. Marilyn Monroe Among Friends by Sam Shaw and Norm Rosten—Bloomsbury, England.	$20–35
1990. Marilyn Monroe Calendar by Athena.	$20–30
1990. Marilyn Monroe Calendar by Culture Shock of England. 12 x 16½"; spiral bound with lamenated pages.	$25–35
1991. Marilyn Monroe Calendar by Culture Shock of England.	$20–30
1991. Marilyn Monroe Calendar by Athena.	$15–20
1991. Marilyn Monroe Calendar by Danilo of England; spiral bound.	$25–30

	Value
1992. Marilyn Monroe Calendar by Archives Alive.	$20–25
1992. Marilyn Monroe Calendar by Culture Shock.	$20–25
1992. Marilyn Monroe Calendar by Coles of Canada.	$20–25
1992/93. Marilyn Monroe Calendar by *Gente* magazine of Italy. 8 x 11". Color pic for each month (Aug. 1992–July 1993).	$20–25
1993. Marilyn Pocket Calendar Set by Rua do salitre, 890 Algarve; has twelve calendars, each with a different photo of Marilyn.	$8–12
1995. Marilyn Monroe Calendar by Culture Shock of England.	$20–30
1995. Marilyn Monroe Calendar by Oliver Books of England.	$15–20

1989 12-month
calendar by
Portal

1992 12-month
calendar by
Coles

Value

1996. Marilyn Monroe Calendar by Scheurkalender of
  Holland; 365 pages! One for each day of the year! $30–35
1997. Marilyn Monroe Calendar by Danilo of
  England. $15–20

Advertising Posters

Value

1956 Color poster measuring 28 x 40"; advertising
  reads, "Pete Martin's candid report on 'The New
  Marilyn Monroe.'" On the bottom it reads, "The
  Saturday Evening Post." This is a poster advertising a three-part series in the *Post* on Marilyn. Pete
  Martin authored the second book published in
  America on Marilyn entitled *Will Acting Spoil Marilyn Monroe?* The photo of Marilyn is a rarely seen
  one and shows her lying on her side with her head
  being propped up with her left hand. She's wearing
  long black gloves and a beautiful red off-the-shoul-
  der dress. A stuning portrait of Marilyn that just
  oozes glamour. $300–500

Ink Blotters

All known examples of these were done by pinup artist Earl Moran. The first were produced in the late
1940s and show a young Marilyn in various poses

1993 16-month
calendar by
Portal

Value

in full color and with catchy phrases. These featured advertising for a company on one end and the artwork of Marilyn on the other. There were at least two sizes made and they were 3½ x 5" and 4 x 9". Some of the phrases used were, "Some People Like Boats", "What You Don't Owe Won't Hurt You"; "Worry Is the Interest Paid by Those Who Borrow Trouble"; "Things Don't Turn Up Unless You Turn Them Up"; "Little Miss Muffet"; "Baa, Baa, Black Sheep"; "Peter, Peter, Pumkin Eater"; "Old Mother Hubbard"; "Little Boy Blue"; "Rosie's Are Red"; "Now This Is Just Between You And Me"; "Don't Hope for the Best, Hop for It"; and "What Little Girls Are Made Of."

Sizes:

3½ x 6"	$25–35
4 x 9"	$35–45

Product Advertisements

Marilyn began modeling for her first product advertisements in 1946 and appeared on the pages of numerous magazines in the U.S. and in foreign countries. These advertisements are coveted by today's Marilyn collectors. By about 1954, Marilyn had ceased to appear in any product ads. Below is a list of ads that she appeared in, along with their approximate values.

Value

Album Color Prints for Tri-Color Prints of Hollywood, CA (Color ad—1946)	$40–60
Argoflex Cameras (1940s)	$20–40
Arnold's of Hollywood (Modeling the new "Star Suit"—1940s)	$20–40
City Club Shoes for Men (Color ad—1951)	$20–40
Close-Up Perfect Kiss-Tested Lipstick (Color ad)	$20–30
Douglas Airlines New DC-6 Airplane (Color ad—1946)	$35–55
Hilton Hair Coloring	$20–30
Hinds Hand Cream	$20–30
Jantzen Swimwear Catalog, 1947	$75–150

1940s ad for Argoflex Cameras

Kyron Way Diet Pills	$20–40
Louis Creative Hairdressers	$20–40
Lustre-Creme Shampoo (Color ad—1950s)	$20–40
Max Factor Cosmetics (1950s)	$20–40

1954 Westmore Tru-Glo Make-Up ad

**1951 "Rayve"
shampoo ad**

Maxell Tapes	$20–40
Nesbitt's California Orange Drink (Color ad—1940s)	$35–65
Rayve Shampoo (1951)	$20–35
Roi-Tan Cigars	$20–40
So-Rite Fall Fashions Catalog (1949—Color pic on cover)	$400–600
Tar-Tan Suntan Lotion	$20–30
Tru-Glo Make-Up by Westmore Cosmetics (Color ad—1952 and 1954)	$20–40

MISCELLANEOUS COLLECTIBLES

(Arranged in alphabetical order)

	Value
Act Now Products—Various products featuring André de Dienes' photos of Marilyn on them; 1995; labeled "The Lost Photos of Marilyn"; consisting of the following items:	
Key Chain	$2–3
Mirror	$2–3
Magnet	$2–3
Button (2½")	$2–3
Button Covers (Set of four)	$2–3
Address Book—Andy Warhol photos on front and back by te Nues Publishing; Item #8083; ISBN-3-82-38-8083-7	$3–5
Ballpoint Pen—Shaped like a match; 1970s; 4"; plastic; head removes to reveal pen; has Marilyn's face etched on it and it says, "Marilyn Monroe Likes It Hot."	$8–12
Balsa Wood Boxes—Three oval boxes with artists' rendering of Marilyn on the top; all glamour shots; each	$15–20
Beach Towels—Each depicting Marilyn in a gold lamé gown, the famous blowing white skirt and in a black gown; each	$30–40
Book Mark—Color painting of MM in a caricature fashion, showing her in the white blowing dress from *The Seven-Year Itch*; glossy surface to paper.	$2–4

Bridge and Canasta Set—1950s; boxed set of two decks of playing cards; one of the *Golden Dreams* pose and one of the *New Wrinkle* pose; includes four metal coasters showing two each of the above poses; came in either a cardboard or a velvet-covered box.

1950s bridge and canasta set

	Value
Cardboard Set	$75–150
Velvet Set	$100–200

Car Deodorizer—1955; 3 x 4"; hanging color car deodorizer sealed in cellophane showing Marilyn in the famous *Golden Dreams* pose with black lace overlay; says, "Hang Glamorette Pamela Wherever A Fragrance Is Desired"; produced by Presto Products Co., Detroit. $30–40

Cedar Box—Approximately 8 x 10"; 1950s–60s; features the famous nude *Golden Dreams* pose of Marilyn laminated to the top of the box; came with a lock and key. $50–75

Ceramic Tiles—1990s; two 7⅞ x 7⅞" tiles; one b/w showing the famous white blowing skirt scene and one in color showing Marilyn in a black negligee; each $15–25

Cigarette Lighters—1992; set of several lighters, each with a photo in b/w of André de Dienes's photos of Marilyn; produced by Weston Editions, Ltd., and labeled DJeep disposable lighters; entitled, "The Lost Photos of Marilyn"; each $5–10

**1955 car
deodorizer**

	Value
Cigarette Lighter—A chrome "Zippo" lighter with the famous pose of MM that Warhol later made famous showing MM in a black halter dress with a white collar; photo is beneath the classic glass dome; vintage unknown (circa 1990s); packaging says, "Zippo-U.S.A.-Lighter-Lifetime Guarantee."	$50–80
Coasters—Set of four; 1991; made by Clay Art; style 1621; feature color glamour shots of Marilyn on each.	$10–15
Coasters—Original 1950s; 4"; metal coasters of Marilyn in the *Golden Dreams* and *New Wrinkle* pose; each	$20–30
Coat Hanger—Full-color face shot of Marilyn mounted on a coat hanger; circa 1980s	$8–10
Cologne Spray—Marilyn concentrated cologne spray; 1983; 3.3 oz. bottle; packaged in a decorative box showing a color photo of Marilyn; made in U.S.A.	$15–20
Color Tinted Portrait—1950s; 5 x 7"; circa 1949 photo of Marilyn that was sold in five & dime stores in a picture frame; bottom has Marilyn's name and "Printed in U.S.A."	$25–35

Assortment of DJEEP lighters, 1992

	Value
Datebook—1974; features many color and b/w photos of Marilyn with commentary by Norman Mailer; printed on slick heavy paper and spiral bound.	$40–50
Datebook—1993 Marilyn Datebook by Cedco Publishing Co.	$15–20
Drawing Aid—1970s, though dated 1956; 8" long; female-shaped plastic drawing form; Marilyn's photo is on the envelope with the phrase "Whether the angle's acute, or the slope is so great, that you need a directional change, you will find what you want on the back or the front of Marilyn's beautiful frame."	$20–30
Earrings—Pair of earrings by Vitreous Co. showing a head shot of Marilyn	$20–30

Ed Weston Fine Art of Northridge, CA; 1992; various items produced for a *Some Like It Hot* New Year's Eve bash at the Riviera Hotel & Casino in Las Vegas on December 31, 1992:

- Pin; 2½"; numbered; limited edition of 5,000; features a b/w photo of MM. — $5–10
- Brochure; 4½ x 11" folded; 8 pages; has 54 photos of MM inside; photos issued in Limited Edition of 99 at $250.00 for a 5 x 7" and $3,000.00 for an 8 x 10"; photos by George Barris, Bert Stern, Laszlo Willinger, and others. — $10–20

Assorted Clay Art and Italian coasters, 1980s

	Value
• Single photo; Limited Edition 7 x 10" photo of MM; only 2,500 made.	$20–30
Emerson Junior High Graduating Class Photo—taken in June 1941; approximately 8 x 25"; showing entire class in front of school in a panoramic view; has a glossy finish.	$1,000–2,000
Exhibition Catalog—Homage to Marilyn Monroe at Sydney Janis Gallery in NYC, December 6–30, 1967; has an MM photo on the cover; features works by Stern, Avedon, Warhol, Rosenquist, Segal, Rotella, Dali, de Kooning, Marisol, and others on the inside.	$30–45
Exhibition Catalog—Marilyn, "The Legend and the Truth"; a photographic retrospective; 10½ x 10½"; softcover with silver cover; small b/w photo of MM; 16 pages with b/w and color pics from the exhibit and a list of photographers.	$80–100
Frame Up!; 1990s; cardboard picture frame that came in two styles with Marilyn's photo in one and two photos in the other. Had easels on the back; 7 x 8" and 7 x 9"; each	$5–10
Gift Bags—Numerous gift bags have been produced in the 1980s and 90s with Marilyn's image on them.	

Value

Some are made just the right size to hold a wine
bottle, and others came in mini to large sizes; each $5–10

Gift Cards—Pack of three cards to include with a gift
that say, "Especially for you" next to Marilyn's
image. $6–10

Gum Case—1989; plastic case with the white blowing
dress scene on it and a facsimile of Marilyn's signature; held gumballs; 3½" wide and 7" tall. $8–12

Halloween Mask—1950s latex mask of Marilyn Monroe; few remain. $50–100

Holograms—Marilyn by Hollywood Legends; 1992;
Harold Lloyd Collection; consists of four Marilyn
holograms in a set (boxed). $20–25

Invitations—Set of eight; 1984; made by Hallmark and
say, "Wanna Party?" $5–10

Jack in the Box—1990; Limited Edition of 10,000 by
Enesco Corp.; beautifully done in a decorative box
featuring pictures of Marilyn on its side; entitled,
"Stars of the Silver Screen"; porcelain. $150–200

Jeans—Marilyn Monroe Signature Jeans; circa 1996;
have tag attached with a color pic of MM in jeans,
along with a phone card featuring her photo on it. $40–50

Kaleidoscope—1988; by Applause, Inc.; says, "Kiss" and
shows many colored Marilyns; 8½" long; Taiwan. $5–10

Key—1970s; solid brass 2" diameter medallion with
the 20th Century Fox logo on one side and "Marilyn Monroe—Dressing Room #5" on the other;
attached to a small ring on a nylon wrist band. $30–50

Key Chain—1950s; 1½ x 2"; clear Lucite plastic with
b/w pics of Marilyn in the *Golden Dreams* pose on
one side and the *New Wrinkle* pose on the other;
has a bead link chain that opens and closes. $30–40

Key Chain-Circa 1970s large plastic key chain in the
shape of the white dress blowing scene; has *Some
Like It Hot* on it, and the face is left empty so you
can insert whatever photo you like. $5–10

Key Chain-Circa 1980s plastic case key chain with a
color photo of Marilyn lying on her side in a two-
piece yellow bathing suit like the one featured on
the earlier Lusterchrome postcard. $4–8

Key Chain—Circa 1996 key chain with two photos of
Marilyn on each side in plastic case. $4–8

Cardboard standee, 1980s

	Value
Korea Photos—Original photos taken by G.I.s while Marilyn performed for the troops in Korea 1954; various sizes with no negative available; each	$40–100
Lapel Pin—1953; small metal pin of Marilyn in a one-piece red bathing suit; dated on back.	$40–60
Lapel Pins—Ceramic hand-painted lapel pins of Marilyn; came with rhinestone earrings or necklace; each	$10–15
License Plate—Pink license plate depicting the 1984 Olympics held in Los Angeles; Marilyn's face and name are on the front.	$15–20

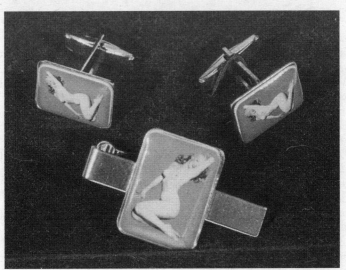

Cuff link and tie bar set, 1972

	Value
Lithograph—Earl MacPherson litho of Marilyn; 1990s; depicts a nude Marilyn standing and bending her left leg up.	$40–60
Lithograph—By Royal Orleans, entitled, *Gentlemen Prefer Blondes* and *Niagara*; circa 1990; 22 x 28"; Limited Edition of 500; signed and numbered by artist; came in museum-quality framing; these were mates to the plates done by Royal Orleans the same year in conjunction with 20th Century Fox; each	$75–150
Lithograph—By JUREK. Printed on litho is Fantazya-Provincetown, MA; 1985; Limited Edition of 500 made; came with a Certificate of Authenticity.	$100–200
Mannequin—Marilyn Mannequin by Dector Mannequin Co., Los Angeles, CA (now American Mannequin Co.); 1990s.	$1,000–1,200
Matchbook Covers—1950s; depict Marilyn art on the front with captions such as, "Look Here Pardner"; usually feature the artwork of Earl Moran (showing Marilyn in a two-piece yellow bathing suit) or T. N. Thompson (showing Marilyn in a white cowgirl outfit, topless); each	$20–30

Value

Metal Sign—Circa early 1990s; reproduces Marilyn's
Lustre Cream Ad in color; 12½ x 16½" $15–20

Metal Sign—1994; reproduces Marilyn's Tru-Glo
Makeup Ad in color; about 12½ x 16½" $15–20

Metal Tray—Circa 1980s/90s; 12 x 16½"; shows b/w
ballerina photo of Marilyn and is titled, "Marilyn
Forever"; made by Tropico of Paris. $10–15

Mirror—1950s advertising mirror with the nude *Golden
Dreams* pose in color on it; approximately 8 x 10". $60–100

Model Car—1993; white convertible (1955) with a red
interior by Solido "Signature Series"; Limited Edition; shows Marilyn's facsimile signature and image
on the car; came in two sizes. $40–80

Movie Script Reprints—Reprints of scripts from some
of Marilyn's bigger films, such as *Some Like It
Hot*. $20–30

Mug—12-oz. ceramic Marilyn mug; 1990; depicts col-
orized Andy Warhol images of Marilyn; made by
Clay Art; style #1620. $12–15

Mug—Late 70s/ early 80s art portrait mug with *Some
Like It Hot* written on reverse; made by Famous
Mugs of Nostalgia Lane. $15–25

Mug—Circa 1980s; entitled, "Marilyn The Cat," showing a white Persian cat with a blue dress styled
after the white dress in the famous skirt blowing
scene. $8–12

Notecards—Boxed set of ten notecards from France; 5
x 7"; early 1990s; features two cards each of five different Eve Arnold photos in color; cards are blank
and came with envelopes. $10–15

Notepad Cube—1990; 3 x 2¾" cube of paper. $2–5

Numismatic Marilyn Items:

- 1 troy oz. silver medallion; .999 FS; Limited Edition; shows Marilyn in the famous white blowing
dress on one side and the reverse says, "Marilyn
Monroe 1926–1962." $20–30

- 1 troy oz. silver coin; .999 FS; shows Marilyn in
the famous nude *Golden Dreams* pose on one side
and the number one on the other. $20–30

- 1 troy oz. silver coin; .999 FS; shows Marilyn in
the famous nude *Golden Dreams* pose on one side
and John F. Kennedy on the other. $20–30

Celebrity win-
dow waver, 1982

Value

- 1 troy oz. silver wafer; .999 FS; shows Marilyn in the famous nude *Golden Dreams* pose on one side and is blank on the other except for a decorative border. $20–30
- Silver Coin Set; 1971; by The Franklin Mint; Marilyn is one of ten coins in the set; each bears a legendary star's likeness; a star's image is on one side and his/her facsimile signature on the other; limited to 500 sets. $200–300
- 2 oz. Bronze Wafer; shows Marilyn in the famous *Golden Dreams* pose on one side and is completely blank on the other. Has the initials T. P. to the right of Marilyn's image. $15–25
- Aluminum Coin; 1985; shows Marilyn's face on one side and the words "Krewe of Jefferson" on the other; came in blue, gold, red, and silver; says, "Famous Americans—A Tribute to Marilyn Monroe 1926–1962." $5–10
- Aluminum Token; 1974; gold in color; shows Marilyn's face on one side and says, "Token of Youth—New Orleans Mardis Gras" on the other, as well as "Token of Youth." $8–12
- Aluminum Token; 1975; shows Marilyn in the famous *Golden Dreams* nude pose on the front with

Ornaments,
1990s

Value

"Marilyn" under it; on the back is a twelve-
month calendar. $8–10
- Tin Coin—Circa 1985; Marilyn's face and a small
  skirt-blowing scene on one side with the caption "Famous Americans—A Tribute to Marilyn Monroe." $8–10
- One Dollar Bill; features Marilyn's face on it. $5–6
- Ten Dollar Bill; features Marilyn's face on it. $10–15

Ornament—MM ornament by Carlton Cards; 1996; depicts Marilyn in a full-length glamour pose wearing
a white glitter gown. $18–20

Paper Mask—1983; postcard-sized mask of Marilyn's
face by artist Betty Levine; made by Intra Dynamics,
Inc., Santa Barbara, CA; original price was $0.85. $2–3

Peep Show TV Set—1970s/80s; 2" tall; color case
shows eight different views of Marilyn inside. $5–10

Peep Viewer—1970s/80s; you look in to see Marilyn in
the nude *Golden Dreams* pose; green case. $5–10

Pendulum Clock—Depicts Marilyn in the famous white
blowing-skirt scene; 1991; made by Kirch of NY;
plastic; Taiwan. $10–20

Perfume—1985; Marilyn Golden Musk; 1.7 oz.; in decorative box; made in U.S. $15–20

Phone Cards—Set of two by Gem International; 1995;
face value of $3.00 each; feature George Barris pho-
tos of Marilyn on them. $30–40

Pendulum wall clock, 1991

	Value
Phone Cards—1995; two sets of three phone cards by Worldlink; all have a $10 face value; feature various glamour shots of Marilyn along with her facsimile signature.	$40–50
Phone Card—1995; a single phone card by Worldlink; special issue for Cardex '95 convention held in the Netherlands; face value of $5; features a Richard Avedon photo.	$5–10
Phone Cards—Set of three Marilyn cards by Global Com 2000; Bernard of Hollywood photos on each; face value of $3 on two and $10 on one.	$40–50
Phone Cards—Set of four cards by Laser Radio; each has a different pic of MM; face values are $10, $12, $15, and $20; came with a Certificate of Authenticity for each and came in a three-ring binder with printing on it.	$50–80
Phone Card—One card by France Telecom Cable; card has a microchip on its front; shows a scene from *The Seven-Year Itch* with Tom Ewell and MM.	$20–30

Value

Phone Card—One card by Pacific Coin Co. of New
  Zealand; 1994; official telecom card; limited to
  5,500; face value of $20. $30–40

Phone Cards—Set of seven by George Barris; feature $20–40
  Barris photos of Marilyn on each; 1994; five have a   and
  face value of $10, one of $20, and one of $1,000 $1,000–
  (which is signed by Barris).   1,200

Phone Cards—Set of two by American National Phone
  Card Co.; circa 1996; one is a jumbo 5 × 7" size
  and is worth 20 units, and the other is a super-
  jumbo size of 8 × 10", is worth 50 units, and both
  feature artwork of Marilyn on them; prices for:
  Jumbo $30–40
  Super Jumbo $45–55

Phone Cards—Set of two Gem International WORLD
  '95 phone cards; produced for the International
  Phone cards Show in Singapore on December
  15–19, 1995; each feature a George Barris photo of
  Marilyn on them; one is worth 8 units and the
  other is worth 88 units; prices for:
  8 Unit $15–20
  88 Unit $35–40

Pin Back Buttons—Numerous examples have been produced over the years, some by fan clubs, others by
  individuals, and several by companies; size varies;
  all are generally worth each $2–12

Playing Cards—Circa 1976; two decks, one showing
  Marilyn in the *Golden Dreams* pose, and another in
  the *New Wrinkle* pose; these being reproductions of
  the two decks done in the 1950s; each $10–25

Pocketknife—1970s; features the nude *Golden Dreams*
  pose of Marilyn encased in hard plastic on the handle of this case knife. $5–10

Pocket Mirrors—Several 2 x 3" mirrors with photos of
  Marilyn or of her film posters were done in the
  1970s; some are dated on the edge and some not;
  though some are dated earlier, they were not made
  earlier; each $10–15

Pool Cue—1993; Marilyn Legend Cue by McDermott
  Cue Mfg. Co., Menominee Falls, WI; features color
  art of Marilyn and came with a choice of nylon, Irish
  linen, or a leather wrap; came in a soft black case with

Assortment of pin-back buttons

	Value
Marilyn's facsimile signature on it in blue; original price was $295.00; case was $34.00; for both	$300–350
Print Portfolios—1990; set of eight hand-colored prints of selected glamour shots of MM; 13 x 15"	$20–40
Print Portfolio—Set of six color images of Marilyn taken by her photographer friend Sam Shaw; 11 x 14"	$20–30

1972 deck of playing cards by NMMM

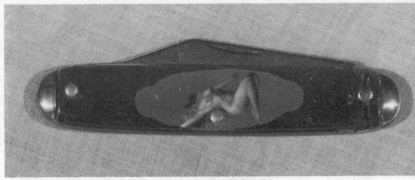

Pocketknife (circa 1972)

	Value

Print Portfolio—1990s; Bernard of Hollywood; set of three color prints by Marilyn's photographer friend Bruno Bernard; 10 x 12"; offered by Int'l Collectors Society, among others; came hand-stamped with a Certificate of Authenticity. — $100–200

Print Portfolio—1991; 16 x 20"; set of four prints by Earl Moran; actual photos from the 1940s; came in a cream-colored slipcase. — $80–100

Assorted pocket mirrors

1,000-piece puzzle, *Forever Ours*, 1986

	Value
Print Portfolio—1990s; set of five prints of Marilyn by George Barris; 11 x 14"; pics taken between June 1 and July 18, 1962; numbered	$125–150
Print—1990s; Earl Moran print entitled *Spanish Girl*; 19 x 24"; print 1; printed on 80 lb. archival acid-free paper; color; Numbered Limited Edition.	$80–120
Puzzle—Circa 1980s/90s; multicolored foam puzzle that you assemble into a standing figure in the famous blowing white skirt scene; 8" tall; from Gift Creations.	$12–15
Puzzle—1973; Playboy Marilyn puzzle; shows Marilyn in the famous nude pose.	$80–100
Puzzle—1972; Playboy Marilyn puzzle; shows Marilyn in the famous blowing white skirt pose.	$80–100
Puzzle—1973; features a Bert Stern photo as the puzzle.	$40–50
Puzzle—Circa 1997; *Memories of Marilyn*; 1,000 pieces; measures 20 x 27"; by Bernard of Hollywood; features a collage of photos.	$15–20
Puzzle Postcard—1970s/80s; British; Pat. No. 8410391; by Hall & Keane Design, Ltd.	$5–10
Puzzle—1967; Marilyn Star Puzzle by Alpsco; Cat. No. 82; by Adult Leisure Products Corp., Locust Valley, NY; a round puzzle in a metal film-type canister; 300 pieces.	$30–50
Puzzle—1986; *Forever Ours—Marilyn Monroe*; 1,000-piece jigsaw puzzle by Springbok; 24 x 30" assembled; shows many pastel-painted images of Marilyn; artwork by Steve Carter; No. PZL6115.	$25–35
Puzzle—250-piece jigsaw puzzle by Jigstars; came put together with collapsed box compressed inside and	

Value

shrinkwrapped; photo is a shot by Milton Greene of
MM in the ballerina outfit; made in England; Marilyn's facsimile signature on bottom right of puzzle. $20–30

Puzzle—1972 jigsaw puzzle showing MM in the nude
Golden Dreams pose and encased in plastic; came
put together and with a gold and red emblem affixed to the front that states "1962–1972—10th Anniversary—Never Before–Never Again"; about 8 x 10". $25–35

Refrigerator Magnets—Numerous refrigerator magnets
have been produced in the 1980s and 90s featuring
Marilyn's photo in color and b/w, among other
MM–related items; price each $3–5

Rubber Stamps—Three different stamps by Rubber
Stampede; 1993; numbered A313-C, A313-D, and
A313-E; entitled *Marilyn Monroe* on first two, and
Glamor Girl on the third; each $7–10

Scent Display—A 12 x 13" cardboard display featuring
four different scent cards called Monroe scent.

300-piece puzzle in canister, 1967

Assortment of magnets, 1980s–90s

	Value
Copyright 1954 by Monroe Manufacturing Company, New Castle, PA	$75–150

Screen Saver—1994; by Sam Shaw; depicts several rare Sam Shaw photos of Marilyn and entitled "Sam Shaw's Stars Photo Screen Saver"; manufactured by Desktop Software, Inc. — $25–30

Sculpture—Life-sized, animated Marilyn, anatomically correct; by a Dutch sculptor; very few were made; depicts Marilyn in the famous white blowing-skirt from *The Seven-Year Itch*, standing above a grate. — $15,000–20,000

Sculpture—Life-sized sculpture of Marilyn in a gold lamé gown; 1991; made by a Canadian sculptor named Chris Rees; constructed of Fiberglas and resin; Limited Edition of ten. — $4,000–5,000

Sculpture—Cast stone bust of Marilyn in the same gown as above and by the same sculptor; 1991; Limited Edition of 100. — $500–600

Serving Trays—Circa 1950s/60s; each have a laminated color photo of Marilyn in either the nude *Golden Dreams* pose or the nude *New Wrinkle* pose; framed in "blond" wood; came in at least three sizes—i.e., 13 x 18", 18 x 24", and 20 x 24"; each — $100–175

Serving Tray—Same style and vintage as above-described trays, only all metal. — $50–80

Value

Shifter Knob—Circa 1970s; a knob for the top of your car's or truck's shifter rod; has the *Golden Dreams* pose on it in color; another version features a head-and-shoulders pic of Marilyn; these were also known as suicide, spinner, and necker knobs. $20–30

Socks—1993; a pair of Marilyn Valentine adult socks by Fan Club Fitwear; made in Korea of cotton nylon elastane; No. C31991; green in color. $10–12

Socks—Ankle socks by Hot Socks, Inc.; 1992; came in white or pink; pair $8–10

Standees—Numerous life-sized cardboard standees featuring blown-up photos of Marilyn were produced from the late 1980s to the present, some in color and some in b/w; not to be confused with the vintage standees produced by the studios for promoting Marilyn's films; each $20–30

Standees—Miniversions of those listed above; 9–12" tall. $4–8

Steins—1991; by Ernst, Inc.; 3¹¹⁄₁₆" wide and 5³⁄₁₆" high; serially numbered; released in conjunction with Ernst's series of Marilyn ceramic plaques by Susie Morton; each $40–50

Sunglasses—1989; entitled *Marilyn Monroe—The Legend Lives*; eyewear by Renaissance; came with a white case; were on an 11 x 16" display board. $30–50

Tapestry—Depicts Marilyn in either a gold lamé gown or in the famous white skirt-blowing scene; each $20–30

Teddy Bear—1984; entitled, *Bearilyn Monroe*; made by The North American Bear Co., Inc., of Chicago; designed by Barbara Isenberg; U.S. material sewn in Haiti; pink fabric with a dress and a headband covered with large black polka dots; 21" tall. $50–70

Thermometer—Circa 1970s; 3 x 7"; reads, "Some Like It Hot—Marilyn Monroe"; boxed $10–15

Thermometer—As above, only 8 x 24" $20–25

Thimble—Fine bone china; made in England by Finsbury; titled, *The Seven-Year Itch*. $10–15

Thimble—Pink plastic construction with Marilyn's image on it. $3–5

Ties:
- "Flying Skirt"; by Bernard of Hollywood; 1993; color. $20–30
- MM in a one-piece bathing suit by Bernard of Hollywood; 1993; color. $20–30

Bearilyn Monroe
teddy bear, 1984

	Value
• MM in a black dress with studded straps by Bernard; 1990s.	$20–30
• MM in three color glamour poses by Bernard; 1990s.	$20–30
• MM in sectional glamour pose by Bernard; 1990s.	$20–30
• Two color ties by Ralph Marlin; 1990s; 100 percent polyester; made in U.S.; each	$20–30

**Assorted ties,
1990s**

Value

Tie Bar and Cuff Link Set—1972; depict the famous
nude *Golden Dreams* pose on them; released on the
10th anniversary of Marilyn's death; came in a
black felt-covered hinged box. $40–60

Trade Cards:
- Set of 20 Marilyn Trade Cards labeled, "Marilyn
  and Her Music"; copyright NMMM; 1963, but
  likely from the early 1970s; numbered 1–20 $15–25
- Set of 100 Marilyn Trading Cards by Sports
  Time; 1993–94; all different, beautifully done
  high-gloss cards featuring many nice pics of
  Marilyn. $20–30
- Set of 100 Marilyn Trading Cards by Sports Time;
  1995; 2nd Series; numbered 101–201; as above. $20–30
- Set of 75 Marilyn Collector Cards by The Pri-
  vate Collection; 1993; feature photos by Joseph
  Jasgur; boxed. $45–55

T-Shirt—Marilyn Monroe T-Shirt with the label
"Marilyn Monroe Signature Jeans"; came with a
phone card and a sample bottle of perfume attached;
Marilyn's image is on the front of the shirt. $20–30

Assortment of trading cards, Sports Time, 1993–95

**1972 series of
20 trading cards
by NMMM**

	Value

Watches:
- One by Bradley; includes color art of Marilyn on the face; has a white band. — $30–40
- A small tin watch with elastic band of 1950s vintage; has Marilyn's image on the face and came in various colors; for children. — $15–20
- Pocket Watch; silver windup; has a glamour shot of Marilyn on the face in a white fur pose. — $20–30
- Ladies Wristwatch—Circa 1970s; has a bust shot of Marilyn on the dial and a flexible gold band, metal case, and stainless-steel back. — $25–35
- Wrist Watch; 1987; part of *The Movie Star Watch Collection*; numbered ASU-876005; depicts a glamour shot of Marilyn on the face; has a black suede band, a fact card, and an artwork box. — $20–40
- Watch by Fossil; postage stamp design in full color; rectangle shape, with a gold finish; packed in a wooden box with same graphic on the box. — $60–80

Wig—Marilyn wig; 1991; by Franco American; one size fits all; flame-retardant; style no. 24-0025-11; made in Korea; sold out of Glendale, NY. — $30–40

Assortment of watches

Window Waver—1982; shrink-wrapped color window
   waver of Marilyn's face by Starpool of Santa Mon-
   ica, CA. $20–30

Wine—Marilyn Merlot Wine; bottled by Nova Partners
   of St. Helena, CA; first appeared in 1988 with the
   sale of a vintage 1985 Merlot. Each June 1 (Marilyn's
   birthday), 3,000 cases are produced bearing Marilyn's
   image in color on the label. The 1986 vintage was the
   only one to also feature a chardonnay. It is important
   to remember that there is a three-year difference be-

Value

tween the vintage year and the release year. Prices
below are for the year printed on the bottle:

- 1985 Merlot; red table wine; featuring MM in
  the color white-fur pose. $500–900
- 1986 Merlot; featuring MM in a color gold lamé
  pose. $350–600
- 1986 Chardonnay; featuring MM in the same
  color white-fur pose as the 1985 Merlot. $100–200
- 1987 Merlot; featuring MM in a black-sequined
  gown and fur stole color pic by Richard Avedon
  (French import). $140–180

Note: The higher value on the above wine (1987) was due to
the fact that there was a shortage of the grapes used in California
that year and, as a consequence, French grape imports were used in
the making of the wine.

- 1988 Merlot; featuring MM in a color gold lamé
  dress with her chin resting on her hand. $110–140
- 1989-Merlot; featuring MM in an off-the-
  shoulder dress. $100–130
- 1990 Merlot $90–120
- 1990 Champagne $60–80
- 1991 Merlot $80–110
- 1991 Champagne $50–70
- 1992 Merlot $70–100
- 1992 Champagne $40–60
- 1993 to 1996 Merlot $60–90
- 1994 Cabernet $50–80
- 1998 Norma Jean Merlot (1st in series) $20–30

Wrapping Paper—by Rock Wraps; with Marilyn's
image all over it. $3–5
Yearbook—Marilyn's original yearbook (not her personal copy) from University High School in Califor-
nia (10th grade-1942); not signed by Marilyn. $1,000–3,000

FAN CLUBS AND COLLECTOR SOURCES

International Fan Clubs

America—None active at the present time, except online.
Australia—"Glamour Preferred," c/o Jane Guy, P.O. Box 539, Camberwell, Victoria 3124 (Founded in 1989)
England—"Marilyn Lives Society," c/o Michelle Finn, 14 Clifton Square, Corby, Northants NN17 2DB
France—c/o Miss Mary Belzunce, 5 Avenue B., Hakeim, 06110 Le Cannet
Germany—"Some Like It Hot Fan Club", c/o Marina Muller, Link Str. 2, 31134 Hildesheim

Poster/Paper Restorers in the U.S.*

Jim Ashton, Indianapolis, IN. PH: 317-354-2308
Igor Edelman, 7466 Beverly Blvd., #205, Los Angeles, CA 90036. PH: 213-934-4219
Roger Fenton, 3440 Butler Ave., Los Angeles, CA 90066. PH: 310-391-1078 or FAX: 310-390-9824
J. Fields, 25 West 17th St., NY, NY 10011. PH: 212-730-7821
Garo, West Virginia. PH: 304-291-5299
Gary Goss, 320 Riverside, Northampton, MA 01060. PH: 413-586-0778
Herman Poster Mount. PH: 212-730-7821
Judy Jones (Poster Patch), San Francisco, CA. PH: 510-791-8209
Ron Moore, 2005-A Gates Ave., Redondo Beach, CA 90278. PH: 310-379-5327

*Note: the author lists the restorers' names as a reference only and has not had personal dealings with them.

Eric Panelle, 1217 E. San Joaquin, Sierra Tulare, CA 93274. PH: 209-686-4006 or 209-686-2369

Jim Sanchez, 484 Frederick St., Apt. A, San Francisco, CA 94117. PH: 415-752-0881

Dan Strebin, 644 Landfair Ave., 102, Westwood, CA 90024. PH: 310-208-8482

Collectible-Related Publications

Antiques & Collecting Hobbies Magazine
1006 S. Michigan Ave.
Chicago, IL 60650
PH: 312-939-4767
FAX: 312-939-0053
Rates: US: $24.00/year; foreign: $34.00/year
Features all types of collectibles and has very nice articles. Lots of color.

Antique Trader Weekly
100 Bryant St.
Dubuque, IA 52003
PH: 319-588-2073
FAX TOLL FREE-800-531-0880
Canada/Foreign FAX-319-588-0888
Rates: US: $19.00/6 months; $35.00/12 months; $58.00/2 years; Foreign: $58.00/year
Lists auctions by region and features great articles, along with classified ads. Newspaper format.

Collectible Madness
483 Federal Rd.
Brookfield, CT 06804
PH: 203-740-9472 or 800-784-7796
Catalog issued on TV and movie collectibles.

Collecting Hollywood
2401 Broad St.
Chattanooga, TN 37408
FAX: 423-265-5506
Rates: US: $16.95/six issues; $22.95/12 issues; $40.00/24 issues; Foreign: add $6.00 per issue; Canada: add $3.00 per issue.
Features poster- and film-related items for sale and has very nice articles. Items are consignable.

Country Accents COLLECTIBLES Magazine
P.O. Box 336
Mt. Morris, IL 61054-7535
Rates: US: $18.97/4 issues; foreign: $23.97/4 issues (US funds only)
Published quarterly. Features lots of color and very nice articles on
  a wide variety of collectibles.

ebay Auction On-line
This is an Internet auction where you can buy and sell any number
  of Marilyn items and anything else you can imagine!
Just type in "ebay auction" in your search engine, and they'll come
  up. You'll have a blast!

Heather Holmberg Auctions
3727 W. Magnolia Blvd., #247
Burbank, CA 91505
PH: 818-557-7435
FAX: 818-557-7436
Features auction catalogs of Hollywood-related collectibles.

Manion's International Auction House
P.O. Box 12214
Kansas City, MO 66112
PH: 913-299-6692
FAX: 913-299-6792
e-Mail: collecting@manions.com
Catalogs that are priced reasonably and cover a wide variety of collect-
  ible items in both U.S. and foreign categories.

Movie Collector's World
Box 309-P
Fraser, MI 48026
PH: 800-273-6883 for VISA/MASTERCARD ORDERS
e-mail: www.mcwonline.com
Rates: US: $25.00/12 issues; $45.00/26 issues; foreign: $85.00/26 is-
  sues (Surface Mail)
Features nice articles and movie-related collectibles wanted and/or for
  sale. Classifieds as well.

Norma's Jeans Celebrity Memorabilia
3511 Turner Lane
Chevy Chase, MD 20815-3213
PH: 301-652-4644

FAX: 301-907-0216
Features original Hollywood costumes/personal items and autographs.
  Catalog issued.

The Paper and Advertising Collector
P.O. Box 500
Mount Joy, PA 17552
PH: 717-653-4300
Rates: US: $12.00/year
Published monthly and features a wide variety of collectible items.

Paper Collector's Marketplace
470 Main St., P.O. Box 128
Scandinavia, WI 54977
PH: 715-467-2379
FAX: 715-467-2243
Rates: $10.95/six issues (for new subscribers only); $19.95/12 issues;
  $36.95/24 issues
Wide variety of paper and related items wanted and for sale. Classified.

Paper Pile Enterprises
P.O. Box 337
San Anselmo, CA 94979-0337
PH: 415-454-5552
FAX: 415-454-2947
Rates: US: $20.00/1 year (Canada included); Foreign: $25.00
Various collectibles offered in categories.

Postcard Collector
P.O. Box 1050
Dubuque, IA 52004-1050
PH: 800-482-7151
FAX: 800-531-0880
e-mail: Traderpubs@AOL.Com
Rates: US: $23.95/12 issues
Various collectibles offered with an emphasis on postcards.

Profiles In History
345 N. Maple Dr., Suite 202
Beverly Hills, CA 90210
PH: 800-942-8856
FAX: 310-859-3842
Periodic Hollywood memorabilia auctions.

Southern Antiques
P.O. Drawer 1107
Decatur, GA 30031-1107
Rates: Sample copy is $2.00
Published monthly and covers various collectibles.

Startifacts
3101 East Hennepin Ave.
Minneapolis, MN 55413
PH: 612-331-6454
FAX: 612-331-8083
e-Mail: startifacts@earthlink.net
Feature authentic costumes and Hollywood memorabalia.

Trap Door Spider
531 S. Prescott
Memphis, TN 38111
Send $0.52 for a list of various collectibles.

Warman's Today's Collector
c/o Krause Publications
700 East State St.
Iola, WI 54990-0001
PH: 800-258-0929 (Subscription Services)
Rates: US: $21.95/12 issues; $41.95/24 issues; $60.95/36 issues
Covers the gamut of collectible items in all categories. Has great
    articles and classifieds.

AUTHOR'S NOTE

If you have questions regarding Marilyn Monroe memorabilia, you can contact the author via email at *ckidder@jvlnet.com*